Towards a Critical Existentialism

Intersections in Continental and Analytic Philosophy

Series Editors
Jeffrey A. Bell, Paul Livingston and James Williams

Drawing on different traditions for new solutions to philosophical problems

Books in this series will bring together work in the analytic and continental traditions in philosophy. Although these traditions have until recently been thought of as separate, if not irreconcilable, these books will show how key philosophical problems can be addressed by drawing from work in both.

The intersections on display here will demonstrate the strength and vitality of a pluralist approach to philosophy, as well as its wide relevance to contemporary philosophical concerns.

Books available

Language and Process: Words, Whitehead and the World, Michael Halewood

Dynamic Realism: Uncovering the Reality of Becoming through Phenomenology and Process Philosophy, Tina Röck

An Inquiry into Analytic-Continental Metaphysics: Truth, Relevance and Metaphysics, Jeffrey A. Bell

Towards a Critical Existentialism: Truth, Relevance and Politics, Jeffrey A. Bell

Visit the Intersections website at edinburghuniversitypress.com/ series-intersections-in-continental-and-analytic-philosophy

Towards a Critical Existentialism

Truth, Relevance and Politics

Jeffrey A. Bell

EDINBURGH
University Press

For Elizabeth, Rebecca
And to the Memory of
Leah Bell
Whose Life Will Always Inspire Me

Edinburgh University Press is one of the leading university presses in the UK. We publish academic books and journals in our selected subject areas across the humanities and social sciences, combining cutting-edge scholarship with high editorial and production values to produce academic works of lasting importance. For more information visit our website: edinburghuniversitypress.com

Edinburgh University Press Ltd
The Tun – Holyrood Road
12(2f) Jackson's Entry
Edinburgh EH8 8PJ

Typeset in Bembo
by R. J. Footring Ltd, Derby, and
printed and bound in Great Britain

A CIP record for this book is available from the British Library

ISBN 978 1 3995 0832 2 (hardback)
ISBN 978 1 3995 0834 6 (webready PDF)
ISBN 978 1 3995 0835 3 (epub)

Contents

Acknowledgements

There are many people to thank for the opportunities I was afforded that made it possible to write this book, as well as its companion volume (*Towards a Critical Existentialism*). I thank the Leverhulme Trust for having awarded me a Leverhulme Visiting Professorship that I served at Royal Holloway, University of London, during the second half of 2019. I also thank my Dean, Karen Fontenot, and Department Head, Bill Robison, for supporting the sabbatical leave that enabled me to serve my Visiting Professorship in London. Much of this book was written during an enjoyable stay in London, and in a wonderful flat (thank you Sarah). I especially thank Nathan Widder and Henry Somers-Hall for inviting me to come to Royal Holloway, for working tirelessly on my behalf to complete the Leverhulme application, and for all their helpful feedback and comments on rough drafts of these books. I must also thank James Williams and Paul Livingston for their invaluable comments on the books, and for enabling me to make them better than they would have been otherwise. Michael Della Rocca's encouraging feedback and comments let me know I was not chasing windmills; and Peter Gratton's perceptive comments and unequalled copy-editing skills helped me to clean up some bad writing habits and express myself more clearly. I also received invaluable feedback on drafts to chapters from these books that I gave as talks throughout the UK and in Europe during my stay in London. Many thanks are due for invitations from Frank Ruda and Dominic Smith at the University of Dundee; Chris Henry at the University of Kent; Christopher (Tiff) Thomas at Manchester Metropolitan University; Craig Lundy at Nottingham Trent University; Keith Ansell-Pearson and Stephen Houlgate at the University of Warwick; Eckardt Lindner at the University of Vienna; and Martin Procházka at Charles University, Prague. From them and their students and colleagues I received invaluable comments and suggestions, many of which ended up in what I wrote.

Both books have been long in the making, and many people have provided grist for the mill. Most important among these are my former colleagues at the NewAPPS blog, especially John Protevi, whose friendship before and since NewAPPS has been a treasure, and Eric Schliesser, whose omnivorous approach to philosophy has been an ongoing inspiration for my own work, and whose collaboration on posts at NewAPPS set into motion many of the key themes that ended up in this book. John, Eric and the rest of the crew at NewAPPS – Mark Norris Lance, Edward Kazarian, Roberta Millstein, Catarina Dutilh Novaes, Jon Cogburn, Mohan Matthen and Eric Winsberg – provided me with many opportunities to engage in the type of analytic–continental crossover work that has come to fill the pages of these books. My colleague Peter Petrakis has had many long conversations with me on themes to be found herein as well, themes he will no doubt recognise.

I have also benefited from many informal conversations as I worked on parts of these books. The 'Communication Problems' chapter of *Towards a Critical Existentialism*, as well as some themes in this book, were prompted by a conversation I had in London with Brent Adkins. Andrew Cutrofello offered helpful guidance after reading an earlier version of this book, and his own work exemplifies how one can successfully bridge the divide between analytic and continental philosophy. Thanks to Dan Smith's invitation to speak at Purdue, and to the feedback from Dan and his colleagues (especially Michael Jacovides), I was given encouraging suggestions early in the process of writing. Craig Lundy, Paul Patton, Sean Bowden, Ian Buchanan, Dan Fineman, Audrey Wasser, among many others, have all provided helpful feedback along the way as the books came together.

I also want to thank Carol MacDonald at Edinburgh University Press for her support and guidance over the years, and especially for her efforts to see these books through the process of getting them to press. The anonymous readers, especially the second reader for *Towards a Critical Existentialism*, provided very helpful feedback and suggestions, most of which I acted on, and as a result the books are better for it. Tim Clark's perceptive and discerning copy-editing of these books has made them both better than they would have been otherwise. And most of all I want to thank my wife, Elizabeth, whose untiring support has been a continual source of strength for me in more ways than she can ever know.

Introduction

In the preface to *Unpopular Essays*, published in 1950, the same year he was awarded the Nobel Prize in Literature, Bertrand Russell introduces his collection of essays by claiming that they were 'written at various times during the last fifteen years, [and] are concerned to combat, in one way or another, the growth of dogmatism, whether of the Right or of the Left, which has hitherto characterized our tragic century' (Russell 1950, preface). Russell indeed witnessed a tragic century – two world wars, a holocaust and a Cold War that threatened nuclear annihilation. He did not hesitate to speak out against these tragedies, even suffering the loss of his job at Cambridge and six months in prison in 1918 for a speech he gave criticising the US entry into the First World War; forty-three years later, at the age of eighty-nine, he would be imprisoned for seven days for participating in a London anti-nuclear demonstration in 1961. Speaking truth to power, to the dogmatism, partisanship and irrationality Russell saw in society and politics, was thus a lifelong passion and commitment that he took more seriously than most. Writing now, seventy years after the publication of *Unpopular Essays*, and in the midst of a global pandemic, one could argue that Russell would be just as concerned about today's society as he was about his own. In fact, Russell himself saw this possibility when, as he began his Moncure Conway Lecture for 1922, 'Free Thought and Official Propaganda', he noted that 'unless a vigorous and vigilant public opinion can be aroused in defence of [freedom of thought and freedom of the individual], there will be much less of both a hundred years hence than there is now' (Russell 1996, 125). With the hyper-partisan rhetoric gripping contemporary US politics, the rise of autocratic regimes throughout the world (Russia, Hungary, Poland, Brazil, etc.), and antisemitic hate crimes and white nationalism on the rise, the latter often with the tacit approval of the former US President Donald Trump, it seems quite apparent that we do not have, in 2022, the 'vigorous and vigilant' defence of freedom that Russell called for in 1922.[1]

---

1. Among the many examples one could point to as evidence for Trump's pandering to, if not tacit approval of, white supremacists, there was the conspiracy theory he supported that alleges Barack Obama was born in Kenya rather than the United States, and thus was not eligible to be President. In April 2017, after a deadly clash between white supremacists and

1

Some may challenge this characterisation of the present scene. After all, there is a lively and vigorous debate and defence of various freedoms and rights in contemporary society. For instance, the freedom of religion, the right to bear arms, the right to work and the right for same-sex couples to marry are among the many freedoms and rights that have been vigorously defended in recent decades, and with a number of successes, such as the 2015 Supreme Court decision, *Obergefell v. Hodges*, that legalised same-sex marriage (to be discussed below, in the context of the politics of the family [see §5.2.a]). Despite these successes, however, or perhaps because of them, as will be discussed in later chapters, Russell would still likely claim that what is missing in contemporary society, or what seems to be increasingly on the decline, is what he refers to as 'Liberal tentativeness' (Russell 1950, 17). Stated more fully, 'Liberal tentativeness' is for Russell 'The essence of the Liberal outlook', which means that it 'lies not in what opinions are held, but in how they are held: instead of being held dogmatically, they are held tentatively, and with a consciousness that new evidence may at any moment lead to their abandonment' (15). This tentativeness and conscious willingness to abandon opinions when the evidence merits, or to dump one's 'whole cartload of beliefs' as Charles S. Peirce put it (Peirce 1955, 47), is for Russell, as it was for Peirce, what comes as a matter of course as one adopts the spirit and methods of science. Russell thus contrasts what is the case for 'Every man of science whose outlook is truly scientific [and who] is ready to admit that what passes for scientific knowledge at the moment is sure to require correction with the progress of discovery', with what happens 'in religion and politics ... [where] everybody considers it de rigueur to have a dogmatic opinion, to be backed up by inflicting starvation, prison, and war, and to be carefully guarded from argumentative competition with any different opinion' (Russell 1996, 129).

This last point is key and it brings us to an assumption that underlies the 'Liberal tentativeness' Russell and many others call upon – namely, the assumption that it is the marketplace of ideas, the free exchange of opinions and evidence, that drives the process of inquiry whereby opinions come to be abandoned in favour of opinions that offer a better explanation of the evidence. Russell openly embraces this view, arguing that 'thought is free when it is exposed to free competition among beliefs, i.e., when all beliefs are able to state their case, and no legal or pecuniary advantages or disadvantages attach to beliefs. This is an ideal which, for various reasons, can never be fully attained. But it is possible to approach very much nearer to it than we do at present' (Russell 1996, 127). In short, it is politics and religion that most

---

protesters in Charlottesville, Virginia, where a supremacist killed one of the protesters, then President Trump claimed there were 'some very fine people on both sides'.

often stand in the way of the 'free competition among beliefs', as Russell himself found out, and thus if liberalism is to flourish with the progress this marketplace of ideas brings about, then one's thinking must be left free to pursue the evidence and the arguments wherever they may lead. Russell thus echoes John Stuart Mill's assumption that although a true opinion 'may be extinguished once, twice, or many times', in the end 'there will generally be found persons to rediscover it, until some one of its reappearances falls on a time when from favourable circumstances it escapes persecution until it has made such head as to withstand all subsequent attempts to suppress it' ('On Liberty', in Mill 1991, 34). Given freedom of thought and the absence of interference in this thought from religious and political authorities, the truth will eventually come to be revealed, and with this truth will come advances that stand to benefit individuals and society as a whole.

Connected with the marketplace of ideas is the commercial marketplace, and it is the competition of the market itself that is also, according to Russell, integral to the emergence of the liberal tradition. Russell is clear on this point: 'the liberal theory of politics is a recurrent product of commerce ... The reasons for the connection of commerce with Liberalism are obvious' (Russell 1950, 14). He then goes on to note that people engaged in commercial and trading activities must work with people from different cultural backgrounds, with different customs and beliefs, and this 'destroys the dogmatism of the untraveled'; there is 'negotiation between two parties who are both free ... [and] it is most profitable when the buyer or seller is able to understand the point of view of the other party' (15). Societies that allow for vibrant commercial activities and free trade are also most likely to exemplify what Russell calls the 'Liberal creed', which adopts the perspective of 'live-and-let-live, of toleration and freedom so far as public order permits, of moderation and absence of fanaticism in political programs' (15). Sadly, however, Russell saw little evidence in his day that the widespread adoption of the 'Liberal creed' was on the horizon, and given the rise of intolerance and autocratic regimes in contemporary society it still seems to be far short of being generally adopted.

At this point we could fault Russell for pinning his hopes on the 'Liberal creed', ignoring the many problems that come with commercial society, or with capitalism as it has come to be discussed more widely, and as we will see below (for example, in §3.1.b). There is an enormous body of literature that could be placed in this camp, from Marx and Marx-inspired critiques, to Carl Schmitt, critical theory, poststructuralism, postmodernism, among many others one could list who would argue in one way or another that it is a failure of liberalism itself that accounts for why Russell's vision has not materialised. To simplify greatly, a common claim in a number of these arguments is that the mechanisms of free market capitalism tend towards the dissolution of many of the customs and traditions that provide for the well-being and welfare of members of a society. While Russell saw the tendency for commercial society to bring about the dissolution of the 'dogmatism of the untraveled' as an advantage, many others see it as a tendency that destroys more than just the dogmatism of beliefs but tends also towards the dissolution of the very foundations of society itself. In his well-known arguments for the double movement of social history since the nineteenth century, Karl Polanyi claimed that the tendency of free market liberalism to the dissolution of society is countered by a move to shore up and protect society (see Polanyi 2001, 79–80, and §5.2.a below). For Polanyi, the rise of both fascism and socialism were examples, the first in an extreme form, of this movement against the damaging effects of self-regulating markets (267). The irrational extremes of politics that Russell thought would be mitigated by the widespread adoption of the Liberal creed are thus, on this view, natural consequences of the self-regulating markets and economic liberalism that made the perspective of the Liberal creed possible. On the other side of this issue, proponents of self-regulating markets will argue that what has kept Russell's vision of liberalism from succeeding is not the liberal institutions themselves, but rather the failure to be patient and allow the markets to work as they are best suited to work, which is, as Friedrich Hayek argued, when they function in accordance with the price system and without political interference (discussed below in §5.2.c). It is the use of political power to intervene in markets that fosters, Hayek argued, the conditions which ultimately becomes manifest in the forms of intolerance and repression that Russell spoke out against.[2]

In the arguments to be developed here, we will touch upon a number of these debates regarding liberalism, or more precisely the relationship between capitalism and liberalism. Our primary focus, however, will not be on rehearsing or revisiting the many ways liberalism has been challenged and supported, although this will indeed be part of the discussions to follow; rather, we will take on the problem of meaning as this relates to the nature and processes of capitalism. More to the point, we will be extending the arguments of this book's companion volume, *An Inquiry into Analytic-Continental Metaphysics* (hereafter, *Inquiry*). In that book I developed a Deleuzian theory of problematic Ideas in order to address a number of metaphysical problems that

---

2. See Hayek 2011. In his book *The Great Transformation* (1944), Polanyi refers to a double movement wherein the tendency to further commoditise goods and services, to the detriment of social customs and traditions, provokes a counter-movement to defend society. It is the latter movement that can lead to forms of intolerance, Polanyi argues (discussed below, §5.2.a). Foucault (2008) also offers a very detailed and prescient account of the history of neoliberalism, focusing on the rise of Ordoliberalism in Germany.

have been common throughout the history of philosophy, with a particular focus on more recent arguments in both analytic and continental philosophy. Extending these arguments in this current work, the focus shifts from the metaphysical nature of problems to the problem of making sense. With this shift to investigating the implications of the problem of making sense, we will provide an extended explication of the practical relevance of problematic Ideas to a number of different issues. While the *Inquiry* does provide a metaphysical framework with which to frame the current discussion, the present book can be read independently, exploring as it does the relevance of problematic Ideas to a number of issues that affect everyday life. Rather than being simply a defence of liberalism, therefore, or a further justification of Russell's Liberal creed, what we will be developing here is an understanding of the problem of making sense as a way to clarify many of the concepts and ideas that come to populate discussions concerning the place of liberalism in modern society. This is the task I will call critical existentialism.

One of the ways we will do this is by bringing the problem of making sense to bear on three ideas in particular – namely, freedom, law and progress. Restating Russell's point in the simplest of terms: a society that vigorously defends and encourages freedom of thought, with laws, customs and sensibilities that enable the securing of this freedom, will be a society that advances and progresses. Adding the problem of making sense to this way of formulating Russell's understanding of liberalism will complicate this picture in two distinct ways. First, by focusing on the nature of problems, and again extending the arguments of the *Inquiry*, what will be stressed is that a problem does not presuppose its solution, the solution that makes the problem disappear. Solutions are indeed solutions to problems, but the solution is not predetermined by the nature of the problem, as if the problem already anticipates the determinate nature of the solution itself. A solution also does not exhaust the nature of the problem, and thus other solutions continue to subsist in the solution. To take an everyday example, a kindergartener who is learning to tie their shoes is confronted with the problem of arranging and tying the laces such that, among other things, (1) the laces remain tied together and do not unravel, (2) the shoes are tightened and don't fall off, and (3) the laces can be easily untied. As anyone who has watched several children learning to tie their shoes will know, there are multiple solutions to this problem, and the solution a particular child comes to does not exhaust the problem and thus the possibility of other solutions.

The second way in which we will complicate the elements of freedom, law and progress is to connect problems to the processes involved in 'making sense', and we will do so by drawing from the work of Gilles Deleuze, and in particular his book, *The Logic of Sense* (Deleuze 1990b). More precisely (and to be discussed below in §1.1–2), meaning or sense, following Deleuze, consists of two tendencies, a dedifferentiating and a differentiating tendency (hereafter, de/differentiating when referring to both). The differentiating tendency is the aspect of sense or meaning that is infinitely determinate and determinable; it is the sense or meaning of an expression that can be referred to by another expression, an expression with its own sense that can be referred to, and so on *ad infinitum*. The dedifferentiating tendency is the tendency to the indeterminate and indeterminable that is abstract and not to be confused with anything already determinate and differentiated. These two tendencies are tendencies, meaning that neither the dedifferentiating tendency towards the indeterminate and indeterminable, nor the differentiating tendency towards the determinate, are fully realised. It is common, however, as we will see, to assume the determinate ends of these tendencies – the indeterminate or the determinate – and then think of these tendencies as predetermined processes to an already determinate end, or as necessarily moving from the indeterminate to the determinate. Stated in terms of the theory of problems to be pursued here, this subordination of tendencies to a determinate end will be referred to as the illusion of a solution without a problem. Moreover, the very identification of the two tendencies as distinct – that is, the differentiating and the dedifferentiating – is itself a result of an abstraction (dedifferentiating tendency) that strives to determine (differentiating tendency) and make sense of what is going on, and thus the claims made here could, if we are not careful, become another instance of promoting a solution without a problem.

The determinate thoughts and concepts used in setting forth one's theory, therefore, are never definitive, and so, in the spirit of the 'Liberal tentativeness' Russell praised, one ought to work with an awareness of the illusions we are susceptible to. Maintaining this awareness of, and attempting to avoid, the illusion of a solution without a problem will be how we read the existential tradition's stress upon authenticity and good faith (in §3.2.a and §4.1). Our approach to a theory of sense and meaning is thus inseparable from our understanding of problems, or, as referred to earlier, and for the sake of simplicity, it is the problem of making sense. Bringing the problem of making sense into dialogue with the existential tradition, which will be a central task of this book, will allow us to demonstrate the relevance of Kierkegaard's discussions of freedom to a number of questions relevant to the nature of life in modern society, and this in turn will highlight the affinity of Kierkegaard's thought to several other writers in the 'existential' tradition (§4.1.a for Kierkegaard, §3.2.a for Nietzsche, §4.1.b for Sartre and §4.1.c for Camus). The discussion will also illustrate the relevance of Deleuze to the existential tradition and further support our efforts to think through and ultimately rethink the problems inseparable from liberalism.

To begin to clarify these points, to make sense of them as it were, and to set the stage for the arguments to be developed in the book, in the remainder of the Introduction I want to highlight two key themes that motivate the problem of making sense as it will be understood here. First, we will return to Russell's call for a vigorous defence of the freedoms of thought and individuals, and in particular his hope that a socially encouraged and protected intelligence will allow us to avoid 'the intoxication of power' that Russell claimed (in the waning days of the Second World War in his *History of Western Philosophy*) was 'the greatest danger of our time' (Russell 1972, 737). This will lead us to more recent discussions of the relationship between meaning and Wittgenstein's famous rule-following paradox, which will in turn lead us to a discussion of infinitism, or the view that affirms some infinite regresses, a view that will allow us to clarify the manner in which meaning involves the de/differentiating tendencies. The discussion of infinitism will also motivate a move to incorporating a theory of relevance into our understanding of meaning, or how the problem of making sense is always inseparable from conditions of relevance that are infinitely determinable. In this context we will draw from the work of Aleksandr Luria and more recent studies in the philosophy and psychology of cognition. We will then summarise the chapters that will develop the themes sketched here.

a) Rule-following and infinitism

To counter the propensity to irrationality and a dangerous intoxication with power, Russell calls upon intelligence. Intelligence is more than just tolerance, more than tentativeness and the other virtues Russell identifies with liberalism; these are, rather, virtues that intelligence makes possible. As for the nature of intelligence itself, Russell distinguishes it from having information, which is a 'definite knowledge, [such as] reading and writing, language and mathematics'; intelligence, however, consists of the 'mental habits which will enable people to acquire knowledge and form sound judgments for themselves' (Russell 1996, 135). Reading, writing, language and mathematics will give us a stock of determinate information, but it is intelligence that weighs the information given as evidence for a particular judgment, and it is the development of a discerning judgment, or intelligence, which produces both more information and enables us to assert or deny what is the case. An inability to discern what is the case, to see what is really going on, is precisely the problem, Russell claims, and thus it is 'to intelligence, increasingly widespread, that we must look for the solution of the ills from which our world is suffering' (39). What is needed, therefore, is an expanded education that

7

will increase people's 'powers of weighing evidence and forming rational judgments', in contrast to the standard procedure wherein most students are inundated with 'patriotism and class bias' (201). As an example of what should be taught, Russell suggests that learning how to read newspapers critically would be a good place to start:

> The schoolmaster should select some incident which happened a good many years ago, and roused political passions in its day. He should then read to the school-children what was said by the newspapers on one side, what was said by those on the other, and some impartial account of what really happened. He should show how, from the biased account of either side, a practiced reader could infer what really happened, and he should make them understand that everything in newspapers is more or less untrue. (141)

There is an immense body of literature on what is involved in 'weighing evidence and forming rational judgments'. During the Covid-19 pandemic, for instance, these issues were quite pressing – what evidence justified the judgment that we ought to lockdown much of our daily lives, to the ruin of economies and livelihoods? There was much discussion of the evidence, the nature of the tests, the assumptions built into various models, etc., that were then brought to bear in justifying judgments regarding what was really happening and the best path forward given what was happening. Rather than delve into these issues, however, the question I want to focus on is what one is learning when one learns to weigh evidence and form rational judgments. Rather than detailing the mechanisms involved in forming judgments, for example by using Bayesian analysis among other things, the question here begins with where the process ends, in a judgment, and what it is one learns when one is able to apply a judgment to a new, novel case. Do we apply the same judgment to the novel scenario, or do we need to form a new judgment? If we take Russell to be extending a Fregean understanding of judgment, whereby a judgment consists of relating a concept or predicate to a subject, then coming to learn a concept is in effect coming to learn a rule that one applies to novel cases, if appropriate.[3] For example, if my wife asks me

---

3. In the case of Frege, for instance, the concept 'planet', he argues, 'has no direct relation at all to the Earth, but only to a concept that the Earth, among other things falls under', such as Mercury, Venus, Mars, etc. (Frege 1960, 105). The extension of the concept 'planet', therefore, is not to be confused with the singular, particular objects this concept picks out. The relation of the concept 'planet' to the Earth 'is only an indirect one', Frege claims, a point he summarises as follows: 'The extension of a concept does not consist of objects falling under the concept, in the way, e.g., that a wood consists of trees; it attaches to the concept and to this alone' (106). And the way in which the extension of a concept attaches to the concept alone is as a function, as Frege makes clear in his essay 'Function and Concept' (31–2), wherein a concept is an unsaturated function or rule that those who

to water the gardenias outside, then my knowing what a gardenia is entails being able to follow a rule which guides my behaviour such that I water the gardenias and not the azaleas. If I am unsure which plants the gardenias are, and which the azaleas, I may water them all, at which point I will have gotten it wrong, which could be consequential if, for instance, the azaleas should not have been watered. It thus appears that one is learning a rule when one learns a concept and how to apply it correctly to different particulars and in novel circumstances.

It is at this point that the scepticism associated with Wittgenstein's famous rule-following paradox enters the scene. In his *Philosophical Investigations*, Wittgenstein states the paradox as follows: 'This was our paradox: no course of action could be determined by a rule, because every course of action can be brought into accord with the rule ... if every course of action can be brought into accord with the rule, then it can also be brought into conflict with it' (Wittgenstein 2009, §201). In his famous study of this passage, Saul Kripke offers the example of arithmetic to drive Wittgenstein's point home. If I've learned the plus rule, what have I learned? Presumably I've learned to give the answer 125 when given the problem, 68 + 57 (see Kripke 1982). On Kripke's understanding of Wittgenstein, the scepticism arises when we cannot determine, from the rule itself, whether or not it extends to a new case. Let us say that there is another rule, the quus rule, which gives us the answers we would get from the plus rule when the number is less than 57, but if 57 or greater, the answer is always 5. If someone has always followed the plus rule up to the present moment, meaning they had never added a number equal to or greater than 57, then how do we know whether or not they were following the plus rule or the quus rule in the past? Since all previous cases are in accord with either rule, how can we know, in the case of 68 + 57, whether the answer is 125 or 5? In short, how do we know whether or not a rule extends to a new case. As I walk from one gardenia to the next, watering hose in hand, how do I know that the application of the predicate, ' ... is a gardenia', applies to each of the different plants I come upon. If it is a matter of interpreting a rule in each new case, an interpretation that tells us whether the rule does or does not apply, then the question becomes one of whether or not our standard of interpretation is correct, a standard that will require

---

grasp the concept can then act in accordance with in picking out the particular objects that do or do not fall under the concept; that is, the objects that fulfil or saturate the unsaturated function and give the resulting proposition a truth-value. Russell will largely follow and extend Frege on these points (see his famous essay, 'On Denoting' [Russell 1905]). For an important commentary on this point, and one that includes recognition of Wittgenstein's critique, see Burge 1984.

another interpretation, and so on *ad infinitum*. Wittgenstein, however, avoids this regress, for in the paragraph immediately following the one where he gives us the rule-following paradox, he claims that the paradox rests on a mis-understanding; namely, it assumes that there is a 'chain of reasoning [where] we place one interpretation behind another, as if each one contented us at least for a moment, until we thought of yet another lying behind it' (Witt-genstein 2009, §201). This is a mistake, Wittgenstein adds, for he claims that 'there is a way of grasping a rule which is not an interpretation, but which, from case to case of application, is exhibited in what we call "following the rule" and "going against it"'.

It is around this that much of the debate regarding the rule-following paradox has gravitated. The issue, in short, boils down to whether one should accept the sceptical conclusion of the rule-following paradox, and then turn to external factors such as social norms and customs to account for rule-following, or deny the sceptical conclusion, as Wittgenstein appears to, and then show what it means for there to be 'a way of grasping a rule which is not an interpretation' (this sceptical/anti-sceptical debate will be discussed below [§5.2.d]). One way to grasp a rule which is not an interpretation is through a primitive intuition, an intuition that is basic and requires no further justifications or interpretations – it is where one's spade is turned. Wittgen-stein, however, pours cold water on this approach: 'If intuition is an inner voice – how do I know how I am to obey it? And how do I know that it doesn't mislead me? For if it can guide me right, it can also guide me wrong. (Intuition an unnecessary shuffle.)' (Wittgenstein 2009, §213).

Wittgenstein also pours cold water on the argument that it is solely by human agreement and convention that we follow rules, that we know which way is the right way to proceed in a novel case: '"So you are saying that human agreement decides what is true and what is false?" – What is true or false is what human beings *say*; and it is in their language that human beings agree. This is agreement not in opinions, but rather in form of life' (Wittgenstein 2009, §241). In other words, the right way to follow a rule is not the result of established opinion regarding what is or is not the case, nor is it the result of a primitive intuition, and nor is it the result of interpreting an independent rule that then guides our actions. Wittgenstein, however, is unclear as to precisely what does constitute following a rule correctly, though we do know that it is based on a form of human agreement, on a 'form of life'. The ambiguity and lack of clarity on this point is a likely reason why there continues to be a debate between those who affirm (including Kripke) and those who deny the sceptical implications of the rule-following paradox. Crispin Wright nicely summarises the state of play Wittgenstein has left us in:

So we have been told what does *not* constitute the requirement of a rule in any particular case: it is *not* constituted by our agreement about the particular case, and it is *not* constituted autonomously, by a rule-as-rail, our ability to follow which would be epistemologically unaccountable. But we have not been told what does constitute it; all we have been told is that there would simply be no such requirement – the rule could not so much as exist – but for the phenomenon of actual, widespread human agreement in judgement. I fear that it is probably vain to search Wittgenstein's own texts for a more concrete positive suggestion about the constitutive question. (Wright 2002, 127)

The constitutive question, therefore, is how we come to follow the rules we do, and do so correctly, in accordance with the normative require-ments of the rule (e.g., I correctly water the gardenias and not the azaleas). Wittgenstein clearly admits that we do do so – there is 'following the rule' and 'going against it' – but the standard which determines what is right is neither a pre-existent rule nor a Platonic rule-as-rail which predetermines our future actions in accordance with the rule; nor is there an already estab-lished custom or agreement relevant to a particular case, a novel case, which determines what is the correct way to proceed; and nor, finally, is there a primitive intuition that simply tells us, without further need for justification, how to obey the rule, for this too reintroduces the scepticism of knowing whether or not this intuition is misleading us. Wittgenstein would likely be unbothered by Wright's suggestion that he has left us without a clear answer to the 'constitutive question'. Wittgenstein's primary concern was to disabuse philosophers of the problems they felt their questions generated. If we know what rule-following does *not* entail, then we can avoid falling into certain philosophical arguments and debates. In developing our notion of making sense, however, we will avoid the presuppositions Wittgenstein rejected while also providing a way of understanding the nature of rule-following that does address the constitutive question. To state my conclusion up front, I shall argue that we should not seek to end the regress in a transcendent, autonomous, rule-as-rail, or end it in the established habits and agreements of human beings; rather, I will argue that rule-following is to be understood as inseparable from the process of making sense. Instead of bringing regresses to an end, therefore, a consequence of my argument will be the acceptance of the infinite regresses the rule-following paradox brought to light.

b) Infinitism

As noted earlier, a key issue surrounding the sceptical outcome of the rule-following paradox was whether or not there is a regress of interpretations of the rule, a regress that casts doubt on any interpretation being the correct one to use in determining how to follow a rule. Wittgenstein rejected the regress (a point missed by Kripke, as has been widely noted[4]) and thus avoided the sceptical consequences it implied. The regress in question was made famous by Sextus Empiricus when he listed it as one of the 'Five modes leading to suspension [of belief] that have been handed down by skeptics' (Sextus Empiricus 1933, I.166). This particular mode, he goes on, is 'based upon regress *ad infinitum* ... whereby we assert that the thing adduced as a proof of the matter proposed needs a further proof, and this again another, and so on *ad infinitum*, so that the consequence is suspension, as we possess no starting-point for our argument'. If we need to interpret a rule to know how to proceed in any particular case, and if our interpretation implies a standard or rule that is itself subject to interpretation, an interpretation open to yet another interpretation, and so on *ad infinitum*, then we can never be sure we have correctly extended a rule in any particular case. What we need, as Sextus Empiricus himself notes, is a 'starting-point', a definitive, non-arbitrary interpretation that requires no further interpretations and justifications. The sceptics, unsurprisingly, denied there were any such starting-points.

Since Wittgenstein does not accept the sceptical implications of the rule-following paradox, the question then is how he avoids scepticism. If we accept the premise that avoiding scepticism was an important motivation in Wittgenstein's thought, then this can shed further light on why he turned away from a Platonic understanding of rules as transcendent rules-as-rails, and also why he refused to accept a primitive, self-sufficient intuition that needs no further justification. With respect to the latter, we end up with the scepticism of knowing whether or not this 'intuitive voice', this brute, self-sufficient fact, 'doesn't mislead me? For if it can guide me right, it can also guide me wrong' (Wittgenstein 2009, §213). In the former case, by avoiding Platonic rules-as-rails, Wittgenstein avoids another famous regress, and the scepticism this entails. This is the regress made famous in the *Parmenides*:

> 'I [Parmenides] fancy your reason for believing that each idea is one is something like this; when there is a number of things which seem to you to be great, you may think, as you look at them all, that there is one and the same idea in them, and hence you think the great is one'.
>
> 'That is true', he [Socrates] said.

---

4. Alexander Miller states the point explicitly: 'as many commentators have pointed out, the paragraph in *Philosophical Investigations* which follows this one [i.e., the first paragraph of §201] shows that contrary to what Kripke claims, Wittgenstein does not accept the skeptical paradox that there is no such thing as a fact about meaning' (Miller 2004, 132). What the nature of this fact is, however, remains a question – it's the 'constitutive question' Wright mentions.

'But if with your mind's eye you regard the absolute great and these many great things in the same way, will not another great appear beyond, by which all these must appear to be great?'

'So it seems'.

'That is, another idea of greatness will appear, in addition to absolute greatness and the objects which partake of it; and another again in addition to these, by reason of which they are all great; and each of your ideas will no longer be one, but their number will be infinite. (*Parmenides* 132a-b)

If a rule functions like an Idea, and it is a single rule that can be iterated infinitely many times in the particular cases of following the rule, then the problem is that we need another rule to relate this rule to the particular case before us, and then a rule to relate that rule to the rule that relates the rule to the particular case, and so on. The implication being that if we are to avoid scepticism and ever be justified in how we use a rule, then the assumption is that we must also avoid a regress. Wittgenstein appears to accept this assumption, hence the anti-sceptical moves he makes. What we will argue here, however, is that if we understand rule-following as a process of making sense, then we can both avoid scepticism and address the 'constitutive question'. Central to this approach is the embrace of an infinite regress, and it is at this point that I will adopt Deleuze's theory of sense. In particular, I will take on Deleuze's claim, early in *The Logic of Sense*, that sense entails a paradoxical infinite regress:

> Sense is always presupposed as soon as I begin to speak; I would not be able to begin without this presupposition. In other words, I never state the sense of what I am saying. But on the other hand, I can always take the sense of what I say as the object of another proposition whose sense, in turn, I cannot state. I thus enter into the infinite regress of that which is presupposed. This regress testifies both to the great impotence of the speaker and to the highest power of language: my impotence to state the sense of what I say, to say at the same time something and its meaning; but also the infinite power of language to speak about words. (Deleuze 1990b, 28–9)

The 'infinite power of language to speak about words' reflects the differentiating tendency of sense, the power of sense to open an infinite regress of further attempts to express the sense of what was said. At the same time this infinite regress reflects the dedifferentiating tendency of sense in that each time something meaningful is said by way of a determinate expression or statement, the sense of this expression moves contrary to the determinate, differentiating nature of expressions and statements, and it is this dedifferentiating move that accounts for the need to say something more and hence for the infinite regress of attempts to express 'the sense of what I am saying'. This infinite regress, however, is not fatal to the act of saying something meaningful, nor to feeling justified in believing you have understood the sense of what someone else has said. One can express one's thoughts clearly. That said, however, the determinate nature of our thoughts and expressions presupposes an infinite regress, and there are important implications that follow from this. To see how this is so, although this theme was also explored at great length in the *Inquiry*, we can turn to the work of Peter Klein, who has also embraced infinite regresses while maintaining that this does not lead to scepticism.

According to Klein, there are two principles at work in the classic infinite regress arguments that support the assumptions that Wittgenstein and most others make in concluding that a regress ought to be avoided. The first is the 'Principle of Avoiding Circularity' (PAC), which Klein states as follows: 'For all x, if a person, S, has a justification for x, then for all y, if y is in the evidential ancestry of x for S, then x is not in the evidential ancestry of y for S' (Klein 1999, 299). To take an example from Hume's *Dialogues Concerning Natural Religion*, Philo (Hume's surrogate) challenges accounts where it is claimed, for instance, that 'bread nourished by its nutritive faculty, senna purged by its purgative … In like manner when it is asked, what cause produces order in the ideas of the supreme being, can any other reason be assigned by you, anthropomorphites [meaning Cleanthes], than that it is a rational faculty, and that such is the nature of the deity?' (Hume 2007, 4.12). In other words, if the justification given by S, or Cleanthes, for x, x being here the cause that produces order in the ideas of the supreme being, y, or x being the cause that produces nutrition, y, etc., and if x is the rational nature of the deity, then one would have violated PAC since the rational nature of the deity, or x, is simply another way of referring to the order in the ideas of the supreme being, or y, just as citing the nutritive faculty as the cause that makes bread nourishing is simply another way of saying that bread is nourishing. To state the problem here in Klein's terms, x is being used as evidence for x.

The second principle at work in the classic regress arguments is the 'Principle of Avoiding Arbitrariness' (PAA), which Klein states as follows: 'For all x, if a person, S, has a justification for x, then there is some reason r_1, available to S for x; and there is some reason, r_2, available to S for r_1; etc.' (Klein 1999, 299). Returning again to Hume's *Dialogues*, we find this principle being implicitly used against Cleanthes. In response to Cleanthes' argument that one can account for the material world by grounding it in the ideas of God, Philo asks Cleanthes how we can account for 'the ideal world, into which you [Cleanthes] trace the material? Have we not the same reason to trace the ideal world into another ideal world, or new intelligent principle? But if we stop, and go no farther; why go so far? Why not stop at the material world? How can we satisfy ourselves without going *in infinitum*?' (Hume 2007, 4.9). If the justification for the material world is the ideal world, or some reason r_1, then if we are to avoid simply stopping, arbitrarily, at reason r_1, there must be another reason r_2 for r_1, and another reason for r_2, and so on *ad infinitum*. But then we never get to the reason which accounts for the material world, Hume argues, and thus sceptical doubts come to haunt Cleanthes' claims.

With these two principles in play, infinite regress arguments can then be used to justify either scepticism, as Sextus Empiricus did, or foundationalism when one calls upon a brute fact or a primitive intuition, both of which require no justification and yet serve as the justification or reason for everything else (in the manner of Aristotle's unmoved mover). For Klein these arguments generally take the form of a *reductio* (drawing from Klein 2007, 3–4). Beginning with the assumption that (1) everything we know is the result of reasoning from premises to conclusions, then (2) this series either does or does not have a first premise. If (3) it does not have a first premise, then knowledge is not possible, as Sextus Empiricus and the Pyrrhonian sceptics concluded. If there is a first premise, then (4) either it has appeared earlier in the series or it hasn't. If it has appeared earlier, then (5) a reason or premise is being used in the justification of its own use. At this point we have violated PAC and thus knowledge is not gained. If the premise or reason has not appeared earlier in the series, then (6) it is simply being assumed to be true without justification, which in turn does not bring about knowledge that is justified by reasons. Here we have a violation of PAA. As Klein draws the argument to a close at this point, it seems that if knowledge is indeed what we come to acquire through reasoning from premises to conclusions, then (7) there would be no knowledge; but since (8) there clearly seems to be knowledge, we thus come to the conclusion, from a *reductio* of 1–8 above, that knowledge is therefore not the result of reasoning from premises. It is at this point that one of two approaches is taken, according to Klein. One can accept the sceptical conclusion, as Sextus Empiricus does, or one can call upon a form of knowledge that is not the result of reasoning from premises, but is instead the result of an intuitive grasp of brute facts that require no justifications or reasons (this was an important theme in the *Inquiry*). Wittgenstein, as we saw, wants to avoid scepticism, and the regresses he likely assumed to be the source of the sceptical consequences, but we were left with the constitutive question of precisely what justified, for Wittgenstein, how we follow a rule, especially in a novel situation. Wittgenstein appealed to a form of life that is not to be confused with shared opinions or beliefs, beliefs that are taken to be either true or false, nor with a primitive 'intuitive voice'. But what is a form of life?

Klein provides us with an opening through which we can begin to offer an account of what a form of life might entail, at least on the arguments to be developed below (and with full recognition that Wittgenstein might not countenance these arguments as extensions of his own). The first step in this account is to accept Klein's embrace of what he calls infinitism. Key to Klein's understanding of infinitism is the rejection of the third premise mentioned above, namely the assumption that if a series of reasons does not have a first reason, if it is not a finite series of reasons and premises, then knowledge is not possible. For Klein there is always another reason to be given, or as he puts it, the 'infinitist is claiming that a normatively acceptable set of reasons must be infinitely long and non-repeating if we are to avoid the pitfalls of foundationalism' (Klein 1998, 922). The main pitfall for a foundationalist, Klein argues, occurs when one appeals to a reason that needs no further support and justification – in short, the issue is one of avoiding PAA. For Klein this is achieved simply by accepting that there is an infinite series of reasons, an infinite regress; in other words, rather than undermining knowledge, as the sceptics do, or moving to a foundationalism to avoid the regress, Klein bites the bullet and accepts the reality of an infinite series. But how does this help us with the constitutive question, with justifying how one follows a rule, and how one does so without falling into scepticism all over again?

Klein's solution is bold – he simply rejects the assumption that an infinite series of reasons undermines the possibility of having a legitimate justification for a knowledge claim. The assumption that an infinite series does undermine such a claim only works, Klein argues, on the basis of a false dilemma which asserts that *either* one has a complete list of reasons to justify one's knowledge claim, what Klein calls the 'completion requirement' (Klein 1999, 314), *or* one does not have a legitimate claim to know something. For Klein there is a third possibility, namely that there may be sufficient justifications or reasons *relevant* to the circumstances at hand. To use Klein's own example, the claim 'that a snowstorm is likely' may well be justified if certain 'objective availability constraints' are satisfied, and the belief 'that dark clouds are gathering over the mountains and it is mid-winter in Montana' (300) satisfies these constraints. What Klein has in mind here regarding objective availability constraints is rather straightforward. Among the constraints he lists (there are seven in all [299]) is that the reason for a particular belief be of sufficiently high probability and, a further constraint, that an impartial and informed observer would also accept the reason given as justification for the claim being made. The claim that it is likely to snow would satisfy these constraints if it is indeed highly probable that the gathering of dark clouds over the mountains in mid-winter Montana is evidence for the claim, and that an impartial, informed observer such as a Montanan, for instance, would also accept this as evidence for the claim. In addition to these objective availability constraints, Klein also claims there are subjective availability constraints: 'There might be a good reason, r, that is objectively available for use by any person [the dark clouds billowing in the west for instance], but unless it is properly hooked up with S's own beliefs, r will not be subjectively available to S' (300). A person unfamiliar with Montana weather patterns may well not make use of a reason that is objectively available to others (i.e., to Montanans). Klein's arguments are more complex and nuanced than I have presented them here, but the basic point is that although there may well be an infinite series of reasons that one could continue to offer, at some point the *relevant* reasons will have been provided, given the context, and so a knowledge claim will be justified for all intents and purposes. All that infinitism entails, Klein concludes, in an echo of Russell's 'Liberal tentativeness', is that

> Nothing is ever completely settled, but as S engages in the process of providing reasons for her beliefs they become better justified – not because S is getting closer to completing the task, but rather because S has provided more reasons for her belief. How far forward in providing reasons S need go seems to me to be a matter of the pragmatic features of the epistemic context. (Klein 2007, 10)

To clarify Klein's point regarding the 'pragmatic features of the epistemic context', and how these features determine whether the relevant reasons are both subjectively and objectively available, we can turn now to some recent work in the psychology of reasoning. This work traces its lineage back to Aleksandr Luria, whose 1931–2 studies of illiterate villagers in the remote regions of Uzbekistan and Kirghizia provide insights into the relevance of epistemic contexts (e.g., literate or non-literate contexts) and how this relevance affects the manner in which one reasons.

c) Relevance

In his 1931–2 studies, Aleksandr Luria set out to determine the extent to which cultural factors affect how one thinks about oneself and one's world. Extending the work of his colleague, Lev Vygotsky, Luria hypothesised 'that people with a primarily graphic-functional reflection of reality would show a different system of mental process from people with a predominantly abstract, verbal, and logical approach to reality' (Luria 1976, 18). Since the villagers Luria studied were illiterate, he believed they would most likely think in a graphic-functional manner than in an abstract, verbal and logical manner. His studies were intended to test this hypothesis. In one experiment concerning the use of categories, Luria found resistance among illiterate villagers who, when shown pictures of a hammer, saw, log and hatchet, were asked which three of the four could be grouped together, hence leaving one of the pictures out. A villager from Yardan, for instance, said "'They all fit here! The saw has to saw the log, the hammer has to hammer it, and the hatchet has to chop it ... You can't take any of these things away'" (58). Those with an education and an ability to read would readily exclude the log, given that the other three are all tools and the log is not. The villager, apparently, lacked the abstract category 'tool' as a way of categorising their world. Luria found that solving reasoning problems was equally difficult for the villagers. When given the following syllogism – 'In the Far North, where there is snow, all bears are white. Novaya Zemlya is in the Far North. What color are bears there?' – a typical response was either to refuse to make any inferences at all or to add qualifiers such as pointing out that 'they "had never been in the North and had never seen bears; to answer the question you would have to ask people who had been there and seen them'" (107). The conclusion Luria draws from this and other examples along these lines is that 'the formal operation of problem-solving presents major, sometimes insurmountable difficulties for these subjects' (132).

More recent studies have come to a different conclusion regarding Luria's observations. Sylvia Scribner, for instance, has argued that there is no failure or lack in the reasoning and problem-solving abilities of the villagers; they were simply unfamiliar with the *closed* nature of the formal language genre, or language-game to use a Wittgensteinian term, in which the problems were posed. When given a problem the villagers looked beyond what was given and considered other relevant possibilities from which a conclusion could be drawn, rather than simply drawing their conclusion solely from the premises, as is done in a closed argument. For example, take the problem:

All people who own houses pay a house tax.

Boima does not pay a house tax

Does Boima own a house?

In cases such as this, Scribner found that those who were familiar with the language-game of formal problem-solving would usually provide a theoretical justification such as "'If you say Boima does not pay a house tax, he cannot own a house'", while those less familiar with the genre would provide an empirical justification: "'Boima does not have money to pay a house tax'" (Scribner 1977, 489). They would thus look beyond the premises themselves to find a reason why Boima does not pay a house tax. Familiarity with the formal language-game, however, is not the only factor at work here. In one of his studies of the Kpelle tribesmen, Joseph Glick found that the relevance of the reasons to the situation at hand is often the overriding factor. When

Glick asked the tribesmen to group objects in accordance with the abstract categories of food and tools, they would instead group the potato with the hoe, the orange with the knife, etc. This observation was in line with Luria's, but out of curiosity Glick asked them 'how a fool would do it?' (Glick 1975, 635), and they promptly grouped the food together and the tools together. In short, while the Kpelle tribesmen were familiar with the abstract categories of tools and food, they simply saw these categories as irrelevant to their concerns and to the problem before them. Such categories were only relevant to fools.

More recent work in philosophy and cognitive science reinforces many of the claims Scribner, Glick and others have made. In their book *Human Reasoning and Cognitive Science* (2008), Keith Stenning and Michiel van Lambalgen argued that traditional views of classical logic need to be supplemented with a semantics that determines the relevance or significance of the situation at hand. For Stenning and Lambalgen this first entails reasoning to an interpretation of the situation, to the relevant scope and domain that is at issue, and only then, they argue, do we begin with the more traditional reasoning from this situation to the inferences and conclusions that follow. To clarify, we can take a standard classical example. If it is true that all cats are mammals and true that all mammals are animals, then the logical conclusion one can draw from these two claims or premises is that all cats are animals. As Stenning and Lambalgen point out, one can abstract a schema from classical logical arguments such as this. With the example just given, the schema would be as follows:

All A are B

All B are C

Therefore, all A are C.

The validity of this schema is taken to mean something like 'whatever you substitute for A, B and C, if the premises are true for the substitution, then so is the conclusion'. (Stenning and van Lambalgen 2008, 20)

Instead of cats, mammals and animals, I could substitute anything – say baseball, sport and non-essential pastime – and as long as the premises are true, the conclusion, in each and every case, will logically follow. If we look at our earlier example of whether or not Boima owns a house since he doesn't pay a house tax, one could think, as Luria likely did, that the villagers do not understand the formal schema associated with this argument. The formal schema in this case would be the standard modus tollens argument, where the substitutions would go as follows: If you own a house, then you pay a house tax. Boima does not pay a house tax. Therefore, Boima does not own a house. The modus tollens schema has the following form:

19

$$A \supset B$$
$$\underline{\sim B}$$
$$\therefore \sim A$$

As one of the basic rules in classical logic, the modus tollens schema will give us a valid conclusion no matter what we substitute for A or B, as long as the premises are true after the substitution. If I substitute 'it rains this afternoon' for A and 'get wet' for B, and if it is both true that if it rains this afternoon then I get wet and true that I do not get wet, then the logically valid conclusion is that it did not rain this afternoon. For Stenning and Lambalgen, the relevant point is that 'This schematic character of inference patterns is identified with the "domain-independence" or "topic neutrality" of logic generally, and many take it to be the principal interest of logic that its laws seem independent of subject matter' (Stenning and van Lambalgen 2008, 20). Moreover, the fact that the villagers do not immediately jump to the conclusion that follows by the modus tollens schema, namely that Boima does not own a house, would seem to lend support to Luria's own conclusion that the 'formal operation of problem-solving presents major, sometimes insurmountable difficulties for these subjects' (Luria 1976, 132). In short, they lack a grasp of an important formal schema associated with classical logic.

This conclusion would be mistaken, however, for as Scribner, Glick and others have shown, what is important is not whether the formal schema is known or not, but whether it is deemed relevant to the problem at hand. This is just the point Stenning and Lambalgen will claim is critical, and it is at the heart of their semantic approach to logic. As they put it, rather than being domain-independent or topic neutral, 'logic is very much domain dependent in the sense that the valid schemata depend on the domain in which one reasons, *with what purpose*' (Stenning and van Lambalgen 2008, 20). In other words, the schema to be used is dependent upon its relevance to the situation at hand. There are many instances where people do not follow the modus tollens formal schema, as the many Wason selection task studies have shown,[5] but given the domain at hand other relevant factors may come into play. For example, given an inference equivalent to the Boima example – if you drink alcohol here (A), then you have to be over 21 (B); this person is not over 21 (~B); therefore, they are not drinking alcohol here (~A) – one could find at college campuses many in the bars who would not draw this conclusion, and the relevant domain would lead them to consider factors beyond the premises alone.[6]

---

5. For the classic study, see Wason 1968. Stenning and van Lambalgen (2008) discuss a number of the experiments this one inspired.
6. This was indeed the result of an experiment conducted by Griggs and Cox (1982), cited by Stenning and van Lambalgen 2008, 46.

Returning to the problem of rule-following, and to the constitutive question Wittgenstein left us with: rather than worry about the justification or interpretation that tells us how to follow a rule, an interpretation that needs another, and so on *ad infinitum*, we can accept this regress and focus instead, as Klein argues, on the pragmatic features of the epistemic context, or the 'domain dependent' nature of the reasoning and justification one is providing. Stated in the terms we introduced earlier, the nature of the problem as the problem of making sense is what provides the pragmatic epistemic context that allows us to determine the rule that is then used to guide one's actions. The rule-as-rail is thus the result of reasoning to an interpretation or solution of the problem; and yet the problem remains – another interpretation or solution is always possible, just as the infinite regress remains inseparable from the reasons listed.[7] To mention briefly an example that will become prominent below (at §1.3.c): after discussing an experiment in which monkeys learned to find food under boxes of a particular colour, Deleuze makes the point that 'Learning is the appropriate name for the subjective acts carried out when one is confronted with the objecticity (*objectité*) of a problem (Idea), whereas knowledge designates only the generality of concepts or the calm possession of a rule enabling solutions' (Deleuze 1994, 164). Before they come to know that the food is always under boxes of a particular colour, for the monkeys there is 'a paradoxical period during which the number of "errors" diminishes even though the monkey does not yet possess the "knowledge" or "truth" of a solution' (164). This paradoxical period is precisely when one encounters the nature of the problem, or the problem of making sense as we have put it, and thus there occurs here both the movement of dedifferentiation – the un-learning of established habits, routines and expectations – and the movement of differentiation – differentiating the elements that are relevant to the given problem (the coloured boxes, food, etc., in the case of the monkey experi-ment). Neither movement attains the full realisation of its tendency, and yet the solution can and often does come to be seen as a rule separate and distinct from the actions done in accordance with the rule. This latter tendency to see rules as separate and distinct from the actions done in accordance with them is especially relevant to thinking about politics, and this will become the focus of our attention in the final chapter. What emerges, as we will

---

7. There is a key difference between the understanding of problems we will be using and the infinite regresses the infinitist embraces. When Klein accepts an infinite regress, he accepts that one could continue to list determinate reasons ad infinitum, but the 'pragmatic features of the epistemic context' ultimately render continuing down this path irrelevant. Problems, by contrast, are not determinate but are rather the condition presupposed by that which is determinate. Determinate solutions, for instance, presuppose the nature of a problem that is indeterminate, and yet is the condition for determinate solutions.

see, is a situation where those who govern have the power to bring people into accordance with their will (or their rules and laws), and this power, this fact that people act in accordance with the rules of those who govern, is itself made possible by the nature of a problem that provides the conditions of relevance (as I will call it). On my reading, these conditions of relevance are what Wittgenstein was gesturing towards when he recognised that there is an 'agreement' that makes knowing how to follow a rule possible, but an agreement 'not in opinions, but rather in form of life' (Wittgenstein 2009, §241). We will return to this theme in the final chapter after having set forth various ways in which the problem of making sense allows us to think through a number of other relevant issues, issues that will set the stage for our discussion of some key concepts frequently associated with liberalism. With this return to politics, and to Wittgenstein, we will also be able to address what Hume takes to be a surprising, if not mysterious fact, as he presents it in a famous passage from the beginning of his essay, 'Of the First Principles of Government':

> Nothing appears more surprizing to those, who consider human affairs with a philosophical eye, than the easiness with which the many are governed by the few; and the implicit submission, with which men resign their own sentiments and passions to those of their rulers. When we enquire by what means this wonder is effected, we shall find, that, as Force is always on the side of the governed, the governors have nothing to support them but opinion. It is therefore, on opinion only that government is founded; and this maxim extends to the most despotic and most military governments, as well as to the most free and most popular. (Hume 1985, 32).

As we will see, the opinions Hume has in mind here are not those that can be stated in propositional form and with a corresponding truth value; rather, the opinion that founds government is rooted in the problem of making sense, and it is this problem that accounts for the power relations between those who govern and those who are governed, relations that emerge as the resulting solutions that express the problem of making sense. Power relations thus speak to the very problems that people encounter, and the forms of power that emerge do not solve or exhaust the nature of the problem, nor is the solution necessarily the one the problem deserves (as we will see §1.3.c). One possible solution to the problem of making sense, for instance, as Polanyi pointed out, is fascism, and this is a solution that continues to subsist within current power relations. Foucault's famous questions from his preface to Deleuze and Guattari's *Anti-Oedipus* thus remain equally pressing for our times: 'How does one keep from being a fascist, even (especially) when one believes oneself to be a revolutionary militant? How do we rid our speech and our acts, our hearts and our pleasures, of fascism? How do we ferret out the fascism that is ingrained in our behavior?' (Deleuze and Guattari 1977, xiii). Although the fascist solution is one possibility, in the pages to follow we will chart a path that reveals the many different ways in which the problem of making sense may come to be expressed and resolved, and often resolved as a solution without a problem. As these themes become interweaved in subsequent chapters, we will by the final chapter be in a position to draw the threads together to provide a critical existentialism, as I will call it, that may help us to 'ferret out the fascism that is ingrained in our behavior'.

d) Chapter summaries

To begin this process, the first chapter will explore the problems of making sense by turning to Camus, Proust and Hume, with the stress here being on the problem of making sense of life. This will set the stage for later arguments where the existential tradition is brought in to reconceptualise and revitalise traditional views of freedom, which in the existential tradition is largely taken to be paradoxically bound to the concrete situation of one's life. In preparation of this theme, we will turn to Spinoza to explain how, for him, a blessed and joyful life consists in understanding our finite selves as expressions of the absolutely infinite nature of God. This will enable us to show how problems are infinite – not in the determinate sense but absolutely infinite in Spinoza's sense – and hence how they entail a form of infinitism. From here we will pick up the thread of Hume, as mentioned above, and shift our attention to his essay 'Of the Standard of Taste'. Turning to Hume at this point will allow us to clarify the relation between problems and solutions, and more precisely Deleuze's claim that 'A solution always has the truth it deserves' (Deleuze 1994, 159). This truth, we shall argue, expresses the nature of a problem and as such is provisional, tentative, and is not a solution or truth without a problem. Truths or solutions understood to be solutions without a problem are not, to use Deleuze's phrase, solutions with the truth they deserve. It is with this distinction in hand that we turn to Hume's essay on taste to show how it is that problems are not there waiting to be discovered but must be constructed amidst and with that which is determinate and given to us in life, in our concrete situations, and constructed with the 'consistence and uniformity', to use Hume's phrase (Hume 1985, 240), that makes solutions possible. Following Hume's lead we will argue that what ought to be developed, in life and in politics, is a taste for problems.

Chapter 2 will begin explicating the nature of this taste by clarifying the relationships between problems and solutions. I will do this by contrasting the problem of making sense with the process of communicating information. Building on Claude Shannon's work I will set forth a distinction between signs and signals in light of the problem/solution distinction being developed here. Whereas Shannon attempted to reduce communication to a signalling of information between endpoints, signs are expressive of problems, and as such communication through signs always entails the possibility of miscommunication. To clarify this point further, and see it in light of the problem of making sense of life itself, I will turn to work on territoriality in animals, highlighting the territorialising process – that is, the use of signs in the process of acquiring territory – rather than, as is more commonly done among ethologists, focusing on the signalling behaviour of animals once they have come to occupy a territory. This focus on the territorialising process will allow us to return to and clarify human communication, and most especially the importance of narratives in making sense of life, including the death and loss inseparable from life. Claude Steele's self-affirmation studies will provide a window onto the role narratives play in making sense of life, while Heidegger's concept of authenticity in the face of death will allow us to develop a distinction between authentic and forced narratives, a distinction that will become increasingly important to the critical existentialism that will be developed and used to discuss some key concepts associated with political theory.

In Chapter 3 we will continue with the Heideggerian theme of the role of authentic narratives in our lives, narratives that will be contrasted with forced narratives. The latter, we shall argue, can be helpfully understood if we think of them along the lines of the forms of arbitrary power that classical republicans challenged. In adopting many of the reasons classical republicans offer against arbitrary power, we will be able to further develop our arguments against forced narratives and in favour of authentic narratives. In this discussion we will begin to see the relevance of classical republicanism for rethinking some key concerns of the existential tradition, and in particular the distinction between good faith and bad faith that is found, in one form or another, in a number of the existential writers. In closing this chapter, and to solidify the distinction between forced and authentic narratives, we will see that conspiracy narratives provide a good example of a forced narrative. The example of conspiracy narratives will also allow us to interweave into the discussion the work on self-affirmation studies that is an important theme in Chapter 2.

In Chapter 4 we will turn to a number of arguments from the writers who have come to be identified as existentialists, and use their work to continue clarifying the relationship between problems and solutions. Beginning with Kierkegaard's understanding of despair as set forth in his *Sickness Unto*

Death, we will argue that Kierkegaard, Nietzsche, Sartre and Camus are each sensitive to a paradoxical, dual tendency in human existence. For Kierkegaard this paradox is bound up with becoming oneself, a becoming that 'must be an infinite moving away from itself in the infinitizing of the self, and an infinite coming back to itself in the finitizing process' (Kierkegaard 1980b, 30). In various ways we will find this double movement at work in each of the existentialists, and as we have seen it is also at work in Deleuze's theory of sense, which entails both dedifferentiating and differentiating tendencies. To clarify the existential tradition's relationship to political critique, we will then discuss Theodor Adorno's criticism of existentialism, and most prominently of Heidegger, in his book *The Jargon of Authenticity* (1964). By understanding the existential tradition in light of the paradoxical double movement Kierkegaard highlights, a double movement that is nothing less than the nature of a problem as argued for here, we will be able to obviate Adorno's criticisms of Heidegger and in fact bring Adorno's thought into the mix as we develop a critical existentialism. As with the critical theory developed and deployed by Adorno, Horkheimer and others from the Frankfurt School, a critical existentialism challenges the traditional understanding of theory as a series of propositions about a subject that is separate from the theory itself. For critical theory, by contrast, and as argued for here, theory is part of a 'dynamic unity' between 'the theoretician and his specific object' (Horkheimer 2002, 215). In response to social injustice, for instance, a critical theorist sets out to facilitate 'a transformation of society as a whole' (219), but there is a tension between the fact that the theorist engages in 'the critique of the existing order' and the fact that this very 'struggle against it [the existing order] ... [is] determined by the theory itself' (229). There is thus a tension for a critical theorist between their aspiration to offer a critique of the existing social order and the inseparability of their efforts, including their theorising, from the order itself. To resolve this tension, Horkheimer calls upon 'more specific elements ... in order to move from the fundamental structure to concrete reality' (225). In other words, an interdisciplinary effort is necessary to connect the lives of individuals in their concrete circumstances to the 'basic form of the historically given commodity economy on which modern history rests' (227). It is at this point that the critical existentialism developed here parts ways with critical theory. Rather than attempt to bring determinate facts, or 'specific elements', to bear in the effort to shuttle back and forth between the social order as a whole and the concrete situations that are part of this order, the existentialism-inspired understanding of problems at play here will show that problems are irreducible to any determinate facts, whether of the whole, parts or specific elements; it is the nature of problems to serve as the condition for the possibility of such determinate facts, and of the relationships between them. Moreover, problems are inseparable from such facts and relations and thus forever threaten to undermine and problematise them, revealing the problems that are inseparable from facts and relations that are taken to be solutions without a problem. Revealing the problems that are inseparable from solutions is the task of critical existentialism, and with that approach in hand I will return, in the final chapter, to the themes with which we began; namely, to Russell's faith in the 'Liberal creed' and the 'tentativeness' this entails.

In the fifth and final chapter we will continue with the effort to rethink and revitalise a number of ideas commonly associated with the liberal tradition – most notably the concepts of freedom, law and progress – by focusing on the problem of making sense. We will highlight the dual de/differentiating tendencies of making sense, and most importantly the illusion that comes with them – what we have called the illusion of a solution without a problem. Starting with Tim Ingold's work, and his important concept of the carto-graphic illusion – the illusion that a map is simply 'a direct transcription of the layout of the world' (Ingold 2000, 234) – we will then return to the constitutive question Wittgenstein left us with, the question of how human agreement as form of life accounts for the possibility of rules, or how it is that 'government is founded on opinion' as Hume put it. The process and problem of making sense, it will be argued, is continually moving in contrasting direc-tions (de/differentiating) without fully realising the immanent tendencies of either, and it is for the problem that is inseparable from this process that the existential philosophers, along with Deleuze and others, have developed an important if underappreciated taste. By drawing from the existential tradition, and highlighting the nature of life as a problem, we will show how politics is one of many provisional solutions to the problem that is life. One solution that will be of particular focus in this chapter, and where Hume's claim that 'government is founded on opinion' becomes salient, is the solution that stresses negative liberty, or the view that we ought to be free to act without interference as long as we act within the limits of the law, which is thought to be external to the actions that are done within the constraints of the law. The solution to Wittgenstein's rule-following paradox that I will develop here, along with the critical existentialism being deployed, will challenge and problematise negative liberty. This in turn will have consequences for how we think about law, government and progress, among other things. In the end, therefore, if we are to follow Foucault's call to 'ferret out the fascism that is ingrained in our behavior' (Deleuze and Guattari 1977, xiii), then the task, I argue, will be precisely that of acquiring a taste for problems, a taste that may well lead us to a point where the life we live stops making sense. This book attempts to provide a way of thinking through the nature of this task.

§1 Making Sense of Life

1. Signs of Jealousy

a) ... to be undermined

Early in his essay, 'The Myth of Sisyphus', Camus offers the example of an apartment manager who committed suicide five years after his daughter's death. It was said that since her death 'he had changed greatly ... and that that experience had "undermined" him'. For Camus, 'A more exact word cannot be imagined' than 'undermined'. 'Beginning to think', he adds, 'is beginning to be undermined' (Camus 1955, 4). We can imagine, in part, what the apartment manager's thinking must have entailed and why it became undermining. He no doubt tried to think through his situation and make sense of it – why did this happen? how have things changed? what will I do now?, among many other questions. As we can also imagine, the apartment manager would not have been satisfied with a simple causal explanation of the event, or with reassurances from others that his affairs were in order. Camus does not tell us how the daughter died. The apartment manager most likely did know, and yet this is not what he wants to know when he wants to know why it happened. What he wants to know goes beyond the concrete details, the specific facts that might fill the pages of a police report or news story. This is why Camus stresses that suicide is a philosophical problem rather than a 'social phenomenon', and why the efforts of the apartment manager to make sense of his situation could not be accomplished through the kind of objective reporting and fact gathering that may be appropriate for those who see suicide as a social problem. Camus thus claims that 'we are concerned here, at the outset, with the relationship between individual thought and suicide' (4). No matter what one might have said to the apartment manager, it would not have been what he was looking for. It was this disparity between his thinking, his efforts to make sense of the situation, and the inadequacy of anything to respond to this thinking, which undermined him.

It is not hard for us to empathise with the plight of the apartment manager. Although we may consider suicide to be an extreme response to the inability to make satisfactory sense of one's situation, we can nonetheless recognise the problem that confronted the apartment manager – the problem of making sense. There are times in most people's lives where circumstances unfold in such a way that one encounters the difficulty of making sense of what happened. Perhaps there were too many strange coincidences to chalk the event up as a random occurrence. There's something more, we may think, that connects the facts and circumstances together such that they make sense. There must be, we may think, an underlying reason or purpose for why things happened as they did. For some, the providential power of God makes sense of situations such as these, as what accounts for the fact that all the events conspired together just as they did, and for a reason or purpose, even if this reason or purpose is one we cannot understand. For others, the laws of nature and the chain of cause and effect are sufficient explanations, even if they do not satisfy our desire to find a meaning or purpose in events. For them, there is just natural causality and things don't happen for a reason or purpose – there is no teleology in nature and our desire for such is just a useless passion, as Sartre might put it.[1] Camus challenges both approaches, and the problem of suicide is a problem for Camus precisely because there is no objective criterion or standard – whether supernatural or natural – that can satisfy the desire to make sense of life. If there were such a standard, a person could be given a reason or purpose for living; but since there is not, Camus argues, one is left wondering and thinking why one should continue living at all, and hence the problem of suicide emerges.

We will return to the problem of suicide below, but I want first to arrive at this problem by another path – this time the path of jealousy and delusion. This will help us to clarify the disparity between the apartment manager's efforts to make sense of his situation and the ways of making sense that Camus rules out as unsatisfactory. Let us take the jealous lover first. In cases of jealousy the ordinary, expected interpretations of facts may well be passed up for more extraordinary, unexpected interpretations. In Luis Buñuel's film *Él*, for example, the jealous older husband is convinced that on their wedding night his new bride is thinking about her former fiancée, and he confronts her with this accusation. His new wife is stupefied, not so much by the fact that her husband is wrong, which he surely is in her eyes, but because of the absurdity of the accusation itself, of the fact that her husband would even entertain such a delusional thought on their wedding night. As the narrative of the film unfolds, the husband's jealousy continues and he begins to be

---

1. Referring here to the famous closing lines of Sartre's *Being and Nothingness* where – after more than 600 pages showing how our consciousness, as a being-for-itself, can never be something in the sense that an inkwell is an inkwell, or we can never become a being-in-itself-for-itself, as he puts it – he concludes that we nonetheless desire to be a being-in-itself-for-itself. Thus his closing line: 'Man is a useless passion' (Sartre 1956, 615).

undermined. While at a hotel on their honeymoon, for instance, he leaps to the conclusion that an acquaintance of his wife is now stalking them; in another scene the laughs of others are interpreted as being laughter at him; and towards the end of the film he succumbs to delusion altogether and sees a crowd of churchgoers, along with the priest, all break out into uproarious laughter at him, even though none of them were laughing at all. What jealousy such as this teaches us, therefore, is that the search for meaning takes us, even if illegitimately so, beyond what is determinately given.

Marcel Proust was well aware of this tendency to move beyond what is given, and of the excesses to which the jealous person may succumb. In his novel *The Prisoner*, the narrator admits that his nature had 'always made [him] more open to the world of the possible than to that of real-life contingencies', and it is this openness that results in the need

> to find within oneself a prefect of police, a clear-sighted diplomat, a head of criminal investigation who, instead of letting his mind wander among all the possibilities between here and the four corners of the universe, reasons logically and says to himself, 'If Germany announces this, it's because she wants to do something else, not any odd thing at random, but precisely this or that …' – 'If such-and-such a person has escaped, he will not be heading for a, b, or d, but for c, and the place to begin our search is, *etc.*' (Proust 2003, 13)

What is needed to counter the undermining tendency of thinking, therefore, and especially the thinking of one who is jealous, is to consider what the probabilities would have us do. What is the expected, usual thing to do in situations such as this? Where do the facts themselves lead, based on similar past circumstances and sets of facts? This was *not* how the jealous narrator of *The Prisoner* thought, however, and he readily acknowledged that 'Reality is always a mere starting-point towards the unknown, on a path down which we can never travel very far. It is better not to know, to think as little as possible, not to feed jealousy on the smallest concrete detail' (Proust 2003, 13). To state this point in Camus' terms, when the jealous person begins to think, each little fact leads beyond the fact itself to an interpretation no longer justified by the fact, and the more facts and details this thinking is fed the more the reality of the jealous person is undermined by the delusional ways in which they make sense of everything around them.

What the thinking of the grieving father and the jealous lover have in common, on the interpretation proposed here, is that they are making sense of signs, and hence making sense of the reality the signs are taken to be signs of (for more on signs, see §2.1). The father treats the facts as signs of a reality that would provide these facts with a meaning or purpose; the jealous lover sees factual details and behaviours as signs of a reality that would justify their jealousy. In both cases, and in many others besides, Camus' caution is warranted: 'Beginning to think is beginning to be undermined.' On this view, thinking is a process that comes with risks – and quite serious ones, as was Camus' point – in that thinking does not hew to the determinate facts that are given but moves beyond them in order to make sense of them, and it is this process of making sense that forever risks succumbing to delusion and delirium, to thinking a thought that undermines one's credibility, social standing and, in the extreme, one's life. This, in short, is the problem of making sense, and Camus and Proust are attuned to this problem. They are far from the only ones, however, for Hume, among others to be discussed in due course, was also attentive to the problem of making sense, to the process whereby thinking and delirium are, at a fundamental level, inseparable.

b) Hume and delirium

Just as the narrator in Proust's *The Prisoner* was aware of his own tendency to be 'more open to the world of the possible than to that of real-life contingencies' (Proust 2003, 13), and subsequently let his imagination run wild in formulating extraordinary realities in line with his jealousy, so too for Hume the imagination is open to infinite possibilities, each one of which, as conceived, is plausible. This is one of Hume's claims that has received the most attention.[2] For Hume, this point is non-controversial,

> 'Tis an establish'd maxim in metaphysics, that whatever the mind clearly conceives includes the idea of possible existence, or in other words, that nothing we imagine is absolutely impossible. We can form the idea of a golden mountain, and from thence conclude that such a mountain may actually exist. We can form no idea of a mountain without a valley, and therefore regard it as impossible. (Hume 1978, 1.2.2.8; SB 32).[3]

As Hume makes clear, there is a line to be drawn between that which is conceivable and that which is not. A mountain without a valley is inconceivable, and a square circle is inconceivable, for by the nature and definition of one it either includes (e.g., a valley) or excludes (square) the other. In infinitely many other cases, however, one can be thought with the other – golden with mountain for instance – and with these cases the imagination

---

2. For some work on this, see Gendler and Hawthorne's edited collection (2002), especially David Chalmers' and Michael Della Rocca's contributions.
3. References to Hume's *Treatise* follow the custom of Hume scholars to reference book, part, section and paragraph, followed by the pagination for the Selby-Bigge text.

can run free. Where and how the line is to be drawn between that which is conceivable and that which is not has been the key subject debated on this theme. For our purposes, however, what is most important is that outside what is inconceivable, and hence not possible, there is an infinite world of conceivable possibilities.

It is here that delirium enters the scene. This occurs for Hume because the principles of association which naturally lead us to connect one impression or idea with another – namely, the principles of resemblance, contiguity and causation – will over time solidify into custom and habit, leading us to have more lively expectations of, and make more lively associations between, some ideas rather than others. The idea of a mountain and being covered with snow, for example, will have more numerous associations, and hence result in a more strongly held belief about reality, or what is true and false about reality, than will the idea of a mountain and gold. In cases of delirium and madness, however, the role that habit and custom play in determining what we are likely to believe comes to be undermined. As Hume describes such a scenario:

> a lively imagination very often degenerates into madness or folly, and bears it a great resemblance in its operations; so they influence the judgment after the same manner, and produce belief from the very same principles. When the imagination, from any extraordinary ferment of the blood and spirits, acquires such a vivacity as disorders all its powers and faculties, there is no means of distinguishing betwixt truth and falsehood; but every loose fiction or idea, having the same influence as the impressions of the memory, or the conclusions of the judgment, is receiv'd on the same footing, and operates with equal force on the passions. A present impression and a customary transition are no longer necessary to inliven our ideas. Every chimera of the brain is as vivid and intense as any of those inferences, which we formerly dignify'd with the name of conclusion concerning matters of fact, and sometimes as the present impressions of the senses. (Hume 1978, 1.3.10.9; SB 123)

In this passage Hume is reiterating a point he made in the first pages of his *Treatise* – namely, that while the distinction between an impression and an idea is quite clear, and 'Every one of himself will readily perceive the difference betwixt feeling and thinking', nevertheless sometimes the distinction between, for example, *feeling* one's leg break and *thinking* about the time one broke one's leg can fail to hold. 'Thus in sleep', Hume argues, 'in a fever, in madness, or in any very violent emotions of soul, our ideas may approach to our impressions' (1.1.1.1; SB 1–2). If we think of the delirium that befell the husband in Buñuel's film, his jealousy led him from one idea to another – from the idea of meeting an acquaintance of his wife in a hotel (not an altogether unexpected phenomenon) to the idea that this person is most

31

certainly stalking them – an inference that was not grounded in probabilities, as Proust's police prefect would think. In delirium, however, this belief is held with the same strength and conviction as if it were an inference 'we formerly dignify'd with the name of conclusion concerning matters of fact'. Thus, although our thinking usually follows the tried and tested patterns laid down by the principles of association and the customs and habits built upon their repetitive application, there is no guarantee that this will occur, and the infinite play of imagination with its threat of delirium is an ever present risk associated with thinking.

It is the inseparability of delirium from thinking that will be a primary focus of Deleuze's interest in Hume. Of particular importance for Deleuze are passages such as the following, where Hume acknowledges 'the liberty of the imagination to transpose and change its ideas', adding that 'The Fables we meet with in poems and romances put this entirely out of question. Nature there is totally confounded, and nothing mentioned but winged horses, fiery dragons, and monstrous giants' (Hume 1978, 1.1.4.4; SB 10). In other words, we only need to read a poem, a romance or a *Harry Potter* book to realise the liberty with which the imagination can combine and change its ideas. As Deleuze takes up this passage he sees the starting point for Hume's project as being one where, 'Left to itself, the mind has the capacity to move from one idea to another, but it does so at random, in a delirium that runs throughout the universe, creating fire dragons, winged horses, and monstrous giants' (Deleuze 2001, 41). As we have seen, though, this delirium comes to be tamed as it is drawn into habitual patterns by way of the principles of association. As Deleuze states this point: 'The principles of human nature … impose constant rules on this delirium: laws of passage, of transition, of inference, which are in accordance with nature itself' (41). The manner in which this delirium plays itself out in Hume's project, despite the efforts of the principles of human nature to tame it, will be discussed on recurring occasions throughout this book. For now, however, and to continue to set the stage for the arguments to follow, what is important to draw from Hume, as well as from Camus, Proust and Buñuel, is that making sense of a situation, of one's life, involves a thinking that is inseparably related to a delirium that may well undermine the very task this thinking sets out to do. To state this point differently, if thinking sets out to think determinate thoughts, thoughts with some determinate content and meaning, then this thinking also involves a problematic tendency which may well undermine the very tendency towards determinate thoughts. To make sense of things is thus to risk invoking the problems that stop making sense.

c) Making sense and problems

As we have seen, the problem with the thinking of the apartment manager, the jealous husband and Hume's delirious person is that whatever may be taken to be the true facts of the situation are not sufficient for making sense of what is being encountered. In encountering the reality of his situation after the death of his daughter, the apartment manager attempts to think through the significance and meaning of the reality that can account for this situation. None of the determinate facts which could fill the pages of a report are adequate to the reality he is encountering and attempting to make sense of. For the jealous husband as well, the inferences he draws in encountering the reality that would make sense of his jealousy 'did not derive from any probability' (Proust 2003, 17), as Proust's narrator admitted, and thus unlike the 'prefect of police' who would confine his inferences to the most likely conclusions, the husband's imagination roams well beyond the facts to the possibilities that make sense of his jealousy. With Hume's delirious person, they too come to conclusions unlike those that are normally 'dignify'd with the name of conclusion concerning matters of fact', and suddenly any random possibility, 'every loose fiction or idea' (Hume 2007, 1.3.10.9; SB 123), has for them the same strength and vivacity as if it were a matter of fact. The delirious person thus poses a threat to the usual weight we give to what we consider to be matters of fact, since for them 'there is no means of distinguishing betwixt truth and falsehood' (1.3.10.9; SB 123). As consequence of the challenge the delirious person poses to our accustomed ways of distinguishing between truth and falsity, other questions become more pressing. Rather than what is the case? what is the truth of the matter? what are the matters of fact?, the questions now more likely to be asked will be who is saying such crazy things? how could they think such things? what circumstances could ever lead them to think that? and so on. The delirious person becomes a problem, though one we could easily dismiss, perhaps, as Hume did, by citing their madness, their 'extraordinary ferment of the blood and spirits' (1.3.10.9; SB 123), as the matter of fact which accounts for the way they are thinking. The jealous person is also a problem, since for them the matters of fact that would satisfy most people do not satisfy them; to the contrary, they are driven on by other questions, such as who is the person I should be jealous of? how many people are there that I should be jealous of? in what circumstances will I find them? and so on. For the jealous person there is no knowing where, when or how they will encounter the person or persons who will make sense of their jealousy. Their jealousy is thus an encounter with a reality that fails to be resolved by anything that may be taken to be true or false. Even if the jealous person does determine that their partner has actually cheated with a particular person, X, their questioning may well only be intensified: how often did they see X, in what circumstances, where, when, and who else besides X? If there was X, there may also be Y, Z, etc. The problem that confronts the jealous person, as with the problem that confronts the apartment manager or the problem the delirious madman poses for society, is a problem which no determinate or determinable facts can resolve, a problem no solution ever eliminates.

For Deleuze, the examples we have been discussing bring us right to the very nature of the problem that motivates philosophy itself, and hence in his own way Camus was right to say 'There is but one truly serious philosophical problem, and that is suicide' (Camus 1955, 3). Moreover, the questions that have most propelled philosophy are not those regarding the truth and falsity of matters of fact, but the questions that come when we encounter, as with the jealous person or the madman, the nature of a problem. Deleuze is straightforward on this point: 'It should be noticed how few philosophers have placed their trust in the question "what is X?" in order to have Ideas. Certainly not Aristotle [or Plato, as discussed in *Inquiry*] ... Once the dialectic brews up its matter instead of being applied in a vacuum for propaedeutic ends, the questions "How much?", "How?", "In what cases?", and "Who?" abound' (Deleuze 1994, 188). For Deleuze these are precisely the questions that best characterise our encounter with the nature of a problem, or our encounter with the Ideas philosophers are attempting to think. Deleuze thus takes the encounters we have described – of various individuals in their problematic situations – and sees them as being at the heart of thinking itself, or at the heart of the effort to make sense of things. This effort confronts the very problematic nature that motivates this thinking in the first place, and for these reasons Deleuze will again stress that, 'Once it is a question of determining the problem or the Idea as such, once it is a question of setting the dialectic in motion, the question "What is X?" gives way to other questions, otherwise powerful and efficacious, otherwise imperative: "How much, how and in what cases?"' (188).

By 'setting the dialectic in motion', Deleuze has in mind the attempt to make sense of the concrete determinacies of reality. It is not a matter of laying out abstract concepts or rules that serve as a guide, as rules-as-rails as discussed earlier (Introduction), that then enable us to navigate and solve whatever issues may arise. This may be good, as Deleuze said, for 'propaedeutic ends', i.e., for teaching the nature of abstract categories and concepts *as* abstract – for example, to clarify what is involved in the relationship between x and y, where x is the nature of justice and y an act done in accordance with x. When Cephalus states such an abstract relationship in the *Republic*, arguing that justice is repaying one's debts (*Republic* 330d–331b), this teaching moment comes to be undermined as Socrates pursues further details. When Socrates adds the detail about a person to whom one is obliged to return a borrowed weapon but who is not in their right mind, and in fact is a danger to themselves and potentially to others, then the abstract relationship of x to y is undermined. Stated differently, this is where the dialectic is set in motion, or where the abstract, dedifferentiating tendency we introduced earlier encounters the differentiating tendency of increasingly determining the concrete possibilities of a situation. It is the encounter with these tendencies, or the problem of making sense, that sets the dialectic in motion and undermines the traditional, rule-as-rail account of rule-following. At this point, other questions become more pressing: rather than asking what the rule is and what is to be done, the problem of making sense leads us to ask how? when? where? and in what circumstances should we act? The abstract rules or solutions that may come to guide conduct in a formal, mechanical way, such that an action is taken in accordance with a rule, are made possible by the questions (what were called relevance questions in *Inquiry*) provoked by the encounter with the problem of making sense.

Such questions were important for Nietzsche as well. For Nietzsche questions of value and meaning were more significant and relevant than questions of truth and falsity, and this is precisely how Deleuze reads him: 'Nietzsche questions the concept of truth', Deleuze argues, and moreover is 'contesting the very notions of true and false. Not because he wants to "relativise" them like an ordinary sceptic. In their place he substitutes sense and value as rigorous notions. You always get the truth you deserve according to the sense of what you say, and according to the values to which you give voice' (Deleuze 2004, 135–6). As Nietzsche understands slave morality, for example, the truths of this morality reflect the values and significance the slave moralist has towards life. Thus for Nietzsche the principle of 'refraining from injury, violence, and exploitation, [of] placing your will on par with the other's', is not a principle whose truth justifies its being the basis for society; to the contrary, Nietzsche claims that once it is 'held to be the fundamental principle of society, it immediately shows itself for what it is: the will to negate life, the principle of disintegration and decay' (Nietzsche 1966, §259). In *On the Genealogy of Morals*, Nietzsche begins the First Essay by claiming that 'the concept "good" has been sought and established in the wrong place: the judgment "good" did not originate with those to whom "goodness" was shown!' (Nietzsche 1969, 25). For Nietzsche it was 'the noble, powerful, high-stationed and high-minded, who felt and established themselves and their actions as good, that is, of the first rank, in contradistinction to all the low, low-minded, common and plebeian' (26). Thus the value and significance the nobles attributed to themselves and their actions was contrasted with the actions of the common and low people they looked down their noses at, a contrast that comes to be expressed in moral judgments regarding what is good and what is bad. It was this 'pathos of distance', as Nietzsche calls it, that the noble and self-affirming seized upon 'to create values and to coin names for values' (26). What is thus more important for Nietzsche than knowing whether our moral judgments are true or not is the attitude towards life these judgments express – is it a life-affirming or life-denying attitude?

Deleuze will parallel Nietzsche's understanding of values as expressions of an attitude towards life by seeing solutions as expressions of a problem. As moral judgments are seen by Nietzsche as expressing an underlying attitude towards life, rather than as independent truths or rules that are separable from the lives that may or may not be lived in accordance with them, so too for Deleuze problems are seen as that which comes to be expressed by solutions, and thus the problems do not disappear with the solutions; rather, the solutions 'give voice' to the problems which subsist in the solutions that express them. Echoing his comments regarding Nietzsche's understanding of truth, Deleuze thus claims that 'A solution always has the truth it deserves according to the problem to which it is a response, and the problem always has the solution it deserves in proportion to its own truth or falsity – in other words, in proportion to its sense. This is what is meant by such famous formulae as "The really great problems are posed only once they are solved"' (Deleuze 1994, 159). In encountering the nature of a problem, therefore, the problem is not to be confused with its solutions, and yet the problem is not determinate and identifiable until it is 'given voice' by the solutions which respond to the problem. This is why Deleuze endorses the standard line that great problems 'are posed only once they are solved'; that is, they are given voice and determinately posed only with the solutions that respond to them. The nature of the problem, however, is not a determinate and/or determinable reality to which a solution responds, thereby fulfilling what was already determinately given and called for by the problem itself. A problem that presupposes its determinate solution, such that the solution eliminates the problem, is a false problem, or an inauthentic problem, whereas a true problem will give rise to questions that move beyond the determinate, beyond the 'What is X?' questions, to the questions the jealous lover can identify with – 'who, how many, in what circumstances?' – questions that do not vanish once a determinate answer is given. This then is the sense in which, for Deleuze, a solution 'has the truth it deserves ... in proportion to its sense'; that is, in responding to or encountering the de/differentiating tendencies of sense, the questions that come once the dialectic gets set in motion follow from an encounter with a problem, a true problem we might say. 'The power of the questions', as Deleuze elaborates, 'always comes from somewhere else than the answers, and benefits from a free depth which cannot be resolved' (188). Deleuze and Guattari will repeat this point, years later, in their final collaborative work, *What is Philosophy?*, when they challenge philosophy's common approach to truth as being about the truth of propositions. Echoing Nietzsche (and Camus, though perhaps unknowingly), Deleuze and Guattari argue that:

> Instead of a string of linked propositions [and propositions with a truth value], it would be better to isolate the flow of interior monologue, or the strange forkings of the most ordinary conversation. By separating them from their psychological, as well as their sociological adhesions, we would be able to show how thought as such produces something interesting when it accedes to the infinite movement that frees it from truth as supposed paradigm and reconquers an immanent power of creation. (Deleuze and Guattari 1994, 139–40).

Rather than attempt to makes sense of our propositions by determining their truth value, along with whatever relevant psychological and sociological facts may help in the determination of that value, Deleuze and Guattari instead call for a move beyond the discrete, determinate nature of propositions and their truth values to an underlying depth and continuity, a 'free depth which cannot be resolved' and which sets thought free so that it 'reconquers an immanent power of creation'. What is at work here, therefore, is a distinction between the continuous and discrete, or the dedifferentiating and the differentiating. For Deleuze and Deleuze and Guattari we have discrete propositions that are linked together, like a string of pearls, and linked in turn to other determinate facts and realities, to the arguments that make propositional functions true, including psychological and sociological facts, among others; and then more importantly we have an immanent, continuous 'flow of interior monologue' whereby thought 'produces something interesting' rather than something true, and in doing so gives to a solution the truth it deserves. This relationship of something interesting to something true, of problems to solutions, and the priority Deleuze gives to the former over the latter, becomes most evident, as we have begun to see, in making sense of life, and in the questions that cannot be resolved during this process. There is nonetheless a distinction to be drawn between the true and the interesting, or, in a related way, between how, when and in what circumstances a delirium allows the powers of creation to flourish, and when this delirium undermines life to the point of self-destruction. We can see this question as following up on the one with which Nietzsche concludes *Beyond Good and Evil*:

> Oh, what are you anyway, my written and painted thoughts! It was not long ago that you were still so colorful, young and malicious, so full of thorns and

secret spices that you made me sneeze and laugh – and now? You have already lost your novelty, and I am afraid that some of you are ready to turn into truths: they already look so immortal, so pathetically decent and upright, so boring! (Nietzsche 1966, §296)

The question, then, is how, in what circumstances, etc., our thoughts become truths, become so boring, and what the meaning and significance of this process might be. To begin to take up these questions, and in turn those regarding where, how and when a creative delirium becomes destructive, we can turn to Spinoza, in whom Nietzsche saw a precursor to himself. In doing so we will further clarify what is involved in making sense of life.

2. Making Sense of God

a) Spinoza and the 'inmost essence' of God

Spinoza's philosophy arguably begins with the effort to make sense of life. In his early, never to be completed work, *Treatise on the Emendation of the Intellect*, Spinoza begins by claiming that experience has taught him 'that all the things which regularly occur in ordinary life are empty and futile' (Spinoza 2016, 7; TdIE II/5[4]). In particular, he lists 'wealth, honor, and sensual pleasure' (7; II/6) as among the motivations in life that are 'empty and futile', and thus those things we pursue in the hope that they will satisfy these motivations are ultimately lacking in meaning and significance. As Spinoza adds, the fleeting, perishable nature of these things which we think will satisfy our 'empty and futile' motivations only make things worse, since the pursuit of them sets us up for suffering and sorrow. More precisely, it is the love we have for these perishable objects that becomes, in the end, the cause of our sorrow. As Spinoza puts it:

> all happiness or unhappiness was placed in the quality of the object to which we cling with love. For strife will never arise on account of what is not loved, nor will there be sadness if it perishes, nor envy if it is possessed by another, nor fear, nor hatred – in a word, no disturbances of the mind. Indeed, all these happen only in the love of those things that can perish, as all the things we have just spoken of can do. (Spinoza 2016, 7; II/6)

What Spinoza thus sets out to do is to think through the possibility of a love that is not of perishable objects, and so correct (i.e., emend) our intellect in

---

4. This reference is standard among Spinoza scholars and refers to the Carl Gebhardt edition of Spinoza's posthumous works: Spinoza, *Opera*, 4 Vols. TdIE refers to *Tractatus de Intellectus Emendatione*, in Gebhardt, Vol. II, p. 5.

order to put an end to our meaningless, futile life of suffering and sorrow and set us on a meaningful path to a life filled with joy. Spinoza is quite forthright in setting this out as his goal: 'But love toward the eternal and infinite thing feeds the mind with a joy entirely exempt from sadness. This is greatly to be desired, and to be sought with all our strength' (9; II/7). In his *Ethics* as well, Spinoza will continue to identify human misery and suffering with a life that is too attached to perishable things. As he puts it in this context: 'it should be noted that sickness of the mind and misfortunes take their origin especially from too much love toward a thing which is liable to many variations and which we can never fully possess' (Spinoza 1985, 605; II/293. The task of the *Ethics*, therefore, is also that of showing how one can live a blessed, joy-filled life (we will return, in the final chapter, to see how freedom, for Spinoza, realises the joy-filled life [in §5.2.e. freedom]).

While Spinoza would complete this project in the *Ethics*, the reason he never finished his *Treatise on the Emendation of the Intellect*, I would argue, is that he became dissatisfied with how he was going about correcting the manner in which we make sense of our lives. In short, in his effort to show how a love of God, 'the eternal and infinite thing', would feed the mind with 'a joy entirely exempt from sadness', he was not quite able to break free of Descartes' approach to making sense of God as the eternal and infinite thing. In particular, Spinoza followed in the footsteps of Descartes by understanding the nature of the eternal and infinite on the basis of a determinate property, in this case the determinate nature of one's own finite mind. Spinoza was aware of the difficulties of doing this, and in the *Treatise* he acknowledges the inadequacy of attempting to understand the nature of something through its properties or *propria*. He offers the example of a circle, which we could define as 'a figure in which the lines drawn from the center to the circumference are equal'. Although this is true, Spinoza argues that it 'does not at all explain the essence of the circle, but only a property of it'. As he puts it: 'To be called perfect, a definition will have to explain the inmost essence of the thing, and to take care not to use certain propria in its place' (Spinoza 2016, 39; II/34). What we need, he adds, is 'a concept, or definition, of the thing such that when it is considered alone, without any others conjoined, all the thing's properties can be deduced from it', which can be done with the definition of a circle Spinoza offers: 'it is the figure that is described by any line of which one end is fixed and the other movable' (40; II/35). To begin with the thing's properties, by contrast, puts us in a position much like that of the merchant Spinoza discusses early in the *Treatise*. 'Suppose', he says, 'there are three numbers. Someone is seeking a fourth, which is to the third as the second is to the first. Here merchants will usually say that they know what to do to find the fourth number, because they have not forgotten that procedure which they simply heard from their teachers, without any demonstration' (14–15; II/11). In other words, the merchant may get the correct answer by following an established rule or 'procedure', just as it may be correct to say that God is infinitely perfect, omniscient, etc.; but that is not the same thing as understanding the 'inmost essence of the thing' from which these answers, rules or properties follow. Stated in terms of our earlier discussion (in the Introduction), the nature of a rule is not to be confused with the conditions that make the rule itself possible.

We can now understand how and why Spinoza parts ways with Descartes, for Descartes does indeed move, in the *Third Meditation*, from the clear and distinct idea we have of certain properties or propria of God as 'eternal, infinite, immutable, omniscient, omnipotent and creator of all things that exist apart from him', to the conclusion that God must exist. The link that brings us from the ideas of God to the conclusion is Descartes' assumption that the ideas we have of God have more 'objective reality than the ideas that represent finite substances' (Descartes 1984, 28). Since human beings, as finite, cannot be the cause of the idea of an infinitely perfect being, there must be a being that does have the objective reality capable of doing so, namely God. The problem with this argument, however, is that it relies on properties or *propria* of God – a being that is infinitely perfect, omniscient, etc. – properties, as Spinoza recognised, that do nothing to explain or make sense of the nature of God, the 'inmost essence' from which these properties follow. In short, Descartes' approach does not get us to a proper understanding and love of God as the 'eternal and infinite thing' that will 'feed our minds with a joy entirely exempt from sadness'.

Despite highlighting the futility of understanding the 'inmost essence of a thing' by way of the propria of the thing, Spinoza in the end left the *Treatise* unfinished since he encountered the problem of understanding the inmost essence of God by way of our own finite mind. Spinoza's motivation for going about it this way was reasonable enough. We seem to know our own thoughts, or what it means for us to think, better than almost anything else. This was certainly what Descartes thought too! As Spinoza puts it, 'from the fact that I know something, I know what it is to know something' (Spinoza 1985, 14; II/11). Deleuze will criticise this assumption, what he calls the dogmatic image of thought, for presupposing that we do indeed know what it is to know something. But Spinoza will encounter the limits of this dogmatic image, to continue with Deleuze's phrase, when he attempts to account for the inmost essence of God by beginning with the nature and truths of our own mind. The problem is that this will not give us a real definition of God, a definition of the essence from which everything, including finite minds, follows. Spinoza thus begins again in the *Ethics*, but this time he starts with the nature and definition of God, and only later does he come to the nature of our finite minds.

We can now begin to summarise and take stock of Spinoza's effort to make sense of God. In our desire to make sense of the eternal and infinite reality that will in turn make sense of our own lives, and hence fill us with 'a joy entirely exempt from sadness', it is understandable that we would begin with that which is determinate, identifiable, and thus capable of being the subject of determinate thoughts that can be shared and re-presented to others. But for Spinoza it is critical that we distinguish and do not confuse the thoughts and words we use to understand and make sense of things, and the things themselves. This concern becomes the basis for Spinoza's distinction between real being and being of reason. We need to be cautious here, however, for by saying *being* of reason we might be led to think it has being like real being, which would be a mistake. For Spinoza 'it is easy to see how improper is the division of being into real being and being of reason. For they divide being into being and nonbeing, or into being and mode of thinking. Nevertheless, I do not wonder that Philosophers preoccupied with words, or grammar, should fall into such errors. For they judge things from words, not words from things' ('Descartes' Principles of Philosophy', Spinoza 1985, 301; I/235). It is thus important for Spinoza that 'we should be on guard in the investigation of things, lest we confound real beings with beings of reason' (302; I/236).

But how do we avoid doing this? It is at this point that our earlier discussion of the relationship between problems and solutions returns. As was pointed out, a problem, as understood here, is not to be confused or confounded with the solutions it makes possible. In other words, a problem is not a determinate prefiguring of a solution such that the solution fulfils the problem and the problem thereafter vanishes from the scene. To the contrary, a problem is precisely the 'free depth' (Deleuze 1994, 188) which engenders the questions that cannot be resolved, a free depth that subsists despite the determinate answers and solutions that may be given. For Deleuze, a comparable relationship occurs between signs and expressions. 'A sign', Deleuze argues with respect to Spinoza's reading of the Bible in his *Tractatus Theologico-Politicus*, 'always attaches to a *proprium*; it always signifies a commandment; and it grounds our obedience. Expression always relates to an attribute; it expresses an essence, that is, a nature in the infinitive; it makes it known to us' (Deleuze 1990a, 57). In making sense of God through reading the Bible, therefore, we come only to signs of God, or *propria*, which may well be true to the nature of God but they do not give us the understanding of God's inmost essence that will provide us with joy. What such signs are suited for is order – a determinate order and ordering of people and things. The

41

commandments, therefore, as well as the many other signs to be found and interpreted in the Bible, are well suited for providing that which 'grounds our obedience'. Deleuze anticipates the potential counter-argument:

> Should one say, at least, that commandments 'express' the wishes of God? But that would in turn prejudge will as belonging to the nature of God, take a being of reason, an extrinsic determination, for a divine attribute. Any mixing of the two domains is fatal. Whenever one takes a sign for an expression, one sees mysteries everywhere, including, above all, Scripture itself. (Deleuze 1990a, 57)

As with the jealous lover, and the delirium of questions that balloon as we feed jealous thinking with concrete details (as Proust's narrator warned), so too if we mix a being of reason with a divine attribute, or *propria* with God's real being, we are unable to draw limits but continue, without respite, in a futile attempt to make determinate sense of God's nature, multiplying along the way the interpretations of signs as well as the questions that go with these interpretations. It is for this reason that Spinoza differentiates between God's nature as absolutely infinite and the infinitely many determinate *propria* of God. God's infinitely perfect being, and the infinitely many things that can be said of God, follow from God's absolutely infinite nature. The same can be said of the relation between problems and solutions. In fact, we could say God is a problem, or God is the reality we encounter when we encounter the nature of a problem. As such, to make sense of God is not to compile a list of determinate properties and adjectives that could be said of God. This would be to 'confound real beings with beings of reason' (Spinoza 1985, 302), as Spinoza has warned us not to do, and would then simply lead us to address our questions and questioning to the items on our list, thereby diverting us from truly making sense of the inmost essence of God, and hence of the reality which will provide us with 'a joy entirely exempt from sadness'. A problem is nonetheless related to solutions and is in fact only determinate and identifiable in the solutions that 'give voice' to a problem. The nature of this relationship was a primary theme of my *Inquiry*, but to help prepare the way for understanding the ethical and political implications of making sense, let us briefly highlight and summarise some of the key aspects of this relationship.

b) The ultimate elements of nature

As we saw earlier, Deleuze follows Nietzsche's attitude towards truth in developing his own understanding of the relationship between problems and solutions. Just as Nietzsche understood moral judgments as giving voice to values and attitudes towards life, so too Deleuze will argue that 'You always get the truth you deserve according to the sense of what you say, and according to the values to which you give voice' (Deleuze 2004, 135–6). We can now shed further light on the implications of deserving the truth or solution we get after having encountered Spinoza's concern about confounding beings of reason with real being, a concern that derives from his critique of using the properties or *propria* of a thing to understand and make sense of the thing. In particular, it is precisely the values that moral judgments give voice to that make sense of those judgments, and it is the problems that solutions give voice to that make sense of those solutions. It is not the solutions or moral judgments which make sense of the problems and values, for this simply opens a regress of seeking further judgments and further solutions – the endless, differentiating quest for further signs. What then is this sense? Put simply, it is the dual tendency of making sense towards delirium (dedifferentiating), the thinking that undermines any and every determinate identity, on the one hand, and towards the determinate (differentiating) on the other, towards the beings of reason, *propria* and descriptors that become the focal points of our efforts to make sense of something. This latter tendency can likewise undermine established habits and expectations by flooding the system, so to speak, with increasing differentiations that do not allow us to solve the problem (or to learn), much as the jealous lover feverishly continues to search for signs to justify his jealousy. What is to be done instead? How are we to correct and emend our tendency to confound real being with beings of reason, our tendency to succumb to the illusion of a solution without a problem? Stated simply, we are to draw limits and boundaries, or to create the conditions that will make solutions possible, or establish a paradoxical period whereby the de/differentiating tendencies maintain a consistency that allows for the possibility of solutions.[5] But are we not violating the Spinozist maxim in doing this – namely, Spinoza's claim that we are not to confound the determinate with the conditions for the determinate, or the *propria* of something with the inmost essence of something? We also appear to be violating Deleuze's own version of this maxim: 'The foundation can never resemble what it founds'

---

5. This understanding of de/differentiating tendencies is similar to the edge of chaos states one finds in dynamic systems theory. A dynamic system is one that is neither locked into a repetitive cycle nor operating chaotically and unpredictably. Rather, dynamic systems at the edge of chaos maintain a dynamic equilibrium state that maintains both the tendencies to chaos and order. Similarly, the differentiating tendency, if taken too far, can undermine established identities by overwhelming the order and predictability necessary to such identities; and the dedifferentiating tendency that moves towards the abstract and away from emerging differences can also be undermining by failing to adjust to changing circumstances. For more on these themes, and on the manner in which dynamic systems theory offers a way of reading Deleuze, see Bell 2006.

(Deleuze 1990b, 99). However, drawing limits need not entail setting forth a determinate problem to which a determinate solution gives voice, or setting forth a determinate rule for others to follow. We have already seen, and will continue to see, the difficulties of this approach, of assuming rules are autonomous guides to action. What we are to do, and do in a way that does not bypass the distinctive nature of problems and yet draws limits to problems, is to understand problems as non-mereological parts of the solutions that have given voice to them.[6] What it means for a problem to be a non-mereological part of a solution is that it is not a determinate part of the solution, a part that can be separated off from that of which it is a part. There is no determinate part of the solution of which one can say, there's the problem that's being responded to, and from there separate off the problem from this particular solution and address it independently. If this is done, then one has confounded problems with solutions. To avoid this, we can say that a problem is a part of the solution, for the solution would not be the solution it is, nor would it have the sense it has, without the problem that is a non-mereological part of it, the problem the solution gives voice to. What is to be done, therefore, in order to stave off the undermining quest for more and more signs, is to focus on the solutions at hand, those that are part of life as it is offered to us, and return our enquiries into signs back to the place from which we started, potentially problematising and creating the conditions for new solutions.

Yet another way to avoid confounding problems and solutions is to rethink the nature of the determinate itself. An important theme in this work will be the idea that making sense is not a matter of compiling a list of determinate features, facts, answers to our questions, etc.; rather, the very process of making sense will be the genesis of determinate facts, facts that give voice to that which we are making sense of. Making sense thus entails both the tendency towards delirium (dedifferentiation) and the tendency towards the determinate (differentiation), towards the delirium that undermines identity and towards differentiations and determinations of identity that both resolve and occlude the problem. These are not, however, two distinct realms, one of pure problems freed from the determinate, and the other a realm that consists of nothing but determinate individuals. Both realms are to be understood as abstractions made possible by the nature of problems and the role they play in making sense of things. As a result we could say, with Deleuze and picking up on a theme from my *Inquiry*, that 'problematic Ideas are precisely the ultimate elements of nature and the subliminal objects of little perceptions' (Deleuze 1994, 165).

---

6. See my *Inquiry* §11.11 where I set forth and then borrow D.M. Armstrong's concept of 'non-mereological parts'.

c) Making sense of things

A few things need to be said about problematic Ideas, 'the ultimate elements of nature'. Although there are some similarities to philosophical atomism in the arguments to be developed here, the key difference is that these elements are neither determinate nor particulars. Stated simply, the elements are precisely the paradoxical tendencies towards both delirium and the determinate, towards a simultaneous undermining and assertion of identity. Deleuze's linking of problematic Ideas to 'subliminal objects of little perceptions' is a reference to Leibniz, in particular his famous example of the sound of the wave crashing on the shore, where the clear sound of the wave we hear consists of the sounds of many smaller waves. The sounds of these smaller waves are the little perceptions or microperceptions that go unnoticed except for when a sufficient number of them are brought together; thus a clear perception, for Leibniz, necessarily presupposes a con-fusion of microperceptions. A critical difference between Deleuze and Leibniz is captured nicely by Deleuze's use of the term 'nomadology' for his own project, in contrast to the monadology of Leibniz. For Leibniz, microperceptions become elements of differential series, series that converge at limits which then give rise to the determinate identities that are the subject of representational thought. In contrast to Russell's understanding of logical atomism, where the sense-data that become the sensations of our experience once we become aware of them are themselves determinate and of the same nature as that which we perceive (a position Russell calls neutral monism), for Leibniz the microperceptions are differentials or infinitesimal monads that are of a different nature or kind than that which we perceive in the physical world. The physical world, to use Leibniz's analogy, would be like a rainbow, whereas the true reality behind its appearance consists of the infinitesimal monads, understood as the basic substance but an active, psychic substance, a substance, as Leibniz put it in a letter to Arnauld, 'endowed with a primitive entelechy or, if you permit me to use the concept of life so generally, with a vital principle' (Leibniz 1988, 343). Leibniz thus concludes that all corporeal substances presuppose these monads, and hence 'they are living'. For him, however, the entelechy of the monads, the vital principle that guides their activity, is guaranteed to result in a series of infinitesimals, with all series converging on the one world, the greatest of all the possible worlds that God could have created. It is this convergence of series that enables each monad to express in its own way the world as a whole. Like the rainbow, the world is the phenomenal expression of all the monads, and God's choice has assured that the monads will all converge upon this one expression, this one best of all possible worlds.

45

For Deleuze, problematic Ideas, as the ultimate elements of nature, are, as with Leibniz's monads, processes, and are of a psychic nature if understood as contemplations.[7] Problematic Ideas, as with Leibniz's 'subliminal little perceptions', are also the conditions for, but not to be confounded with, the things that come to be identified and represented in our perceptions and thoughts. Leibniz's thought, however, remains committed to a representational model of thinking, for the monads, each in their own way, come to re-present the one world that God created. For Deleuze, by contrast, there is no predetermined guarantee that the ultimate elements will converge such that things or even the one best world that contains all things will result. Problematic Ideas, as ultimate elements, are thus freed from the predetermining constraints with which Leibniz saddles his monads, and it is for this reason that Deleuze counters Leibniz's monadology with his own nomadology. Whereas Leibniz's infinitesimals consist of differentials that are bound to give rise, at the limit, to something determinate which is different from the series of differentials themselves (the polygons converge, at the limit, to become the circle), for Deleuze problematic Ideas are not assured of converging upon a limit that will give rise to anything determinate. Rather than elements or differentials that converge upon a limit, a limit that then gives rise to something determinate, problematic Ideas are paradoxical elements in that they consist of discontinuous, diverging series (differentiating/dedifferentiating). As Deleuze states this point in *The Logic of Sense*, the differentiating series moves from less to more differentiated while the dedifferentiating moves from more to less differentiated. The past, for instance, entails a differentiating tendency and movement, for in the past we can discern, identify and differentiate what has come to be. The past is already determined and one can continue to differentiate, *ad infinitum*, the determinate traces of the past. The future, by contrast, entails the dedifferentiating tendency and movement, the movement towards that which is not yet differentiated and determinate. The paradox of sense, or the paradox of the event (Deleuze uses these terms interchangeably in *The Logic of Sense*), is thus a 'past-future ... already past and yet in the future, at once more and less, always the day before and the day after' (Deleuze 1990b, 77). A consequence of this paradox is that the problematic Ideas that make sense of the solutions that give voice to them 'have the characteristic of going in both directions at once, and of rendering identification impossible, as they emphasize sometimes the first, sometimes the second, of these effects' (75). For instance, identification is rendered impossible by the differentiating tendency: imagine, Deleuze says, 'if temperatures which were at first indiscernible were

---

7. See Bell 2016, 74–6, for more on the theme of 'contemplation' as Deleuze and Deleuze and Guattari take it up.

to go on differentiating themselves' (75); then we could never foresee what might happen next, never come to identify anything familiar, because before something comes to be identified it becomes other, and before this other comes to be identified it too becomes other, and so on. It is thus the dedifferentiating tendency, coupled to the differentiating tendency, which allows for the emergence of a determinate identity, for as an expectation or habit builds upon the determinations of the past, one is able to move beyond what is determinately given and expect or foresee that which is not yet given, that which is not yet determined and differentiated. Deleuze refers to this process as good sense, which is, as he puts it, 'said of one direction only ... This direction is easily determined as that which goes from the most differentiated to the least differentiated ... Good sense therefore is given the condition under which it fulfills its function, which is essentially to foresee' (75). The paradox of sense, however, renders foreseeing problematic, since it moves in both directions at once: in the direction that renders foreseeing possible (most to least differentiated, or dedifferentiating tendency) and in the direction that undermines our ability to foresee or predict (least to most differentiated, or differentiating tendency). We can rephrase the paradox of sense by drawing from our earlier discussions. The discontinuous, diverging series that are problematic Ideas, and hence the paradoxical sense that solutions give voice to, consist of both the movement towards habit and the emergence of the determinate and identifiable, and the movement towards delirium, towards that which undermines determinate identity. As a result of their paradoxical nature, problematic Ideas are not assured of convergence upon a limit that will allow for the emergence of something determinate; to the contrary, they may well problematise that which is determinate and undermine its identity, an undermining that may well give way to the emergence of another determinate something.

As a result of his vastly different understanding of the ultimate elements of nature, Deleuze is left with a very different problem to Leibniz – namely, how to account for the possibility of the determinate and identifiable without presupposing that which is already determinate and identifiable. On Leibniz's view, the monads already presuppose the identity of the world God created, and it is this world that makes sense of that which the monads express. For Deleuze, however, the determinate and identifiable is made possible by that with which it is not to be confounded – that is, problematic Ideas – and thus the sense that is expressed by determinate things, the problem that is given voice by its solution, is not already determinate and given but needs to be constructed and made. In other words, making sense of things is inseparable from both the things that give voice to problems and from the problematic Ideas which are given, and only given, along with the determinate solutions

47

and things that give voice to them. The key concept Deleuze develops in the metaphysics that accounts for both problems and their solutions is 'multiplicity', and as we will see going forward, making sense of life entails what Deleuze will call an 'art of multiplicities': 'the art of multiplicities: the art of grasping the Ideas and the problems they incarnate in things, and of grasping things as incarnations, as cases of solution for the problems of Ideas' (Deleuze 1994, 182).

The simplest way to understand Deleuze's concept of a multiplicity is to see it as a way of avoiding thinking of things either in terms of determinate individuals, atoms, etc., or in terms of a determinate one, whole, set or totality which either contains these determinate individuals or is simply all that is (as some monists would argue). With the concept of a multiplicity we can clarify our earlier point about how to avoid the endless, meaningless and futile questioning that results when we confound problems with solutions, or real being with beings of reason, as Spinoza put it. As we saw, what needs to be done (and what Proust's jealous narrator, for example, was unable to do) is to correct and emend our tendency to confound the two by drawing limits and boundaries to a problem that then create the conditions that will make a solution possible. A multiplicity is precisely a problematic Idea whose systemic nature allows for the drawing of limits and boundaries, and we thus avoid the difficulties of confounding the problematic Idea with a determinate solution. The ultimate elements of nature, therefore, are problematic Ideas, but more precisely they are problematic Ideas as multiplicities, and as such they are the metaphysical hinge upon which determinate things come to be. Deleuze acknowledges the metaphysical importance of multiplicity, and contrasts this concept most forcefully with the traditional categories of the one and the many. In doing so, he also returns to the questions prompted by an encounter with the nature of a problem, or, as we can now say, with the nature of problematic Ideas as multiplicities. The passage is worth quoting in full:

> multiplicity must not designate a combination of the many and the one, but rather an organization belonging to the many as such, which has no need whatsoever of unity in order to form a system. The one and the many are concepts of the understanding which make up the overly loose mesh of a distorted dialectic which proceeds by opposition. The biggest fish pass through. Can we believe that the concrete is attained when the inadequacy of an abstraction is compensated for by the inadequacy of its opposite? We can say 'the one is multiple, the multiple one' for ever: we speak like Plato's young men who did not even spare the farmyard. Contraries may be combined, contradictions established, but at no point has the essential been raised: 'how many', 'how', 'in which cases'. The essence is nothing, an empty generality, when separated from this measure, this manner and this study of cases. Predicates may be

combined, but the Idea is missed: the outcome is an empty discourse which lacks a substantive. 'Multiplicity', which replaces the one no less than the multiple, is the true substantive, substance itself. (Deleuze 1994, 182)

The important distinction at work in this passage is that between unity and system. In both cases, a many comes to be organised, but for Deleuze a unity provides an organisational framework that is determinate and distinct from the many. Plato's Ideas are often interpreted to be examples of such unities. As Socrates presses Euthyphro in their discussion of holiness, for instance, he doesn't want Euthyphro to give him multiple instances or cases of holiness, but instead reminds him to 'call to mind that this is not what I asked you, to tell me of one or two of the many holy acts, but to tell the essential aspect, by which all holy acts are holy; for you said that all unholy acts were unholy and all holy ones holy by one aspect' (*Euthyphro* 6d-e). As I argued in the *Inquiry*, one can also read Plato's Ideas as multiplicities, and Deleuze will frequently understand Plato in this way, but there is also a clear sense in Plato's early works (of which *Euthyphro* was one) that an Idea provides the transcendent unity that accounts for why the many are the way they are. A systemic unity, by contrast, is on Deleuze's understanding an organisation of the many that does not require a transcendent, determinate unity to predetermine the process. The organisation of the many in this case occurs immanently, as a process of self-organisation. Deleuze's emphasis on a self-organising system that can do without unity has much in common with recent work in dynamic systems theory (for more, see Bell 2006), though for our purposes here the key point to note is that a multiplicity is a systemic organisation that does not presuppose a determinate unity or totality.

The next key point extends the first: not only does the many not need a transcendent unity to organise it, but the very notion of one or unity is itself an abstraction inadequate to the task of dealing with concrete cases. Whatever way we might combine the one and the multiple, or say the multiple is one, we will still leave the most important questions regarding concrete cases un-answered. Let us return to the case of the jealous lover. Will the many facts that feed into their jealousy be resolved if we tell them that their partner has indeed had an affair? In some ways knowing this would certainly settle some issues — divorce proceedings or separation may commence — but the jealous thinking will not be satisfied, as we have seen. The jealous person will seek more details — in what circumstances did it occur, how many times, who else might there have been if there was this person, etc. The concrete specifici-ties of the case are inadequately addressed by attempting to reduce them to a simple 'What is X?' question, even if we get a true, clear answer to this question, e.g., 'What is the nature of my partner's loyalty?', to which we get the answer, 'Your partner is disloyal.'

The same is true, perhaps surprisingly, in the sciences. Let us assume, for the sake of argument, that to the question 'What is temperature?' we get the answer 'Temperature is mean kinetic energy.' As Mark Wilson has shown, and as discussed in greater detail in my *Inquiry*, this definition of temperature is inadequate to determining the temperature in many actual cases. Wilson argues that the definition of temperature as mean kinetic energy is actually 'generally false' (Wilson 1985, 228), but is widely believed in no small part due to the influence of Ernest Nagel's philosophy of science (see Nagel 1961). To the extent that this definition is true, Wilson adds, it is so only in cases where we have a classical ideal gas rather than most other substances, and a classical ideal gas at equilibrium rather than in a dynamic, far from equilibrium state. In other words, the widely accepted answer to the question, 'What is temperature?' fails to account for the temperature of substances in most cases. Things become even more complicated when we try to account for the *measurement* of temperature (for the full details of this story, see Chang 2004). If we assume, for instance, that a thermometer measures temperature, we need to overlook the fact that this is only true in cases that fall within certain limits and parameters. Wilson points out that a mercury thermometer 'will not function properly in an environment full of shock waves or if applied to objects at extremely high or low temperatures' (Wilson 1982, 563). In cases where temperatures reach such extremes, other means of measurement need to be used, but then these too have their own limits. The point to be taken from this example – and it is precisely Deleuze's point regarding the nature of multiplicities – is that the abstract category involved in the answer to a 'What is X?' question is inadequate for anything other than propaedeutic purposes, and that 'once the dialectic brews up' (Deleuze 1994, 188), and we begin to differentiate this abstract category in concrete cases, as multiplicities, we find ourselves with other questions, e.g., 'How are we to take temperature readings in this case?', 'Where and when should readings be taken?', 'In which cases will this method not work?' In drawing out the implications of these questions, in encountering the nature of multiplicities (problematic Ideas), we come upon the necessity of drawing limits and parameters that create the systemic conditions that make a solution possible – such as correctly applying a temperature predicate to a substance.

We can now begin to fill in the details of what is involved in the 'art of multiplicities: the art of grasping the Ideas and the problems they incarnate in things, and of grasping things as incarnations, as cases of solution for the problems of Ideas' (Deleuze 1994, 182). In short, rather than confounding problems and solutions, and hence launching upon a futile and meaningless process of further determining and differentiating the determinate, we instead need to discern the limits and organisation of a problematic Idea (multiplicity)

50

that make sense of the determinate cases or solutions that respond to it. This is not a matter of discerning determinate limits, or an organised unity that is determinate and distinct from other unities. Due to the paradoxical nature of sense, whatever we may identify and discern, whether as unity or limit and boundary, will at the same time be potentially undermined and no longer what we discerned, even though it is not another determinate that can also be discerned. A better way to understand what is involved here, then, is in terms of an art of multiplicities that entails developing a taste for that which cannot be reduced to the determinate and yet remains inseparable from the determinate. In short, the art of multiplicities requires a taste for problematic Ideas that are non-mereological parts of the determinate things that are the subjects of our thinking. Deleuze and Guattari will explicitly acknowledge the importance of taste, what they will call a 'higher taste', and it will be relevant to both philosophy and science. As they put it, 'a problem, in science or in philosophy, does not consist in answering a question but in adapting, co-adapting, with a higher "taste" as problematic faculty, corresponding elements in the process of being determined' (Deleuze and Guattari 1994, 133). This taste for the problematic, for multiplicity, as it occurs in both science and philosophy, will be critical to how we make sense of things, including our lives. It is to this that we now turn.

3. Matters of Taste

a) The truth one deserves

Let us begin with Hume's famous essay 'Of the Standard of Taste'. This will also enable us to return to and clarify an earlier theme – namely, the manner in which, as Deleuze puts it, 'A solution always has the truth it deserves [mérite] according to the problem to which it is a response, and the problem always has the solution it deserves [mérite] in proportion to its own truth or falsity – in other words, in proportion to its sense' (Deleuze 1994, 159). The question to ask here is how, and in what circumstances, a solution *deserves* its truth, or a problem has the solution it *deserves*. To speak of deserving a truth or solution, of gaining it on merit, implies that there is a standard whereby the deserving can be separated from the undeserving. If an employee, for instance, gets a merit-based pay increase or promotion, we assume there is an accepted criterion or standard upon which the judgment of merit is based. This could be one of many standards being applied – amount of sales the person brought in, number of hours worked, or innovative ideas and proposals that they brought to the company, etc. These standards may be criticised and come to be judged by yet other standards, such as a standard of what is good for society and/or the environment; or those who apply these standards may be accused of not applying them fairly – for instance, when women who are equally deserving get passed over in favour of men. But standards are nonetheless critical to judgments about who or what has merit and is therefore deserving of something. Deleuze himself states the criterion whereby a problem has the solution it deserves – it deserves it 'in proportion to its own truth or falsity … in proportion to its sense'.

At this point it will be helpful to turn to Hume's essay on taste, and for a fairly straightforward reason. While recognising the obvious point that there is a 'great variety of Taste, as well as of opinion, which prevails in the world' (Hume 1985, 226), Hume does not accept the conclusion that might be drawn from this point, namely that the criteria for beauty 'exists merely in the mind', or that since 'One person may even perceive deformity, where another is sensible of beauty', then it must be the case that 'To seek the real beauty, or real deformity, is as fruitless an enquiry, as to pretend to ascertain the real sweet or real bitter' (230). For Hume, by contrast, there is a real basis for judgments of beauty, a real standard of taste. With this basis for judgments of beauty we can return to Deleuze, and to the nature of problems, problems that are not to be confused with the determinate, including especially the determinate solutions that give voice to a problem. But if we rule out a determinate criterion or standard for determining merit, how then can there be a proportion of truth or falsity, a proportion of sense that gives problems the solutions they deserve? The manner in which Hume sets forth his argument for the standard of taste will go a long way in helping us to answer this question.

b) Hume's 'Of the Standard of Taste'

In his essay on taste, Hume is not simply arguing for the legitimacy of judgments of taste. His argument is more complicated in that he is challenging *both* the view that the 'various sentiments' cannot be placed in subordination to any rules or standards that are then applied in our judgments of taste, *and* the view that taste itself can be subordinate to a universal rule. Hume's effort to steer clear of these two positions charts the path of human nature. As he makes clear in the Introduction to his *Treatise of Human Nature*, ''Tis evident, that all the sciences have a relation, greater or less, to human nature; and that however wide any of them may seem to run from it, they still return back by one passage or another'. Whatever the science, they are 'under the cognizance of men, and are judged by their powers and faculties', and for this reason Hume argues that our chances of making any 'changes and improvements ... in these sciences' will be improved by a better understanding of human nature, or by the 'science of Man' as he puts it (Hume 1978, Introduction.4; SB xv). The same is no less true, or perhaps even more so, in the case of our judgments concerning beauty in the arts.

Hume is quite up front in arguing that there is a natural affinity between human nature and the things of the natural world such that, under the right circumstances, people will consistently judge and differentiate between what is beautiful and what is not. As he puts it: 'amidst all the variety and caprice of taste, there are certain general principles of approbation or blame, whose influence a careful eye may trace in all operations of the mind'. The reason for this is that there are 'particular forms or qualities, from the original structure of the internal fabric [of human nature] ... calculated to please, and others to displease' (Hume 1985, 233). Hume thus argues that there is indeed a basis for a rule-like standard in determining whether something is or is not deserving of a particular judgment of taste – i.e., approbation or blame. This standard is only rule-like, however, and not a true universal rule or law, and certainly not a rule one can grasp *a priori*. For Hume 'the general rules of art are founded only on experience and on the observation of the common sentiments of human nature' (232), meaning that since we humans all share the same nature we ought also to be struck by the 'forms or qualities' that please or displease. There are, however, numerous obstacles which keep us from realising this potential, and the 'concurrence of many favourable circumstances' that are necessary to good taste do not often fall into place. Much of Hume's essay, in fact, is spent detailing the various impediments to actualising the standard of taste in a manner that would result in our correctly giving merit where merit is deserved.

The minimal condition that needs to be met in order to be able to actualise the standard of taste in our judgments is that the sense organs should be in fine working order. 'A man in fever', Hume notes, 'would not insist on his palate as able to decide concerning flavours; nor would one, affected with jaundice, pretend to give a verdict with regard to colours' (Hume 1985, 233). In addition to having senses that are in a sound rather than defective state, we also need to develop a delicacy of imagination whereby we can differentiate between the different features and elements of objects, as well as the finer emotions that may also be provoked by the 'forms or qualities' of these objects. At this point Hume brings in an example from *Don Quixote* (pt. 2, chap. 13), where Sancho tells a story about two of his kinsmen who respectively sensed 'a small taste of leather' and a 'taste of iron' in a hogshead of wine, which turned out to be justified when they found 'an old key with a leathern thong tied to it' (Hume 1985, 235) at the bottom of the empty hogshead. Hume uses this example to clarify that most people lack the delicacy to discern 'qualities [that] may be found in a small degree' and that are often 'mixed and confounded with each other', and thus for most the 'minute qualities' remain undetected at all. He thus defines the delicacy of taste necessary for accurate judgments of taste as follows: 'Where the organs are so fine, as to allow nothing to escape them; and at the same time so exact as to perceive every ingredient in the composition: This we call delicacy of taste' (235).

Hume also argues that, in addition to the need for proper and finely tuned sense organs, there is another factor that needs to be avoided if we are to discern and judge what's before us accurately. He categorises this obstacle as '*prejudice*', which he sees as standing in the way of assuring that nothing 'enter into [the critic's] consideration, but the very object which is submitted to his examination' (Hume 1985, 239). We can identify two forms of prejudice: one that is primarily social and conventional by nature, and another (which accounts for the first) that results from the application of the principles of association, principles Hume ties to human nature itself. With respect to the first, Hume admits that 'Authority or prejudice may give a temporary vogue to a bad poet or orator; but his reputation will never be durable or general' (233). For sociological and/or political reasons, a person or persons in positions of authority may hold sway on certain subjects and influence people's judgments such that a work may, for a time, achieve undeserved acclaim. Given a different time and place, when the conditions that temporarily gave merit to the work are no longer be active, it will likely cease being acclaimed; however, a work of 'real genius', Hume argues, will continue over different times and in different places to achieve the praise it deserves.

The second form of prejudice which hinders our ability to ascribe merit where it is due is partiality; this prejudice is even more insidious than the first since it follows from the very principles of association that Hume lays down in his *Treatise*. In particular, whereas the principles of association establish relations between ideas – namely, resemblance, contiguity and causality – it is only the relation of causality, or necessary connection, that Hume claims enables us to move beyond what is given to a new idea or belief regarding something that is not given, and the passions are key to this process. For instance, our expectation that the eight ball will roll into the corner pocket once struck by the cue ball that is moving towards it at a particular angle is not simply the result of our having repetitively applied the principles of association to similar situations in the past. This, by itself, would not give us anything new but would simply give us more of the same. The idea of a necessary connection between A (cue ball) and B (eight ball) is not just another version of previous relations between A and B but involves, rather, inferring that the relationship is distinctive in that it is necessary – without

A, there would be no B. Hume is clear on this point: 'From the mere repetition of any past impression, even to infinity, there never will arise any new original idea, such as that of a necessary connexion' (Hume 1978, 1.3.6.3; SB 88). Consequently, what is needed, he claims, is a feeling that comes to be connected with a new idea in the mind. The important passage from the *Treatise* is the following:

> Tho' several resembling instances, which give rise to the idea of power, have no influence on each other, and can never produce any new quality in the object, which can be the model of that idea, yet the observation of this resemblance produces a new impression in the mind, which is its real model, for after we have observ'd the resemblance in a sufficient number of instances, we immediately feel a determination of the mind to pass from one object to its usual attendant, and to conceive it in a stronger light upon account of that relation ... Necessity, then, is the effect of this observation, and is nothing but an internal impression of the mind, or a determination to carry our thoughts from one object to another. (Hume 1978, 1.3.14.17; SB 164–5).

As we saw earlier in discussing the risk delirium poses, but also its foundational role in the mind for Hume, the idea of necessary connection results from a strong feeling or passion that arises over time, through custom and habit. Delirium arises when the strong passion occurs in just one instance and not in the normal, socially legitimate contexts where a regular recurrence of resembling events leads one to a strongly held belief and the expectations that come with this belief. As with the passion and feeling associated with causality, the same happens with the principles of association more generally – the passions hone the principles and give rise to beliefs and commitments which direct the passions in ways that exclude other possibilities, possibilities that may have been realised given other life histories. In other words, a result of the principles of association and the passions is a partiality that is integral to human nature. This is a point that Deleuze stresses in his reading of Hume: 'the passions have the effect of restricting the range of the mind, fixating it on privileged ideas and objects, for the basis of passion is not egotism but partiality, which is much worse. We are passionate in the first place about our parents, about those who are close to us and like us (restricted causality, contiguity, resemblance)' (Deleuze 2001, 46). The same is true, as Hume shows, with respect to our prejudices concerning art, for here as well our partiality inclines us to favour some works over others and perhaps give undue praise to a work that is not deserving. We are thus 'more pleased', Hume argues, 'with pictures and characters, that resemble objects which are found in our own age or country, than with those which describe a different set of customs' (Hume 1985, 245). In fact, we may well, as Hume said in the opening paragraph to his essay on taste, 'call barbarous whatever departs widely from our own taste and apprehension: But soon find the epithet of reproach retorted on us' (227). Our partiality may well keep us from seeing the 'particular forms or qualities' (233) that are by nature calculated, Hume argues, to please or displease, and it may in fact lead us to misjudge and praise that which is undeserving of praise. The effort to overcome this partiality and prejudice in judgments of art is an arduous one, as Hume himself admits, in referring to the task of appreciating the nuances of works from different times and places:

> There needs to be a certain turn of thought or imagination to make us enter into all the opinions, which then prevailed, and relish the sentiments or con-clusions derived from them. But a very violent effort is requisite to change our judgment of manners, and excite sentiments of approbation or blame, love or hatred, different from those to which the mind from long custom has been familiarized. (Hume 1985, 247)

If a critic is able to overcome these prejudices and 'allow nothing to enter into his consideration, but the very object which is submitted to his ex-amination' (239), and if their sense organs are in excellent working order, then we can trust that this person's judgments will accurately give praise and blame to that which is deserving of it. In other words, it is the critic who meets the aforementioned conditions and overcomes the barriers to formulating a proper judgment who provides, for Hume, the standards of taste for determining which artworks are deserving of merit. The critic who successfully realises the standard of taste when they exercise their judgments concerning art sees that 'there is a mutual relation and correspondence of parts ... [a] consistence and uniformity of the whole' (240). It is precisely this 'consistence and uniformity of the whole' that is the earmark of works which deserve the praise they receive, and it is this that the critic is attentive to when their judgments realise the standard of taste. This consistence, moreover, is not to be confused with the mere uniformity of a rule, an abstract rule-as-rail or principle that is then applied to a separate content (as with our earlier, anti-scepticism reading of Wittgenstein's rule-following paradox), nor are the judgments that praise these works random and relative; rather, the con-sistence and uniformity Hume refers to here is simply the tell-tale signature of an imagination that produces an artwork that gives voice to the condition that abstract rules and principles presuppose.

c) Constructing problems

We are now in a position to address Deleuze's claim that a problem has the solution it deserves 'in proportion to its [the problem's] own truth or falsity – in other words, in proportion to its sense' (Deleuze 1994, 159). Put simply,

Deleuze largely reworks Hume's own claim that a work gets the praise it deserves when it has the 'consistence and uniformity of the whole' which is by nature 'calculated to please' (Hume 1985, 233); for Deleuze this means that a problem gets the solution it deserves when it too has a particular 'consistence and uniformity', and, as in Hume, this 'consistence and uniformity' is neither an abstract rule to be applied universally and without exception, nor is it random and arbitrary. In other words, it is multiplicities, as discussed above, which provide the basis upon which a problem gets the solution it deserves. As we saw, a multiplicity provides an 'organization belonging to the many as such, which has no need whatsoever of unity in order to form a system' (Deleuze 1994, 182). To state this differently, the elements that constitute the problem do not, by themselves, constitute the conditions for the solution, just as it is not only the elements of an artwork discerned by the critic which constitute the genius of the work; rather, it is a 'consistence and uniformity', or what Deleuze (and Guattari) will call a plane of consistency, which gives the solution the truth it deserves, and the problem the solution it deserves.

To clarify this point, we can return to a theme Deleuze himself frequently calls upon when discussing the nature of problems – learning. Deleuze is clear that learning is integrally involved with the nature of problems. As we saw earlier, for him 'Learning is the appropriate name for the subjective acts carried out when one is confronted with the objecticity (*objectité*) of a problem (Idea), whereas knowledge designates only the generality of concepts or the calm possession of a rule enabling solutions' (Deleuze 1994, 164). A problem is thus not an objective reality, something to be confused with the determinate objects and things that can be the subject of representational thought. Nevertheless, insofar as objects and things are understood, by Deleuze, 'as incarnations, as cases of solution for the problems of Ideas', there is an object-ness that accounts for the solutions these problems deserve, and it is this object-ness, or objecticity as Paul Patton translates the French in *Difference and Repetition*, that is confronted when learning occurs. Another way of thinking of this object-ness, this objecticity, is that it provides the consistency necessary for the learning that occurs in response to a problem to take place, a learning that then allows for and makes possible 'the generality of concepts or the calm possession of a rule enabling solutions' (164).

It is immediately after Deleuze makes this point about learning that he brings in the example of the 'well-known test in psychology' which involved monkeys finding, among boxes of different colours, food that was always placed under boxes of a particular colour.[8] Initially the monkeys did not

---

8. Deleuze does not cite the experiment he has in mind, but he may be thinking of Wolfgang Köhler's experiments during the First World War. The most famous of these

search for food, much less realise there was food under boxes of a particular colour. They were hungry, however, and when by chance they encountered food under a box they then began to search under the boxes, randomly at first, until a point was reached where, as Deleuze describes it, 'there comes a paradoxical period during which the number of "errors" diminishes even though the monkey does not yet possess the "knowledge" or "truth" of a solution' (Deleuze 1994, 164). This paradoxical period is precisely the consistency that makes a solution possible, the 'consistence and uniformity' that is not yet knowledge or a rule, and yet is that which makes learning, and hence the actualisation of knowledge of a rule, possible. This paradoxical period, in short, is the consistency, or object-ness, that gives the solution or knowledge the truth it deserves, for it is what makes sense of the solution. As we have seen, however, sense is paradoxical, tending both towards the differentiated and dedifferentiated, and this is precisely what occurs in learning. In the case of the monkeys learning the rule about where the food is to be found, for instance, the process of learning entails a differentiating movement in that the now problematised context the monkey finds itself in is one where many different things have become potentially relevant to the problem – e.g., boxes, colours, etc. At the same time, in order for the monkey to learn, there must also be a dedifferentiating movement, a movement towards a yet to be determined solution, the solution the problem deserves. We see this even more clearly in the example of learning to swim that Deleuze brings in immediately following his discussion of the monkey experiment. In learning to swim one is also confronted with a differentiating movement – one's body is suddenly confronted with elements that it must, in the problematic state

---

experiments were the problem-solving experiments with Sultan the chimpanzee who was able to 'figure out' how to attach two sticks together to reach food and, in another experiment, stack boxes on top of one another to reach bananas that were out of reach. Merleau-Ponty cites the latter experiment in his *Phenomenology of Perception*, and hence Köhler's experiments certainly qualify as 'well-known'. Köhler's interpretations of the results to justify what has come to be called insight learning also track the manner in which Deleuze interprets the results of the experiments he refers to in *Difference and Repetition*. Köhler's interpretations have been contested and subject to varied attempts to modify and rethink them (see, for instance, Perkins 2000 and Ohlsson 2011, and Weisberg 2015 for a critical summary and attempt to integrate them with other approaches; the approach to learning offered here follows Weisberg's integrated approach in important respects). Whether or not Köhler's work is what Deleuze had in mind, I could not find the experiments he cites among those Köhler conducted. Harlow's learning set studies with monkeys from the late 1940s and 1950s do more closely match those described by Deleuze (though not exactly), but the results of his own study led, he argued, to a rejection of Köhler's conclusions regarding insight (see Harlow 1949, 1959). Harlow's studies were also well-known, especially his more notorious studies of attachment in monkeys, and what happens when a monkey is placed on a wire mother rather than a fur mother.

of learning to swim, coordinate and organise such that the skill of swimming can be attained. There are the many motions of one's body that need to be addressed, as well as currents, buoyancy, etc. At the same time there is a dedifferentiating movement, a dedifferentiation of one's bodily relationships in that one's established habits and differentiated relations become undone, undermined, and hence less differentiated than they were. This is the sense in which learning entails unlearning. Learning, however, is a risky venture, for unless both de/differentiating tendencies are brought together into a consistency that makes learning a new skill possible, one may fail to learn at all, or simply resort to established habits and routines. For learning to take place, therefore – 'To learn to swim', for instance, as Deleuze argues – it is necessary 'to conjugate the distinctive points of our bodies with the singular points of the objective Idea in order to form a problematic field' (165). In other words, Deleuze is following Hume and arguing that just as judgments of taste are good if they express the 'consistence and uniformity' of a work that is by nature predisposed to please, so too something that is learned (a rule, skill, etc.) is a solution that expresses a consistency or systematicity of elements, what Deleuze calls the objective Idea.[9] This consistency, however, is not already there, waiting to be discovered, but is a consistency that needs to be constructed and produced in the very process of learning. This is the sense in which a problem is constructed, or what Deleuze has in mind when he speaks of conjugating distinctive points 'in order to form a problematic field'. Once constructed, however, a problem is not a solution. As that which makes sense of its solutions, a problem always entails the paradox of sense: the solutions that express sense also express the potential undermining of the solution, and as a result the dedifferentiation that made the solution possible also renders the solution provisional.

It is now clear why, when they return to this theme twenty-five years later, in a book devoted to making sense of philosophy, Deleuze and Guattari will emphasise both the nature of problems and the 'higher "taste" as problematic faculty'. More importantly, they argue that this higher 'taste' for problems is to be found 'in science or in philosophy' (Deleuze and Guattari 1994, 133). Without saying so explicitly, what Deleuze and Guattari are challenging here is the widely held view that philosophy is simply the mother or incubator of the sciences. A version of this argument states that philosophy is good at raising problems, at asking questions, but science comes along once a way is

---

9. The consistency and systematicity of elements that are involved in learning when both de/differentiating tendencies are brought into the mix but not allowed to exceed limits that would undermine learning is another instance where dynamic systems theory offers a helpful example to clarify these points. Again, see Bell 2006, and footnote 4 above.

found to address these problems through quantitative, experimental methods that can be repeated. This point was most famously made by Bertrand Russell: 'as soon as definite knowledge concerning any subject becomes possible, this subject ceases to be called philosophy, and becomes a separate science' (Russell 2001, 90). This view, according to Deleuze and Guattari, excessively abstracts from the tendencies of philosophy and science when the reality is that both are concerned with problems, and both exercise a 'problematic faculty' with a higher 'taste' for problems, a faculty that involves a necessary creativity. There are differences, however. We could say that philosophy stresses the dedifferentiating tendency of making sense, the movement towards the dedifferentiated and infinite, wherein it seeks the condition that is not to be confused or confounded with any determinate matter of fact. That said, however, philosophy ought nonetheless to be actively engaged with states of affairs, facts, the findings of science, etc., since these are precisely the things that the problems make sense of, or the solutions the problem deserves. One cannot have a higher 'taste' for problems without being actively engaged in the world of determinate things. Science, by contrast, emphasises the differentiating tendency of making sense, and it is for this reason that the sciences are necessarily constrained by the limits that must be drawn in order to represent determinate facts by way of functions and equations (recall our earlier discussion of Wilson on temperature). Despite this, science nonetheless flirts with the infinite, with the dedifferentiating tendency that transgresses limits. As Deleuze and Guattari put it, 'science cannot avoid experiencing a profound attraction for the chaos with which it battles ... Science would relinquish all the rational unity to which it aspires for a little piece of chaos that it could explore' (Deleuze and Guattari 1994, 205–6). In other words, science is also drawn towards the dedifferentiating tendency of making sense, the tendency towards less differentiation, towards the infinitude and chaos that is not to be confused with anything determinate. With both science and philosophy, therefore, we have two contrasting efforts to make sense of problems, to give expression to problems in solutions that have the truth they deserve. Both philosophy and science are thus two indispensable sides to the coin that is making sense of life.

§2 Communication Problems

1. Signal–Sign Systems

Shifting our focus slightly from the claim that philosophy and science are two contrasting efforts to the problem of making sense of life, we will turn in this chapter to explore how this problem has been taken up as a communication problem. This shift to communication problems opens up an entire world of research into language and communication. The effort here, however, will not be to encapsulate the many ways in which communication problems have been addressed, but to follow through on the implications of the previous chapter by employing Claude Shannon's well-known approach to communication problems in order to highlight the difference between scientific and philosophical approaches to the problem of making sense. This difference will then be tracked through a variety of contexts in this and subsequent chapters, including (in this chapter) the territorial behaviour of animals, the challenges of narrative comprehension in AI research, Claude Steele's self-affirmation studies, Plato's view that philosophy is prompted by the contradictory nature of perceptions, and finally Heidegger's understanding of authenticity. This varied, sinuous path will provide us with a number of threads that we will then draw together in setting forth a critical existentialism that can provide us with the tools to sidestep the tendency to become overly reliant on solutions without a problem, solutions that may become, as Foucault recognised, 'the fascism that is ingrained in our behavior' (Deleuze and Guattari 1977, xiii).

a) Information theory

In the late 1940s, while working at Bell Labs, Claude Shannon published his landmark essay, 'A Mathematical Theory of Communication'. At the outset of this essay Shannon states the problem his approach sets out to resolve:

> The fundamental problem of communication is that of reproducing at one point either exactly or approximately a message selected at another point. Frequently the messages have meaning; that is they refer to or are correlated

according to some system with certain physical or conceptual entities. These semantic aspects of communication are irrelevant to the engineering problem. (Shannon and Weaver 1949, 1)

For those old enough to remember making phone calls from as recently as the 1980s, especially international calls, the quality of the call would often succumb to an acoustic fog of static noise and distortion that would make communication difficult if not impossible. In the late 1940s, when Shannon worked for Bell Labs, the situation was even worse, and Shannon's problem, as he himself lays it out, was to figure out a way of eliminating the noise in communications from one point to another, or reducing errors.

Key to resolving this problem, for Shannon, was determining and measuring precisely what is being sent at one end so that it can then be determined how much of what was sent has been received at the other end. To do this, Shannon adopted a base 2 logarithm for measuring the quantity of information contained in a message that is being sent. As he puts it: 'If the base 2 [logarithm] is used the resulting units may be called binary digits, or more briefly bits, a word suggested by J.W. Tukey. A device with two stable positions, such as a relay or a flip-flop circuit, can store one bit of information. N such devices can store N bits, since the total number of possible states is 2^N and $\log_2 2^N = N$' (Shannon and Weaver 1949, 1). Stated simply, one bit of information is what we need to know to decide between two equally likely outcomes, such as whether the coin just tossed came up heads or tails. If we learn it came up heads, our 'flip-flop circuit', to use Shannon's phrase, will flip to 1, and if it came up tails it will flip to 0. The more binary questions we need to answer in order to complete a message, such as in a game of twenty questions, the more information is contained in the message.

With this understanding of information in place, the problem of securing communication across the phone network entailed reducing errors, where errors are understood by Shannon to be what happens 'During transmission [when] the noise introduces errors so that, on the average, 1 in 100 is received incorrectly (a 0 as 1, or 1 as 0)' (Shannon and Weaver 1949, 20), which would in this case be an error rate of 1%. Shannon's solution to this communication problem involves the translation of a message – spoken words transmitted across a phone line for instance – through a statistical analysis that results in a string of bits that are less susceptible to noise interference. What becomes important in this statistical analysis is that which is unexpected or surprising, for this provides more information than that which is more expected and less surprising. If we want a personalised licence plate, for example, we can get by with the following – lvs phlsphy. Most people with sufficient grasp of the English language would likely understand the message – the driver of this car loves philosophy. The vowels, in other words, are not as relevant to understanding the message as the statistically less likely arrangement of consonants – the vowels are redundant letters that occur in words at a much higher rate than others, and hence provide less relevant information. By increasing the redundancy of the information that is statistically less likely, and thus more relevant, one can decrease the error rate of communication transmissions. In other words, making sure 'lvs' gets through will assure the message is delivered more so than if one made sure that 'oe' got through.

Although this is a simplified summary of Shannon's solution to the communication problem he lays out, one thing should be clear – what is important is not the meaning of the message that is sent but merely its statistical-mathematical translation into *bits*, into the 1s and 0s that we are now all so familiar with in this age of computers. As Shannon himself said at the outset, and as cited above, the 'semantic aspects of communication are irrelevant to the engineering problem'. This reduction of communication transmission to an engineering problem that could ignore the semantics of the message caught some by surprise. Although Shannon's work paved the way for information theory, and for many other developments as well, at a colloquium in March 1950 Shannon's proposals were met with some scepticism. As James Gleick recounts the event, some of those in attendance wondered whether Shannon's information theory was really about information. Heinz von Foerster expressed a sentiment shared by others, including the anthropologist Margaret Mead, who was at the colloquium, when he wrote in his notes:

> I wanted to call the whole of what they called information theory signal theory … because information was not yet there. There were 'beep beeps' but that was all, no information. The moment one transforms that set of signals into other signals our brain can make an understanding of, then information is born – it's not in the beeps. (cited in Gleick 2011, 248).

Von Foerster raises an important issue, and one which will be the primary concern of this and subsequent sections – namely, what is the relationship between signals and meaning, with meaning taken to be something that one 'can make an understanding of'. The ambient temperature of a room, for instance, may signal to a thermostat to engage the air-conditioning, or the call of a monkey may signal to others that there is a certain predator nearby, a signal that prompts the monkeys to take particular evasive actions; but there is nothing there in either case that the thermostat or the monkey understands – there's just, in von Foerster's words, and speaking figuratively, 'beep beeps'. Now one may challenge my grouping of monkeys in with the thermostat, for who is to say, one might argue, that the monkeys lack a state of mind or awareness that attends their receiving the signal and their subsequent evasive actions? This is indeed an important question, and what it highlights is the fact that there is a distinction between signs, which include a sense or meaning that is capable of being understood, and signals, which may predictably prompt a response but without any corresponding understanding of the sense or significance of the signal itself. To restate the question regarding the monkey's response to another's call: does the monkey receive a signal or a sign?

b) Signal-sign systems (with excursus on ethology)

To provide a basis for answering this question, let us begin with how we will be differentiating between signs and signals. Put simply, a sign will express a problem, or, to restate our earlier arguments, sense has the sign it deserves, in proportion to the problem it expresses. A signal, by contrast, is an exchange that occurs between two or more already determinate systems or entities. To clarify this distinction, let us return to Shannon's communication problem. At first blush it appears von Foerster is right and what we have with Shannon is a signal theory rather than an information theory, or an information theory without sense and meaning, a theory appropriate perhaps for thoughtless machines that send beeps back and forth, but not for those who communicate with and understand one another. At this point our earlier arguments (1.3.c) become relevant. As we said then, problems and solutions are not two separate realms that are to be thought of as being apart from one another, like Plato's Forms adrift in a heavenly intelligible world completely separate and distinct from the many particulars in the physical world that share in these Forms. It was this lack of separation that led us to say that philosophy, although tending towards the problematic, and science, with its tendency towards the determinate and the limits necessary for the equations and functions that represent determinate phenomena, are in the end two sides of the same coin that is making sense of life. In the case of signs and signals, they too are not to be thought of in the abstract, as removed and separable from one another, but as integrally related in what Deleuze calls a signal–sign system.

One way to clarify what Deleuze means by a signal–sign system is to say that signs are integral to processes of making sense (sense as a problem, as *condition* for the determinate), whereas signals and signalling are what occurs between things where the sense has already been determined (sense as *conditioned*). Let us take territorial behaviour, for instance, since this will get us back to our question regarding monkey calls. Whether it is the droppings of a rabbit, the songs of songbirds, or the pushup displays of the western fence lizard, the key to the territorial behaviour is that certain signs are produced in order to establish a determinate territory in relation to other territories that have been produced by the behaviours and signs of conspecifics. In the case of songbirds, for instance, they produce between five and thirteen different song types, often with subtle variations that other birds are able to recognise (see Searcy et al. 2014, 93). This is important, as Searcy et al. point out, for 'In all populations of song sparrows, adult males defend individual territories during the breeding season' (92). What this study also notes, but does not highlight, is the complexities involved as a young male song sparrow sets out to establish a territory. Searcy et al. claim that 'Territory establishment coincides with the onset of adult singing behavior in young sparrows', citing the influential work of M.M. Nice (1937, 1943). They go on to add that 'During this period in which they learn their songs, young males visit as many as 30–40 territories, gradually reducing their home range … [and] [y]oung males learn songs from multiple males during this period, preferring to learn songs that are sung by more than one potential neighbor' (Searcy et al. 2014, 95–6). Despite these observations, much of the experimental research seeks to differentiate the song types that are most effective at functioning as signals, i.e., which predictably announce aggressive behaviour and thereby reduce the likelihood of intrusion into the songbirds' territory. In other words, much of the focus is upon the behaviours that defend an already established territory and much less attention has been paid to the territorialising process itself. But it is with the territorialising process that the relationship between sign and signal becomes most clear.

As the young male sparrow sets out to establish a territory and learn the song that will eventually form the basis for the aggressive signalling behaviour that alerts potential intruders of their transgressions, they begin by moving between territories. As Searcy et al. show, they visit multiple territories (between 30–40) and learn the songs of the sparrows from these territories, 'preferring to learn songs that are sung by more than one potential neighbor'. In other words, the young sparrow will begin between territories, learning and varying the songs of its neighbours until it comes to a distinctive song that will then be associated by its neighbours with the now established territory of the sparrow. In this context, the initial song variations of the young male sparrow are signs, for they are not yet the determinate signals used to defend an established territory, but variations on the songs of neighbouring sparrows. Thus the signs of a territorialising song sparrow always presuppose other signs – other variations, songs, territories – and thus its signs express a multiplicity of songs from already determinate and differentiated territories; in other words, the young sparrow's songs do not yet signal a territory since it is still in the process of establishing a territory by way of dedifferentiating already established relations and territories. In short, a sign expresses sense, or a problem, and hence the paradoxical de/differentiating tendencies discussed earlier (see 1.2.c), whereas a signal expresses a relationship between already established territories.[1]

Before returning to von Foerster's claim that Shannon's theory is simply a signal theory and not an information theory, let us consider one more example – the lizard – and from there move beyond animal behaviour and begin to clarify Deleuze's claim that 'Every phenomenon flashes in a signal-sign system' (Deleuze 1994, 222). In a series of essays, J.A. Stamps and V.V. Krishnan set out to address what is widely recognised to be a lacuna in the scholarship on territorial animals – namely, the specific behaviour associated with acquiring territory. The influential biologist and theorist, John Maynard Smith, for instance, argues that, although 'much is known about how animals behave once territories have been established, we know little about how these territories are established in the first place' (Maynard Smith 1982, 153; cited in Stamps and Krishnan 1995, 679). Despite this lack of knowledge, the general assumption of Maynard Smith and others, according to Stamps and Krishnan, is that animals 'acquire space by winning contests' (679; see Maynard Smith and Parker 1976; Maynard Smith 1982). What Stamp and Krishnan's work has shown, however, is that this assumption is not true in the case of the lizards (*Anolis aeneus*) they studied. Not only was there 'little indication that settlers acquired space by winning first encounters with opponents … [but] in the vast majority of dyads both winners and losers abandoned the site of their first interaction with each other' (Stamps and Krishnan 1995, 683). In other words, a juvenile lizard does not come to a new territory, guns blazing so to speak, and, if successful in defeating the current occupant, displace them and come to occupy the territory themselves. A far more reliable determinant of whether a lizard will come to occupy and eventually claim a territory for themselves is first and foremost the familiarity they acquire with the space. What Stamps and Krishnan's research showed was that individual lizards 'moved away from the location where they first encountered a new opponent', which is a rule they claim holds 'regardless of the type or the outcome of the first encounter'. Win or lose, in other words, both lizards would tend to avoid the place of a first encounter unless, and this point is

---

1. This point is emphasised by Deleuze and Guattari in their 'On the Refrain' plateau from *A Thousand Plateaus*. They do not use the signal-sign distinction in the context of discussing territorial behaviour, preferring the distinction between rhythm and meter instead, but the role of the latter is roughly equivalent to that of signal and sense as argued for here. A rhythm, they argue, 'is located between two milieus, or between two intermilieus, on the fence … [whereas] action occurs in a milieu' (Deleuze and Guattari 1987, 313).

key, 'a settler had already spent several hours in the area in which it first encountered an opponent, in which case the settler was likely to continue to use that area in the future' (690). For lizards, Stamps and Krishnan point out, several hours is an eternity, given that a territory is usually established within three days of entering a new habitat. During these several hours, a lizard will have become familiar with 'escape routes, shelter sites, foraging locations and other settlers' (681). Moreover, Stamps and Krishnan found that, rather than seeking out a conflict in order to take over a territory, many lizards avoided a first encounter 'by hiding and avoiding social interactions until they became familiar with an area' (Stamps and Krishnan 1994a, 1383). Their conclusion is that 'the only factor significantly related to future space use in these analyses was prior space use; that is, settlers were likely to remain in familiar areas' (Stamps and Krishnan 1995, 684).

With Stamps and Krishnan's work we can restate our earlier points about the territorialising process. Rather than beginning with an already established territory that is then subject to aggressive defence, the acquisition of territory involves a process of familiarisation, and it is the familiarity with an area that underlies the aggressive interactions that eventually establish territorial boundaries between neighbours, boundaries that are marked through the various signs that are the subject of so many studies (e.g., bird songs, scent markings, etc.). Stamps and Krishnan refer to this as a 'symmetrical social interaction between neighbors', in that each of the neighbours engage in the same territorial displays – 'neighbouring wolves ... deposit scent marks on opposite sides of the territory boundary ... cichlid neighbours ... engage in mutual frontal displays ... and song sparrow neighbours exchange song types from a repertoire that they share with another' (as we saw above) (Stamps and Krishnan 1998, 462). To state the process in our terms, an animal constructs a problematic space, a space with a consistence and uniformity of relations between the elements relevant to the animal (e.g., escape routes, shelter sites, foraging locations, other conspecifics), and this becomes the familiarity or condition that determines, more than any other factor, the future use and occupancy of a given space. Stamps and Krishnan thus conclude that 'once the settlement process is complete, *A. aeneus* territory owners have stablished symmetrical (co-dominant) social relationships and relatively exclusive home ranges with owners of adjacent territories' (462). Although work on what is involved as animals acquire territory, rather than what they do with already acquired territory, is limited, Stamps and Krishnan point out that studies of song sparrows (they cite Arcese 1987) show that there is 'no indication that space transfers were preceded by a "definitive" contest won by the floater' (a bird without a territory) (Stamps and Krishnan 1995, 690). Rather than definitive contests of aggression where the winner takes all, other factors such as familiarity with the songs and persistence are more integrally involved with how a song bird comes to acquire a territory.

Rethinking this work on song sparrows and lizards in terms of signal-sign systems, the acquisition of territory involves assembling a consistency and uniformity of signs, such as songs and song types, variations, etc., for song birds, and the relevant parts of an area along with encounters with conspecifics for lizards. As signs, the various elements are not yet tied to a given territory, a territory exemplified by the symmetrical relationships of neighbouring animals, and yet at the same time they are tied to a consistent assemblage of already determinate factors and elements. These signs are what is presupposed by the territories that animals will then set out to defend, through the signalling of aggression (see Maynard Smith 1982, and Maynard Smith and Harper 2003), if not outright aggression, though aggression is not the key factor involved in the acquisition of territory. As forming a signal-sign system, however, signals and signs are to be thought of as abstractions within a dynamic system, or as tendencies of the system that are not fully actualised. As numerous studies of animal behaviour have shown (including the Stamps and Krishnan studies used here), occupying a territory is not a guarantee of future occupation – transfers of space occur all the time. Through familiarisation and persistence, an intruder may well displace a current occupant, or carve out part of the space which then becomes the territory they mark off (i.e., signal) from their neighbours. At the same time, the processes of constructing a consistency of relations among signs involved in becoming familiar with a space are indeed related to determinate features of the environment, including the signals and markings of other already established territories, and thus there are no pure signs in a world of their own safely removed from the determinate.

We can now rethink von Foerster's suggestion that Shannon's information theory is really a signal theory in light of what we have said about signal-sign systems. In short, for the sake of addressing the engineering problem he faces, Shannon has reduced language to pure signals without the potentially undermining effects of signs. From the perspective of the engineering problem itself, it is necessary to limit language to the determinate features that can be statistically quantified and then encoded into a language of bits that can then be transmitted with minimal errors. As we have seen, in order to provide the functional relations and equations that represent phenomena, determinate frames of reference need to be found and maintained – recall our earlier discussion of Wilson regarding temperature, where certain determinate conditions were necessary in order to identify the temperature of a substance. From Shannon's perspective as an engineer with a clearly determinate problem, he is perfectly justified in claiming that 'the semantic aspects of communication are irrelevant to the engineering problem' (Shannon 1949, 1). As we have also seen, however, the sciences nonetheless presuppose the conditions for the determinate that bear the potential to undermine the determinate, the signal-sign system that both makes the determinate possible while also rendering its transformation and undermining possible as well. This is the reason for Deleuze's claim that 'Every phenomenon flashes in a signal-sign system' (Deleuze 1994, 222). Every determinate phenomenon, in other words, comes to be given by virtue of a condition that is not to be confused or confounded with the determinate that is the conditioned, the solution that is not to be confounded with the problem. This was the reason, as we have also seen, for the flirtation on the part of the sciences with the chaos that cannot be represented, a flirtation that must not go too far if the sciences are going to be successful in constructing frames of reference. Shannon's approach thus exemplifies the recognition of the need for limits, of reducing the phenomena of communication to signals that can be digitised and communicated without loss of information; information in this case, however, is nothing but signals without sense, or simply the exchange of 'beeps' as von Foerster put it.

A more problematic tendency that follows in the wake of Shannon's work is the general eclipsing of sense as paradoxical by an understanding of sense as a set of determinate qualities and attributes, and determinate such that they can be captured by the algorithm of a computer. To state this in our earlier terms, this is the tendency to confound problems with solutions, the condition for the determinate with the determinate itself, or to think of solutions as solutions without a problem. This confounding is exemplified in the book by John Pierce that introduced information theory to the general public, a book that Shannon himself oversaw for accuracy. Pierce claims that language is 'a sort of code of communication, though 'an imperfect code [wherein] we must refer meaning back to the intent of the user' (Pierce 1960, 118). To grasp the intent of the user, however, Pierce claims that if 'a word cannot offer a table of qualities or signs whose elements can be traced back to common and familiar experiences, we have a right to be wary of the word' (121). One should be able, therefore, to connect a meaningful word to the determinate elements that allow one person to share with someone else a meaning grounded in a familiarity with the elements of lived experiences. As with the territorial behaviour of animals, the exchange of meaningful words – or signals – presupposes a life wherein an assemblage of elements has already been drawn into the consistency of familiarity. This process of drawing an assemblage of elements into a consistency or the process of familiarisation, is precisely the construction of a problematic space which makes sense of the words that are the signals Shannon encodes through his mathematical

techniques. As that which makes sense of the signals, the process of familiarisation, or the process of territorialisation as we have discussed it here, also
presupposes the potential undermining of a territory, the undermining of
what a word is familiarly taken to mean. In short, if the exchange of words is
a form of *meaningful* communication, then it necessarily entails the possibility
of being misunderstood. Shannon sought to reduce language to a medium
that cannot be misunderstood, where errors can be reduced at will; as a
consequence of this effort, the information age Shannon helped to launch
has carried forward the tendency to confound sense with the determinate,
problems with solutions. This tendency becomes even clearer when we
explore the attempts of researchers in artificial intelligence (AI) to program a
computer to understand stories.

c) Making sense of stories

As a prelude to understanding the nature of stories, and the manner in which
AI addresses the problem that is making sense of stories, let us begin with
improvisational jazz. This may at first appear to be a random digression, but
in fact, as we will see, learning to play improvisational jazz brings with it
many of the same problems that give rise to stories, or narratives. In particular, the difficulty with learning to play *improvisational* jazz – jazz that is not
predetermined by an already written score – is precisely the problem. One
confronts the very nature of a problem in this encounter, and with it the
relevance questions appropriate to the nature of a problem – where? when?
in what circumstances? etc. In his book detailing the difficulties he encountered while learning to play improvisational jazz, David Sudnow explicitly
acknowledges the pressing nature of these questions. As he puts it, in the
effort 'to make up melodies with the right hand' – that is, melodies that are
not already written down but improvised – the 'prime question' that emerged
was 'where?' (Sudnow 1978, 15). As he would later put it to his teacher, the
question is 'where to go?', where the hands should go next, which note to
play, in what circumstances should a particular note or chord be played, or
not played, and so on.

Sudnow, trained as an ethnomethodologist under Harold Garfinkel,
was particularly suited to describing the intricate processes involved in his
everyday efforts to learn improvisational jazz. Among the many tasks he
set out to accomplish, and did so successfully, was to be able to move his
hands around the keyboard, playing scales, notes and chords at will, with
his eyes closed as well! Such technical proficiency, however, is not playing
improvisational jazz, as Sudnow well knew. When he pressed his teacher for

more help, the teacher reluctantly gave him a set of scalar devices to learn, such as jazz-sounding scales, runs and chords. Sudnow would then become proficient at putting these scalar devices together; the result, however, while a jazz-sounding performance, was not what his teacher would do when he sat down to play. His teacher, according to Sudnow, 'was flying over the keyboard, producing the jazz I wanted so much to be doing … he was not simply doing the few scalar devices that I had been employing for each of the chord types. He was going to many more places over the keyboard … [and yet he was] "orderly"' (Sudnow 1978, 25). To state this situation slightly differently, and in terms we have been using, the teacher was not simply playing the scalar devices that serve as solutions to the problem that is playing improvisational jazz; rather, he had developed a taste for this problem that is not exhausted by any of the solutions it makes possible, and it was for this reason that he was able to go to 'many more places'. The problem thus became one of embracing the problem rather than the solutions, and this is just what Sudnow was eventually able to do. At first he might find himself hitting upon 'good-sounding jazz that would come out in the midst of my improvisations', but all too often he would then 'latch on' to the melody and his playing 'would be undermined, as when one first gets the knack of a complex skill, like riding a bicycle or skiing, the attempt to sustain an easeful management undercuts it' (83–4). What was undermining, in other words, was his confounding the improvisational playing of jazz with the jazz that was being played, as when one confounds the problem with the solutions then one undermines the creative possibilities of the problem. What Sudnow eventually realised, or learned, was that he had indeed confused a melody with the process of playing a melody, with melodying as he puts it. The more important lesson he learned was that the problematic is the ultimate reality, and solutions are merely provisional or derivative realities ('beings of reason' as Spinoza might put it [recall §1.2.a]). Thus Sudnow concludes that 'there is no melody, there is melodying' (146), and from this perspective he was able to see that, with respect to the question where to go, 'choices could be made anywhere, that there was no need to lunge, that usable notes for any chord lay just at hand' (94). In other words, as the condition for the determinate, the nature of a problem is inseparable from, though not to be confounded with, any determinate note that may 'lay just at hand', and such notes can be brought into an order that is neither predetermined nor arbitrary, but reflects rather the consistency and uniformity of the nature of the problem. A problem is therefore a process, a process that constructs and continually reconstructs the consistency, or the paradoxical period of learning that makes possible the solutions that all too often come to be taken as solutions without a problem.

We can now turn to the role narrative will play in the arguments going forward, for if life itself is a problem, as we have been arguing, then it too will likewise bring with it the relevance questions (who, where, when, in what cases?) we have seen follow upon an encounter with the reality of a problem. A story or narrative will, in short, provide a solution that answers these questions. Stories or narratives, however, as with melodies, are beings of reason (to use Spinoza's phrase again), and thus to restate Sudnow's claim, there are no narratives, there is narrativising, or making sense as we are developing the notion here. But how does this narrativising process work, and in what circumstances, where, when and by whom can it be discerned? To begin to unpack these questions and come to an encounter with the nature of a problem yet again, we can call upon Thomas Schelling's classic book, *The Strategy of Conflict*. In this book, Schelling draws upon game theory to shed light on the processes involved in negotiations that seek to resolve any of a number of conflict situations. One kind of situation that Schelling applied his game-theoretic approach to was that of coordination problems, or more precisely the problems of coordinating the efforts of two or more people to achieve a certain goal when the manner of achieving that goal has not been laid out in advance. To clarify, Schelling provides an example of two parachutists who need to meet up after they have landed, but who had not determined in advance where to meet. They each have a copy of a map of the local area, and consequently the problem becomes, as Schelling puts it, one of determining, 'What would I do if I were she wondering what she would do if she were I wondering what I would do if I were she … ?' (Schelling 1963, 54). In looking at the map with this question in mind, Schelling's question becomes one of determining where on the map she would she go if she were me wondering where I would go if I were her wondering where she would go. Schelling argues that 'most situations – perhaps every situation for people who are practiced at this kind of game – provide some clue for coordination, some focal point for each person's expectation of what the other expects him to expect to be expected to do' (57). In other words, there is usually, Schelling claims, 'some kind of prominence or conspicuousness' in a situation, some particularly *relevant* aspect of the situation which emerges as the key candidate for resolving the coordination problem. With the parachutists, for instance, the lone bridge on the map emerges as a focal point, rather than the many houses, and hence it becomes the likely place each expects the other to expect the other to go to.

Given this example of the role focal points play in resolving coordination problems, I will argue that narratives consist of a series of focal points that respond to the varied questions that confront a person who is seeking to find their way, or to know how, when, where, with whom and in what circumstances, etc., they are to act and feel. A narrative is thus an example of what helps the person in Hume's thought experiment who, 'on a sudden transported into our world … wou'd be very much embarrass'd with every object, and would not readily find what degree of love or hatred, pride or humility, or any other passion he ought to attribute to it' (Hume 1978, 2.1.6.9; SB 293; see also Hume 2005, 5.3 where this example is largely repeated). In other words, a person who has yet to acquire the habits that come with the repetitive experiences of a life lived with others will not be able to expect what comes next, or know what to feel or do in any given circumstance. Through repetitive experience certain relations emerge as particularly distinctive and conspicuous and become, in Schelling's terms, the focal points – causal relations, for instance – that enable us to orient our expectations and make our way through the world. These relevant focal points are precisely what are brought together into the consistency and uniformity that is a narrative.

We can now turn to how researchers in artificial intelligence approach the problem of understanding stories. This is indeed a difficult problem. As Marvin Minsky noted, although computers can process data and follow pre-programmed instructions and algorithms, and as a result beat chess world champions, they are nonetheless limited for, as Minsky puts it, 'Computers couldn't comprehend the simple stories understood by four-year-olds' (cited by Dreyfus 2005, 48). Patrick Henry Winston, Minsky's successor as head of the MIT Artificial Intelligence Laboratory, echoes Minsky's sentiments. As Winston states the situation in 2011: 'A team of dedicated first-class engineers can build systems that defeat skilled adults at chess and Jeopardy, but no one can build a system that exhibits the commonsense of a child' (Winston 2011, 345). In his effort to rectify this situation, Winston extends Chomsky's work in minimalist linguistics, in particular the merge operation whereby we have the ability, as Winston summarises it, 'to combine two concepts to make a third without limit' (346; see Chomsky 1995). In his extension of the merge operation Winston argues that not only does it give us a flexibility we can then use to describe events, but more importantly it allows us to go even further and 'string event descriptions into stories'. This leads to what Winston proposes as the Strong Story Hypothesis, which he states as follows: 'the mechanisms that enable humans to tell, understand, and recombine stories separate human intelligence from that of other primates'. He goes so far as to claim that story understanding is not only distinctive of human intelligence, but also 'the centrally important foundation for all human thinking' (346).

Winston is far from the only person to make such an assertion, as he himself admits. Alasdair Macintyre is among the more prominent philosophers who have made this claim as well, arguing in *After Virtue* that 'man is in his actions and practice, as well as in his fictions, essentially a story-telling animal' (Macintyre 1981, 201). Macintyre's arguments are themselves largely consonant with those of Paul Ricoeur, who adopts the concept of narrativity to further develop Heidegger's critique of the 'ordinary representation of time as a linear series of "nows"', a representation that 'hides the true constitution of time' (Ricoeur 1980, 170). What is hidden, Ricoeur argues, is the nature of time as a narrative whole that is not to be confounded with determinate events and moments, and yet which somehow guides events in an orderly way. A narrative is thus a narrativising, as a melody is a melodying for Sudnow, in that it entails possibilities that are not exhausted by the determinate events that unfold, and yet it accounts, in an orderly but unpredictable fashion, for the fact that things hold together, or the systematicity and consistency to the relationship of events. As Ricoeur puts this point: 'the time of the simplest story also escapes the ordinary notion of time conceived of as a series of instants succeeding one another along an abstract line oriented in a single direction ... the story's conclusion is the pole of attraction of the entire development. But a narrative conclusion can be neither deduced nor predicted ... a conclusion must be acceptable' (174). For a story to be acceptable, it must make sense in the manner in which we have been developing this theme here; that is, the story must involve a differentiating tendency, a move towards the determinate of the story, the many focal points for instance, as well as a dedifferentiating movement that is not to be confounded with these determinate elements, but which nonetheless is critical to the consistency and uniformity that holds together the various events and details of the story (Ricoeur uses the word 'plot' as the 'most relevant' term for that which 'governs a succession of events in a story' [171]). A narrative or narrativising is thus the processual encounter with the nature of a problem, with life as a problem, and thus the undermining tendencies this entails are inseparable from the narratives that make sense of things. As a result, a life that involves making sense of things will also be one that risks undermining the sense that has been made. Our life as a story thus returns us to Sudnow's challenge of melodying, a challenge Nietzsche was himself aware of: 'The end of a melody is not its goal; but nonetheless, if the melody had not reached its end it would not have reached its goal either. A parable' (Nietzsche 1996, 360). To restate Nietzsche's parable, we could say that life as storytelling, as a making sense of things, does not have as its goal the conclusion or end of a story, but a narrative that does not make sense of things, that does not hold things together in an orderly way, will also 'not have reached its goal either'.

Understanding narratives as problems, as that which makes sense of things, thus entails the paradoxical tendencies associated with sense. It is no wonder then, as Winston noted, that although 'first-class engineers can build systems that defeat skilled adults at chess … no one can build a system that exhibits the commonsense of a child'; that is, the common sense of a child whose story-telling makes sense of themselves and their world. In attempting to rectify this situation, Winston in effect hides the problematic nature of narrativising and thus confounds the problem with its solutions, solutions being in this case the determinate events and relations of events, and the determinate questions that hinge upon these determinate matters being understood and recognised. For instance, in working on the program Genesis, Winston and his team began with a simplified story – Macbeth reduced to a few hundred words – and then approached it as a 'computational problem', by which is meant one that addresses the question, 'what representations make it possible to answer questions posed in story understanding?' (Winston 2011, 347). Winston has questions such as the following in mind: 'Why did Macduff kill Macbeth?', 'Was this a story of revenge?', etc. To prepare Genesis to 'make sense' of the story well enough to answer basic questions – and even, surprisingly, come up with unexpected answers when comparing two or more simpli-fied stories – the program included a series of representations which allowed Genesis to categorise key persons and events and then use these categories to follow certain inferential rules that were also written into the program. The representations included those such as class (e.g. a thane is a kind of noble), job (Duncan was king), cause (Macbeth murdered Duncan because Macbeth wanted to be king), and mood (Macbeth became happy); the inferential rules included things such as 'If X kills Y, then Y becomes dead', and 'If X is dead, then X cannot be unhappy', among an ever growing list of rules that have been written into the ongoing project that is Genesis. What is missing here, however, and what we have been arguing is an integral aspect of making sense of things, is the dedifferentiating tendency of sense, the move towards that which cannot be captured within a net of already determined and differenti-ated representations and inferential rules. The approach taken by the Genesis project, therefore, confounds problems with their solution, narrativising with an already told story.

d) A political narrative

One would not have to listen for long to political news commentary before hearing the term 'narrative' brought into the discussion. A narrative is often referred to in terms analogous to a territory, as something to be controlled and fought over, and thus those who control the political narrative stand a better chance of gaining and maintaining power than those who fail to make headway with their narrative of events. Winning the battle over the political narrative is thus often more important than convincing people of certain facts. We can now begin to see why this is the case, for the narrativising process makes sense of facts and events while at the same time being irreducible to them – a problem is not to be confounded with its solutions. If one has a narrative that makes sense of one's life and world, the facts by themselves will be insufficient to change the narrative, for it is the narrative that makes sense of the facts and thus it has priority. That said, the narrativising process is often confounded with that which makes sense, or that which comes to be determinately told, believed and judged concerning a particular state of affairs. An authentic or good faith making sense of things, as will be argued in subsequent chapters, will simultaneously involve a problematising of things which in turn provokes a thoughtful process of making sense. Before turning to these arguments, however, let us first consider a couple of examples that highlight the identity-maintaining role narratives play when the narrativising process has been confounded with a determinate story.

The first comes from David Sherman and Geoffrey Cohen's essay, 'The Psychology of Self-Defense: Self-Affirmation Theory' (Sherman and Cohen 2006), where they extend Claude Steele's pioneering work in affirmation theory. In their study, Sherman and Cohen focus on the psychological processes involved in self-defence strategies in the presence of threat or failure. A professional baseball player, to use Sherman and Cohen's example, will consider their career a success if they get a hit 30 per cent of the time. In fact, such players will become famous and wealthy, given that the all-time career batting percentage is just under 37 per cent (achieved by Ty Cobb). Despite failing to get a hit 70 per cent of the time, this failure does not undermine the player's positive self-image. 'Like major league baseball players', Sherman and Cohen point out, 'people in contemporary society face innumerable failures and self-threats'. We may experience 'substandard performance on the job or in class, frustrated goals or aspirations … illness, the defeat of one's political party in an election or of one's favorite sports team … rejection in a romantic relationship, real and perceived social slights … [etc.]' (Sherman and Cohen 2006, 183). Sherman and Cohen further develop Steele's claim that, in the face of 'failures' that may threaten to undermine one's sense of self, a common response is to construct a narrative that will make sense of oneself and one's world, constructing 'a self-system' that thereby, as Steele puts it, 'essentially explains ourselves … [and allows us] to maintain a phenomenal experience of the self – self-conceptions and images – as adaptively and morally adequate, i.e., as competent, good, coherent, unitary, stable, capable of free choice, capable of controlling important outcomes, and so on' (Steele 1988, 262). Such attempts to maintain a unitary, self-affirming image (or narrative) can, however, take a more sinister turn, as Sherman and Cohen point out:

> After experiencing a self-threat, people may engage in any number of strate-gies to reaffirm self-integrity via social judgment. These strategies include comparing the self with a clearly inferior other, gossiping negatively about a third party, or harshly judging a political ingroup member who fails to demonstrate as much fervor for the cause as one personally does. (Sherman and Cohen 2006, 203)

In the wake of this effort to maintain a positive self-image, an effort that has been described (e.g., by Greenwald 1980) 'as "totalitarian" in its ambition to interpret the past and present in a way congenial to its desires and needs' (Sherman and Cohen 2006, 184), Sherman and Cohen turn to what they see as an important follow-up question – namely, what are 'the circumstances under which people are less ego defensive and more open-minded in their relationship with the social world'? (184) What they found is that if one has recently maintained a positive self-image, or has performed an exercise that involves doing so (such as a written exercise), then one is more likely to be open to negative or challenging information. In an experiment that bore this thesis out, they found that, after a process of self-affirmation, a person was better able to handle negative health information and was able to 'reduce the physiological costs of stress' (198) that come with receiving such information. The cortisol levels of those placed in a self-affirmation setting were noticeably lower than those who were not put in such a setting. In other experiments, Sherman and Cohen found that, more important than an inconsistency with respect to one's beliefs, was a positive sense of self, thus suggesting that self-affirmation is key to the process of changing one's mind and accepting facts that are no longer consistent with beliefs one holds. For example, in an experiment where the subject writes a self-affirming narrative, a story that is a good reflection of their values and of how they acted in accordance with these values, they found that such people were more likely to correct their beliefs regarding new facts and information than those who did not write a self-affirming narrative. On the basis of these and other experiments, Sherman and Cohen conclude that what is of paramount importance in our lives and interactions with others is that we maintain a self-system or narrative that, as Steele puts it, 'persistently explains our behavior, and the world at large, so as to sustain a phenomenal experience of the self as adaptively and morally adequate' (Steele 1988, 266).

In a more recent study, conducted in the years just before and after the election of Donald Trump, Arlie Hochschild lived in southwest Louisiana (the Lake Charles area) among people who were very conservative and more often than not fervent Trump supporters. From one perspective, however, they should not have supported Trump, whose policies promised to lead, and in fact have led, to the loosening of environmental protections and hence to the presence of even more deadly pollution and chemicals in their air and water. Despite being aware of the damage that Dupont chemicals, among other factories, were doing to their water, and of the many friends who had gotten cancer, they nonetheless supported Trump and his policies. We thus have another case of cognitive dissonance and an inconsistency of the type that Sherman and Cohen studied, and Hochschild's explanation for this largely tracks their conclusions. In short, what is more important than the facts is a narrative, or a 'deep story' as Hochschild calls it. A deep story

> is a feel-as-if story – it's the story feelings tell, in the language of symbols. It removes judgment. It removes fact. It tells us how things feel. Such a story permits those on both sides of the political spectrum to stand back and explore the subjective prism through which the party on the other side sees the world. And I don't believe we understand anyone's politics, right or left, without it. For we all have a deep story. (Hochschild 2016, 131)

In Sherman and Cohen's terms, a deep story is part of the self-system that assures us we are morally adaptive, good and adequate, a story that makes sense of the facts and events of our lives. Among the people in the Lake Charles region of Louisiana, Hochschild found that their deep story was one of injustice. The general sentiment or story that the people she met could identify with was that they were 'patiently standing in a long line leading up a hill, as in a pilgrimage ... [they] are situated in the middle of this line, along with others who are also white, older, Christian, and predominantly male, some with college degrees, some not ... Just over the brow of the hill is the American Dream' (Hochschild 2016, 133). Some people, however, are cutting in line, getting an unfair advantage and a shot at the American Dream, an opportunity they do not get since they are still waiting in line. They are following the rules, this deep story goes (hence affirming their moral worth and value), but many others are not: 'Through affirmative action plans, pushed by the federal government, they [blacks] are being given preference for places in colleges and universities, apprenticeships, jobs, welfare payments, and free lunches ... Women, immigrants, refugees, public sector workers – where will it end? Your money is rushing through a liberal sympathy sieve you don't control or agree with' (136). President Obama would be simply the most prominent example of someone who took advantage of the line-cutting opportunities the folk in Lake Charles, those who follow the rules, are excluded from. Donald Trump's candidacy tapped into this deep story; it was the political narrative that his campaign resonated with throughout the

United States, and thus for Hochschild it makes perfect sense that Trump's election played out in the way that it did.

But are all stories created equally? Is one self-affirming narrative as good as any other? The short answer to this question is no, though providing a detailed answer will be what occupies us over the coming chapters. By way of transition to these discussions, I want first to recall three issues touched upon so far that relate to the question of whether or not all stories are created equally. First, to rephrase an earlier point from Deleuze, we can say that a story 'always has the truth it deserves according to the problem to which it is a response' (Deleuze 1994, 159). In particular, a story has the truth it deserves according to the manner in which it responds to the life it expresses and affirms, and on this point we return to the Nietzschean theme of master and slave morality, whereby a set of values is judged negatively, by Nietzsche, if it is life-denying, and judged positively if it is life-affirming, as was the case with master morality, according to him (recall §1.3.a). Similarly, in the account offered here, a story will be more authentic the more it affirms the problem rather than confounds the problem with its solutions. We prefer to use the word authentic rather than true, since 'true' tends to shift the nature of the story to being a determinate matter of fact, and hence to confound the problem with its solutions.

That said, however, and this is the second issue to be recalled, a story that affirms a problem that makes sense of the story does not turn away from the determinate facts that are the subject of representational thoughts, and that are likewise subject to concerns as to whether they are true or not. For a story to be acceptable, as Ricoeur put it, or to be relevant and make sense, it must draw the determinate facts into an orderly consistency that, as the paradoxical nature of sense which a story expresses entails, is turned both towards the determinate facts that may or may not be true, that may or may not have the relations we attribute to them, and towards the Humean delirium, the dedifferentiating tendency that undermines and prevents connections. We find this at work in conspiracy theories, which construct a story that is often quite absurd but which also anchor the story in a set of facts that the story makes sense of. The conspiracy theory regarding the Sandy Hook shooting in December 2012, which some claim was a fabricated event designed to change public opinion regarding gun control legislation in the United States (for more, see below 3.2.b), is just one example. Among the determinate facts that this conspiracy theory claims to make sense of, and in a way better than the mainstream media narrative, is the fact that the emergency response crews stopped for a pizza break, complete with pizza delivery drivers. Conspiracy theorists who focus on the September 11 attacks, sometimes known as 'truthers', will point to the speed with which the twin towers collapsed, and the pancake manner in which they did so, as being best accounted for by the conspiracy narrative that the US government itself planned and executed the attacks, and that part of this plan was to weaken the steel support beams in the tower to ensure their collapse. What these narratives rely on, however, in order to maintain their aura of believability, is a drastic narrowing of the determinate facts that may be related, or an outright refusal to look at all the other determinate facts that would be implied if the few that justify their story were indeed true. For instance, in both the Sandy Hook and 9/11 conspiracy theories, if the basic premise is true then there must be a lot of other determinate facts that are necessarily implicated and yet somehow remain undetected or unknown (e.g., where are all the children at Sandy Hook who are supposedly not dead?). In embracing such highly unlikely scenarios, conspiracy theories thus tend towards the Humean delirium without sufficient or relevant anchoring in the nature of the determinate. Where do we draw the line, however, between a conspiracy theory – a narrative that falls illegitimately into the delirious tendencies of sense – and a story that is acceptable, an authentic story that affirms the nature of the problem and hence has the truth it deserves? In anticipation of answers to be developed below, and by way of transitioning to these sections, the line is to be drawn between those stories that affirm the infinite nature of the problem, and those stories that do not. Those stories that do affirm the infinite nature of a problem, that embrace the form of infinitism argued for here (recall our discussion from the Introduction), are authentic stories, stories that affirm the reality and nature of a problem, and it is the infinite nature of this reality that forces thought by way of an inexhaustible problem inseparable from each and every determinate reality, and hence from a determinate that can be problematised and provoke one to think, or force one to make sense of things. These stories are to be contrasted with those that foreclose the nature of a problem and assume, from the start, a finite, determinate nature that constrains and predetermines the manner in which the problem is to be affirmed.

This brings me to the third issue, the self-affirmation associated with narratives, especially political narratives. To affirm life as a problem is to affirm the infinite nature of the problem and hence to allow oneself to be provoked into thinking. An authentic political narrative will encourage a critical engagement with the determinate, an engagement that calls one to think through the determinate nature of political reality and thereby open up the possibility of a transformed political reality, and with this transformation an ever-changing process of making sense. Politics should thus provoke thought and in turn express the implications of the thought thus provoked. It is to this theme that we now turn.

2. To Think Against One's Will

a) Plato on contradictory perceptions

To state our conclusion at the beginning, what provokes thought is the infinite nature of our being, our problematic nature as infinite. What is thought, therefore, is not our nature, but it is our nature that provokes thought. It is this relationship between our nature that is not thought and the thoughts we have which is critical to understanding our conclusion. Moreover, this was also Plato's concern. For Plato, what provokes thought is the infinite, or the unbounded (*apeiron*), whereas what is thought is finite, bounded and determinate. To understand what is at work here, let us first begin with what Plato takes to be the provocateur of thought – namely, contradictory perceptions.

This point is stressed in Book VII of the *Republic*, where Socrates and Glaucon set out to determine the best way to educate the guardians of the city, or more precisely how to draw their souls 'from becoming to being' (521d), and decide that they need 'a study that will be naturally conducive to the awakening of thought' (523b). Such a study, they claim, will involve experiences that are to be contrasted with 'The experiences that do not provoke thought ... those that do not at the same time issue in contradictory perception' (523b). If one looks at the fingers of one's own hand, to use the example Socrates offers, then 'Each one of them appears equally a finger, and in this respect it makes no difference whether it is observed as intermediate or at either extreme, whether it is white or black, thick or thin, or of any quality of this kind ... the faculty of sight never signifies to it at the same time that the finger is the opposite of a finger' (523d). In other words, regardless of the context in which the finger is observed, whether close up or at a distance, or even with the potentially contradictory qualities that may be attributed to it – thick or thin, black or white, long or short, etc. – the perception of a finger is simply the perception of a finger and does not involve its opposite. Such perceptions and experiences, Plato claims, 'do not provoke thought'. The perceptions of qualities that entail their contradictory opposite, however, do provoke thought. For example, the perception of something that is 'hard is of necessity related also to the soft, and it reports to the soul that the same thing is both hard and soft to its perception' (524a). The same is true for other qualities such as 'the bigness and the smallness' of objects, the hot or cold temperature of something, etc., for they too involve an experience that necessarily entails its opposite – one cannot experience hot without it being contrasted with cold, likewise with big and small, or hard and soft; stated differently, the subject of the experience necessarily entails what it is not.

But what precisely is it in the nature of contradictory perceptions that provokes thought? In short, it is the infinite nature of becoming, or its unbounded, indeterminate nature, that provokes the processes of thinking which then seek to limit that which is without limits. Becoming does indeed seem to entail a relationship of opposites, but in this case between 'is' and 'is not', rather than between a determinate quality and its necessarily related opposite (e.g., hard and soft). As one who 'is' young becomes old, one becomes what one 'is not' now, and when one 'is' old, or has become old, then one 'is not' young anymore. Becoming, it seems, necessarily entails a relationship between 'is' and 'is not'. Moreover, as Plato stresses in the *Philebus*, this relationship is one that is without limits, such as in the case of more and less. As Socrates states the argument, whenever the 'more' and 'less' are present, 'they do not allow any definite quantity to exist' (24c). Every time the 'more' and 'less' appear, in whatever form this might take (e.g., hotter, colder, gentler, quieter, etc.), 'they always introduce in every instance a comparison – more emphatic than that which is quieter, or vice versa – and thus they create the relation of more and less, thereby doing away with fixed quantity' (24c). But how so? If we were to say that my coffee, brewed at 190°F, is colder than yours, which was brewed at boiling point (212°F), then how have we done away with fixed quantity while saying that one cup of coffee is hotter than another (yours is hotter than mine, for instance)? For Socrates, however, in this case we no longer have hotter and colder but we have definite temperatures instead, and the judgments that follow from this. Socrates thus states quite explicitly that 'once they had accepted definite quantity, they would no longer be hotter or colder; for hotter and colder are always progressing and never stationary; but quantity is at rest and does not progress. By this reasoning hotter and its opposite are shown to be infinite (*apeiron* [without limit])' (24d). As something is getting progressively hotter or colder, it is constantly changing its nature, it never is what it is but is constantly becoming more or less. In other words, what Plato is concerned with here is the nature of becoming, the reality that is not fixed but forever becoming what it is not – e.g., hotter, colder, gentler, etc. – and it is this aspect of hotter and colder, more and less, that is contra-dictory in the etymological sense of the word, as that which is opposed to what can be said. When Plato refers to contradictory or opposing perceptions (ἐναντίαν αἴσθησιν), therefore, this is not a contradiction between determinate elements. What is being opposed in the contradictory perceptions that provoke thought is the very nature of the determinate itself, or precisely what one seeks to have in having a thought, and it is this opposition that provokes thought for Plato, and with it the very thinking that gives rise to the determinate thoughts that bring an end to thinking.

But this brings up a crucial problem for Plato, perhaps the guiding problem of his philosophy, for if becoming always necessarily entails both 'is' and 'is not', or a 'more' and 'less' that is 'always progressing and never stationary' (*Philebus* 24d), then how will we ever come to have a thought of what is, a determinate thought that does not provoke thought but is, so to speak, the resolution of the problem that provoked thought in the first place? Plato notes this problem in the *Philebus* when Socrates asks, 'How can we gain anything fixed whatsoever about things which have no fixedness whatsoever?' (59b). The problem is especially pressing since the 'fixed and pure and true and what we call unalloyed knowledge has to do with the things which are eternally the same without change or mixture, or with that which is most akin to them; and all other things are to be regarded as secondary' (59c). How can that which has 'no fixedness whatsoever', that which is without limit and bounds (*apeiron*), come to be thought and acquire the fixedness and limits that come with knowledge? Or, how can the contradictory nature of becoming which provokes thought become that which no longer provokes thought? To address this question, we can turn to that which, in human experience, is often a source of undermining and a provocation of much thought – namely, death and loss.

b) Coping with loss

If the nature and reality of our life as becoming, a life that is 'always progressing and never stationary' (*Philebus* 24d), is infinite and without limit as Plato understands it, then the awareness of death and loss, of a life cut life short by death, which limits it and marks its end, would thus appear to be an awareness that opposes the infinite, limit-less nature of life. This oppositional or contradictory awareness will in turn provoke thought, the consequences of which one can find throughout the history of philosophy, beginning with Plato and Socrates, for whom philosophy is precisely the practice necessary to realise that death and loss are merely the appearance of a limit and end, whereas the ultimate reality is limitless and without end. As Socrates says in the *Phaedo*, 'the true philosophers practice dying, and death is less terrible to them than to any other men' (67e). Philosophy, we can say, is the result of the encounter with that which provokes thought, and a consequence of philosophy, for Socrates, is reconciliation with a reality that is both limitless and without end *yet is also* a reality that can be thought.

With this move we can begin to see the way in which an encounter with death and loss can provoke a thinking which ultimately thinks the reality that provoked the very act of thinking, and hence addresses Plato's question:

'How can we gain anything fixed whatsoever about things which have no fixedness whatsoever?' (*Philebus* 59b). In particular, and as Socrates elaborates upon his claim that death is nothing to fear, death is nothing but the 'release and separation [of the soul] from the body', and 'true philosophers and they alone', he adds, 'are always most eager to release the soul, and just this – this release and separation of the soul from the body – is their study, is it not?' To which Simmias replies, 'Obviously'. By doing what they do – that is, seeking to grasp the truths of a soul that is separable from the body – philosophers are engaged in a practice that is no less than the practice of dying. When death arrives, therefore, it would be 'very foolish', Socrates claims, 'if they should be frightened and troubled', for the true philosophers have been embracing this moment all along. The practice of philosophy – the practice of philosophical thinking in response to an encounter with a contradictory experience or perception – is thus for Socrates a process that is always already beyond the determinate, mortal limits that death appears to bring. If the task of philosophical thinking is to recollect the eternal, death-less truths that the soul forgot when it entered the body, then it entails recollecting a reality that was never present, was never a determinate, finite reality. As we will see below, this process of recollection is better understood in a manner analogous to learning something new. Rather than engaging with a process of recalling and recollecting something one once knew, something that was once present to one's mind and thought (such as a word or name that is on the tip of one's tongue), the process of philosophical thinking entails an encounter with a problem that has never been fully present, and was never fully a determinate, finite reality, and it is this encounter that brings about the emergence of something new, as when one learns a new skill (such as swimming).

As we will see, the process of learning and making sense of life can be seen to be following in Plato's footsteps in that here too we are attempting to come to terms with a reality that is not to be confused or confounded with anything determinate and finite. If fear of death is taken to be the consequence of recognising the nature of life as finite, limited and mortal, then as with Socrates we too will argue that death is nothing to fear. There are many others, of course, who also follow in Plato's footsteps. The Epicureans and Stoics, for instance, will also argue that death is nothing to fear, although for very different reasons. As materialists, the Epicureans rejected the Platonic appeal to an immortal soul that is separable from the body, and yet they were nonetheless agreed that death is nothing to fear. In a famous quotation attributed to Epicurus, he claims that 'Death is nothing to us. When we exist, death is not; and when death exists, we are not. All sensation and consciousness ends with death and therefore in death there is neither pleasure nor pain.' Epicurus' conclusion: if there is neither pleasure nor pain, there is nothing to fear. The more we understand our nature as material beings, therefore, or the more we learn from philosophy, the less we have to fear death. Despite their avowed rejection of much of Epicureanism, the Stoics will also argue that the key to life is to come to recognise and live in accordance with our nature. As Seneca puts it, 'I follow the guidance of Nature – a doctrine upon which all Stoics are agreed. Not to stray from Nature and to mould ourselves according to her law and pattern – this is true wisdom' (*On the Happy Life* 3.3). Moreover, such moulding in accordance with Nature entails, for Seneca, a withdrawal from social customs and expectations and involves turning within instead, a turning to one's self that also enables us to live well in the face of loss:

> Most of all, the mind must be withdrawn from external interests into itself. Let it have confidence in itself, rejoice in itself, let it admire its own things, let it retire as far as possible from the things of others and devote itself to itself, let it not feel losses, let it interpret kindly even adversities. Zeno, our master, when he received news of a shipwreck and heard that all his property had been sunk, said: 'Fortune bids me to follow philosophy with fewer encumbrances.' (*Tranquility of Mind* 14.2–3)

To take one last example, we can return briefly to our earlier discussion of Spinoza (§1.2.a). As we saw, a good argument can be made that Spinoza's philosophy begins with the effort to think in a way that brings contentment and joy to a life that involves death and loss. Key to achieving that joy and contentment in the face of death and loss is developing a love of the eternal instead of the perishable. As Spinoza puts it, a 'love toward the eternal and infinite thing feeds the mind with a joy entirely exempt from sadness. This is greatly to be desired, and to be sought with all our strength' (Spinoza 2016, 9; TdIE II/7). Critical to the moves Spinoza makes here was his shift away from Descartes' attempt to ground our understanding of God on the properties or attributes of God (i.e., *propria*, such as infinite perfection, wisdom, etc.) and towards an account (as developed in his *Ethics*) that understands properties, attributes and modes such as our finite minds in terms of the reality or nature of God's infinite power.

With this move to an infinite power that is not to be confounded with anything finite, determinate and limited, we can both return to our earlier claim that a narrative has the truth it deserves and relate this to the manner in which narratives make sense of death and loss. Put simply, a narrative that has the truth it deserves will be an *authentic* narrative that expresses our nature as a boundless, indeterminate problem, whereas a narrative that begins with a presupposed solution to a problem will be a *forced* narrative. This distinction comes into play with the awareness of our mortality, where the limited, finite nature of our life appears to contradict our encounter with life as boundless, indeterminate problem. A common narrative that emerges as a result of this encounter is one which claims that the limited nature of our lives is overcome when we grasp an eternal reality or nature that is always already present, a reality that is simply waiting to be recollected, as Plato understands it. If this eternal reality is understood to be an already determinate reality, a Platonic Form for instance – that is, a distinct, determinate reality that exists eternally and independently of the many things we experience in our lives that may or may not participate in the nature of this Form – then this is a forced narrative. It is forced precisely because it forces the narrativising process into a solution or narrative that is predetermined from the start rather than allowing, as authentic narratives do, for a problem to be expressed in solutions that are neither predetermined nor final, and are not final precisely because the nature of a problem is infinite and boundless, and thus determinate solutions presuppose problems they do not exhaust, problems that may undermine the solutions they deserve. With this distinction between authentic and forced narratives, we can now turn to the existentialist tradition, within which the concept of authenticity is important for reasons similar to those that have been argued for here. This is especially the case with Heidegger, as we will now see.

c) Authenticity

At first sight it may seem entirely inappropriate to bring the existentialist tradition into a discussion that aims, in part, to defend the claim that death is not to be feared because life itself expresses a problem which is infinite and without end. Is this not simply a repackaged and rebranded Platonism, a reworked Christian thought as a 'Platonism for the "people"', as Nietzsche put it (Nietzsche 1966, 4), in that it appeals to an eternal reality in order to allay the fear of death? As Nietzsche's comment regarding Christianity implies, the appeal to an eternal, transcendent reality finds little purchase with him, and this is true for other writers who are identified with the existential tradition, such as Sartre, Heidegger and Camus. For them, appealing to an infinite, eternal reality or nature in order to appease our anxiety and fear regarding death, or our being-toward-death as Heidegger puts it, just does not do the job, or involves a forced narrative, as we have argued. A closer look at Heidegger, however, will clarify the difference between the infinite, endless nature of a problem and the determinate reality of the eternal forms and natures that the existential philosophers find forced and inadequate.

Heidegger quite clearly draws a sharp dividing line between an authentic attitude towards one's own nature as being-toward-death and an inauthentic, everyday attitude that in essence eclipses and turns away from that nature. When we think of death in the abstract, as an objective event that befalls everyone, for instance, which is a common Stoic strategy in reconciling oneself to one's mortality, we do not encounter what is unique to the reality of death. As Heidegger puts it, 'Dying, which is essentially mine in such a way that no one can be my representative, is perverted into an event of public occurrence which the "they" encounters' (Heidegger 1962, 297). The 'they', Heidegger claims, is the world of everydayness, a world that 'is constituted by the way things have been publicly interpreted, which expresses itself in idle talk' (296). If the 'they' helps us to confront death, it is only through denial, or by turning away from the distinctive reality that is our being-toward-death. The 'they', Heidegger concludes, *provides a constant tranquilization about death*. (298, emphasis in original). What one is turning away from, what is being tranquilised and anaesthetised, is the anxiety Heidegger claims is integral to our being as being-toward-death. As he puts it, anxiety is 'the state-of-mind which can hold open the utter and constant threat to itself arising from Dasein's ownmost individualized Being' (311). But rather than fleeing this anxious state of mind and getting lost in the everyday, in the objective cultural patterns and expectations of 'the they-self', an 'authentic Being-towards-death' will become, instead, 'an impassioned freedom towards death – a freedom which has been released from the Illusions of the "they", and which is factical, certain of itself, and anxious' (311).

What an 'authentic Being-towards-death' will entail, for Heidegger, is embracing a fundamental non-relation at the core of our nature and being, a non-relation that is rooted in the fact that there is no determinate reality that is death to which one could relate as one relates to the determinate things of everyday existence. Death, to use Heidegger's terms, is never present or ready to hand, never a determinate something with which we might enter into a relation. It is this non-relation that provokes anxiety. Rather than tranquilise this anxiety through a forced narrative, Heidegger instead argues that the proper, authentic way to confront the anxiety that comes with the awareness of death and loss, and more precisely the death and loss of the very being (namely, Dasein) that dies, is to embrace a realm of possibility to which nothing actual can or ever could correspond. Heidegger is crystal clear on this point. 'The closest closeness', he argues, 'which one may have in Being towards death as a possibility, is as far as possible from anything actual' (Heidegger 1962, 307). An authentic embrace of our being as being-towards-death will thus be an anxious embrace of the problem that is our existence, a problem no solution can resolve, and no distractions in and among the everyday can satisfy. In the manner of the Stoics, therefore, an authentic being-towards-death will entail an embrace of one's own nature, or living a life that is in accordance with nature. For Heidegger, however, this nature is not, as it is for the Stoics and others discussed above, a matter of reconciling with an already determinate reality and nature that is eternal and deathless, but is rather a matter of reconciling with our 'ownmost non-relational possibility', or with our nature as Dasein, as a being-towards-death involving a reality that is not to be confused or confounded with anything determinate or actual.

This distinction between authentic and everyday attitudes towards death, as with the distinction being made here between authentic and forced narratives, may appear to rely upon a difference that is itself problematic. In particular, in both Heidegger's case and by extension in the argument offered here, there appears to be an unquestioned acceptance of a difference between the pure and the impure that is far from uncontroversial. Given Heidegger's own well-documented affiliation with the Nazi party, we do not need to look far for a case where the dominance of one group over another was justified by appealing to the dominant group's authentic or pure nature – the pure Aryan race – in contrast to the impure nature of those who suffered at their hands (Jews, Roma, homosexuals, etc.). By turning to the notion of authenticity in order to address our earlier question regarding how we might distinguish the relative merits of one narrative from another, or determine which narratives do or do not have the truth they deserve, such as a delusional conspiracy theory, have we not called upon a distinction that can be used for the very purposes of supporting the types of narratives we initially sought to rule out? The short answer to this question is that yes, indeed, authenticity has been used in political contexts to justify any number of actions, but this, we shall argue, is precisely the nature of the political itself; that is, the nature of the political is the effort to encounter the nature of a problem, but with this encounter comes the risk of forced narratives. It is in making sense of the various contesting interests and powers that are encountered among and within assembled individuals and groups that the art of the political, we shall argue, involves a taste for the problematic that makes sense of the determinate practices and structures one encounters in these situations. The art of the political, in short, entails developing a taste for the authentic as problematic, in a task I will call critical existentialism. Understood in this way, the authentic is not a purity that determines (*forces*) in advance what is or is not to be included in any given political context; to the contrary, the authentic as a problem both makes sense of the current political situation while simultaneously risking its undermining or problematisation, a problematisation which can result in another emergent solution, a solution that is in turn, and endlessly so, subject to further problematisations. At the same time, there is the ever-present risk that a forced narrative could also emerge as a solution, a final solution without a problem. To explore this possibility of forced narratives further, we will turn to relevant discussions within political theory where the concern is with forced, arbitrary power, and with this in hand we will then return to the existential tradition. This will prepare the way for showing how that tradition provides an important perspective that can be brought to bear on much of contemporary political discourse.

§3 Making Sense of Politics

1. Arbitrary Power

In this chapter I will continue to develop the distinction between forced and authentic narratives, or what I will also call free narratives. To provide a context that will enable us to clarify this distinction, and then connect the discussion to politics, we will begin by focusing on classical republicanism. With the emphasis it places on doing what is necessary to avoid arbitrary power, or situations where one is at the unpredictable mercy of another, classical republican thought has focused heavily on determining how to resist such arbitrary forms of power, such as through an institutionalised system of checks and balances. In what may seem to be a surprising connection, we will find important parallels between these concerns and efforts of classical republicans and those of Deleuze and the existentialists. Exploring these parallels, and then discussing arguments from recent work on Marxism and the history of capitalism, will provide us with further tools to be deployed in the next two chapters as we develop a critical existentialism.

a) Forced narratives

In his classic book, *Natural Right and History*, Leo Strauss sets forth an important analysis of the difference between classical and modern natural right. In relation to the former, Strauss claims that '[i]t is the hierarchic order of man's natural constitution which supplies the basis for natural right as the classics understood it' (Strauss 1953, 127). In other words, human beings possess a higher faculty which is capable of accessing a reality that is irreducible to the everyday reality of experience – the Forms or Ideas for Plato – but this can only be achieved as humans come to realise the perfection that is essential to their nature, and, according to the classical tradition, this perfection occurs only when individuals subordinate their individuality to the identity of the polis, or to civil society. Strauss is clear on this point: 'Man cannot reach his perfection except in society or, more precisely, in civil society ... or the city as the classics conceived of it ... a closed society' (127). The city or polis thus functions as nothing less than the condition for

90

the full realisation of the individual, and the moral obligations and duties of the individual are inseparable from what is good for the city as a whole, or for the common good: 'The city has therefore ultimately no other end than the individual. The morality of the state is the same as the morality of the individual' (134). In the ideal of classical republicanism, as this view has come to be known, an individual's duty is to realise their own moral perfection by realising the perfection of the city. What thus becomes most important in this context is that an individual be allowed to develop their moral perfection as necessary to the good of the city itself, and a common obstacle to this process is arbitrary power, for arbitrary power interferes with and disrupts the connection between an individual's actions and the good of the city, a good that serves as the goal or *telos* of these actions. A subsequent concern among classical republicans will thus be with the procedural mechanisms that limit the capacity of those with power to exercise arbitrary power, a limit that may be achieved, for instance, through the institution of checks and balances provided by the separation of legislative and executive powers.

From the perspective on narratives that has been argued for here, how are we to understand the concerns of classical republicanism? Is the classical republican pursuit of freedom from arbitrary power based on a forced or an authentic narrative? If our actions are not to be interfered with arbitrarily – so that we can predictably attain our goals and realise our moral perfection through the exercise of a civic virtue that serves the ends of the polis – does this not mean that our actions are to be predetermined by the nature of the city itself and forced to bend to its needs? It was the critique and subsequent abandonment of the teleological nature of classical republicanism that led, according to Strauss, to the non-teleological account of the modern conception of natural right, an account that sees the passions, and most notably the fear of violent death, as the efficient cause that leads to the emergence of civil society. Despite this, however, I would argue that classical republicanism is not a forced narrative. In fact, a key thesis of this book is that the existential tradition, with its notion of authenticity (among other concerns to be discussed below), can be seen as reinvigorating the case for classical republicanism without relying on teleological accounts that would make sense of politics by way of forced narratives. If Strauss were correct – i.e., if it is the case that 'Man cannot reach his perfection except in society or, more precisely ... a closed society', and if the closed nature of this society is itself guaranteed by a set of already determinate values and truths, as he implies – then this would indeed be a forced narrative. Moreover, if the closed nature of a society is determined by certain actualised features or characteristics that predetermine who is included in it or excluded from it – determinant features such as language, ethnicity, religion, etc. – then the nature of that society is indeed forced upon, and canalises the efforts of, those who are seeking to live in accordance with their nature within this society. Yet this is not the classical republican ideal as I will be developing it here, for one could argue that the classical republican critique of arbitrary power is more accurately described as an attempt to undermine and resist forced narratives.

To clarify this latter point, namely the way in which the discussion of forced narratives both tracks and differs from classical republicanism (a point I will return to in the next chapter), we can turn to a key moment in Nietzsche's argument in *Beyond Good and Evil* where he points out that the good/bad distinction is different from the good/evil distinction: 'It should be noted immediately that in the first type of morality [i.e., master morality] the opposition of "good" and "bad" means approximately the same as "noble" and "contemptible"' (Nietzsche 1966, §260, 204). In other words, 'noble' or master morality is self-affirming, meaning it is good to have 'noble' traits, to be strong, independent, fear-inspiring, etc., and bad to lack these traits, to be weak, dependent and fearful. From the perspective of classical republican- ism, it is the nobles who are able to realise their own moral perfection, who are self-affirming and have the means to act without being at the mercy of arbitrary power, all of which is good, while it is bad to be in a situation where, like a slave, one is *forced* to act in accordance with the arbitrary will of another. As I will argue in the next chapter (§4.1), Nietzsche will not follow the classical republicans with respect to what it means to be self-affirming, but will call for affirming one's nature as an infinite problem in Spinoza's sense (recall §1.2.a), and in Kierkegaard's as well (see §4.1.a and §5.2.d). This understanding of one's self as a problem will allow us to clarify (see §3.2.a) Nietzsche's point that those with 'noble' traits should not consider '[r]efraining mutually from injury, violence, and exploitation and placing one's will on a par with that of someone else', for to refrain from doing so is, as Nietzsche puts it, nothing less than a 'will to the denial of life' (§259, 203). In other words, from the perspective of master morality, exercising arbitrary power is simply, as Nietzsche argues, 'a consequence of the will to power, which is after all the will of life' (§259, 203), and it is only from the perspective of slave morality, consequently, that one becomes concerned to limit arbitrary power and appeal to freedom as non-domination, as classical republicans traditionally understand it. Such concerns and appeals may thus appear to be nothing other than another manifestation of what Nietzsche calls the 'slave rebellion in morals' (§195, 108).

Despite these differences between Nietzsche and classical republicans, there are important resonances, and these become most pronounced around the theme of forced narratives as I have been developing it here. This is a point Eric MacGilvray has also stressed in his recent book, *The Invention of Market Freedom*, where, knowingly echoing Nietzsche, he notes that 'the word "freedom" [was once] ... used to distinguish members of a social and political elite from those – women, slaves, serfs, menial laborers, and foreigners – who did not enjoy their privileges or share their ethos' (MacGilvray 2011, 1). What is important about being a member of the 'social and political elite', MacGilvray argues, is that their 'status shields [them] from the influence of arbitrary power, that is, from power that can be exercised at will by those who possess it' (34). When individuals are shielded in this way they are then able to develop and act in accordance with their own nature rather than being forced into a predetermining mould. In elaborating on this theme of not being forced or dependent, MacGilvray notes that Machiavelli also understands freedom in a republican manner, in terms of the independence that goes with the absence of arbitrary power: 'Machiavelli does not associate freedom with the absence of constraint, or as negative liberty as this has come to be called, but rather with the absence of dependence, and above all with the political independence of a city.' For Machiavelli, therefore, 'to live as a free citizen is to value the freedom of one's city above all else – to love one's country, as Machiavelli famously put it, more than one's soul' (47). What is thus key to the tradition of classical republicanism, MacGilvray argues, is not the end pursued so much as the means to the end, a means that is not *forced* to act in accordance with arbitrary power.

Restating the concerns of classical republicanism in the terms being developed here, and touching again on the differences with Nietzsche, we could say that what is realised when someone is freed from arbitrary power, or from being *forced* into a predetermined mode of living, is that they then encounter their nature as a problem. A consequence of this encounter is that through their nature as a narrative/problem they make sense of the determinate situations of their lives, a making sense which involves the paradox of sense and its dual de/differentiating tendencies (recall §1.2.c). In making sense of one's situation, therefore, one does not begin in the midst of delirium, in chaos, but *in media res*, in the midst of things that are already given, expected and laid down before one, and with the partialities, biases and affects of those involved with these things. The dedifferentiating tendency moves from this determinate situation to one where the previously differentiated relationships, habits, customs, etc., come to be problematised. This problematising, however, also entails the differentiating movement of sense wherein determinate matters and states of affairs become relevant where they may not have been relevant before. Recalling Deleuze's example of learning to swim, dedifferentiation entails problematising the established motions, expectations, habits and relations that one's body has become accustomed to in its encounters with other things. These established motions,

93

etc., no longer work when one is in the water learning to swim, since one is now engaged in the differentiating movement of sense, attempting to identify the relevant elements and relations that will, when drawn into a consistence and uniformity, make the new skill of swimming possible. Many determinate elements then become relevant that were not relevant before – the buoyancy of the water, the various new ways one might move one's legs, arms, etc., among many other things – and, as Deleuze puts it, these elements need to be 'conjugated' such that they 'constitute the Idea' (Deleuze 1994, 165), or are brought together such that they create a plane of consistency, or a problem (or Idea; Deleuze will often uses the two terms interchangeably [see 164, 179, 197, 201]) that is not to be confused with any of the determinate elements themselves and yet which allows a determinate phenomenon to emerge (in this case, the skill of swimming).

We can now begin to clarify the distinction between forced and authentic narratives, or between what we might call, following Spinoza, problems that are held in bondage and those that are free. Put simply, an authentic narrative enables one to live in accordance with one's nature as a problem, rather than being forced by an already established solution without a problem. In the former case, our determinate situations are forever open to problematisation, to further differentiations to be addressed and encountered, *ad infinitum*; in the latter case our situations reflect a solution to which nothing more can be added since it is a solution without a problem. Returning to our earlier example of the jealous husband from Buñuel's film, his narrative is in bondage and illegitimate, rather than authentic and free, since it does not enhance his powers and allow him to increasingly engage and connect with the things of his world. As a result of his delusional narrative, he is led to a near complete and total withdrawal from life. The film ends with the husband largely isolated in a monastery. In short, rather than attaining an enhancement of his powers, or joy in Spinoza's sense, defined as 'the passion by which the Mind passes to a greater perfection', the husband attains only sadness, which occurs for Spinoza 'when the Mind passes to a lesser perfection' (Spinoza 1985, 3P11 Schol.; II/149). The life-denying aspects of forced narratives, their tendency to limit our powers and promote mediocracy, will be a concern for Nietzsche as well, as we will see in the next chapter.

Returning to another example discussed earlier – the deep story Hochschild found to be crucial for those in Louisiana (see §2.1.d), which allowed them to make sense of their situation – the question to ask is whether this narrative enhanced their power to connect with the things of their world. At first blush it may well appear that it did just that, for not only did they have an account of their political reality that made sense of their situation, they also gained the support of a number of political figures, including President

94

Trump, who gave voice to their concerns. To the extent that this deep story enhanced their reality, allowing them to connect with others and feel empowered, it should not be dismissed, even if one's own narrative is at odds with it, leading them perhaps to want to excise it from their own life. If, however, we are to act upon Hume's call that our thought should have 'direct reference to action and society' (Hume 1999, 1.6) and not fall into abstruse, largely irrelevant forms of thinking, or into a shallow thought that simply repeats expected patterns, then we should continue to pursue the elements of our own narrative, fleshing out the details, looking into the genesis of these and other elements. This is another sense in which the infinitism embraced here comes into play – the sense in which the elements of narratives are open to continuing analysis and differentiation, *ad infinitum*, so that the critical question to ask is why someone stops where they do. In short, one should continue to pursue and push the attachments and partialities one has, and especially those that bear on action and society, and to reveal other attachments, make explicit other commitments, that remain implicit. Rather than simply taking our already established commitments, our already determinate patterns of behaviour, belief, etc., as sufficient for making sense of life and politics, following Spinoza we should seek the genetic conditions of such facts, a pursuit that will no doubt lead to further elements that in turn can be given a genetic account. In a late letter written to Tschirnhaus, Spinoza claims that when it comes to knowing 'which of the many ideas of a thing is sufficient for deducing all its properties, I pay attention to one thing only: that the idea or definition of the thing expresses the efficient cause' (Spinoza 2016, Letter 60, 432–3). He then offers the example of a circle to clarify:

> For example, in investigating the properties of a circle, I ask whether from the idea of a circle according to which it consists of infinite rectangles, I could deduce all its properties. I ask, I say, whether this idea involves the efficient cause of the circle. Since it doesn't, I seek another: viz. that a circle is the space described by a line one end of which is fixed and the other moving. Since this Definition now expresses the efficient cause, I know I can deduce all the properties of the circle from it, etc. (433).

In relation to the determinate facts, situations and states of affairs that narratives/problems make sense of, the task of keeping these narratives free rather than in bondage thus entails understanding the genetic, problematic conditions of these facts and situations, conditions that will be open to further analysis, and so on *ad infinitum*. If we assume things are the way they are because this is how they are supposed to be, then this is to propose a solution without a problem. In other words, it is to assume that the problem that led to the current state of affairs is one that was solved from the start and simply needed to be recognised as such, or that the implicit solution only needed to be explicitly realised in order to make the problem vanish. This is what we have called a forced narrative, one which confounds, in Spinoza's terms, a property of a thing, a solution, with the genetic conditions of the thing, or a problem. Returning to the Louisiana residents' deep story, the key is to push the narrative so that it continues to account for or to offer up the genetic conditions for the determinate facts that are the direct concern of action and society. In the case of every narrative, at least as I am arguing here, the shift to a genetic account will at some point problematise some of the current elements of the narrative. What will be revealed, in other words, is a solution with a problem rather than a solution without a problem. It is what happens next that is crucial. The options, as we will see, fall largely in two directions, repeating the nature of sense. One option is to embrace the narrative as problematic, including the problematic state of the phenomena that give voice to the narrative; the other option is to foreclose the genetic inquiry at the point where a determinate state of affairs is taken to be a solution without a problem, and thus removing any need for further inquiry. It is this latter approach that Hume challenges, as does Spinoza, on the reading offered here. To begin to clarify the manner in which the first option might be pursued, we can turn to what is perhaps the most important narrative of our time – namely, the narrative that makes sense of our current economic system, capitalism.

b) Making sense of capital

A key point MacGilvray stresses in his book on the emergence of a market economy is that one of the enticing aspects of this economy, as intellectuals saw it in the eighteenth century, was the manner in which it fulfilled the aspirations of classical republicanism – that is, the market served as a check on arbitrary power. It was this resonance with the arguments of classical republicanism which legitimised, MacGilvray claims, the sense that markets were the key to freedom. As he points out, 'where Montesquieu and Constant had argued that commerce depends on freedom, Hume and Smith insist that freedom depends on, and may even arise from the pursuit of commerce' (MacGilvray 2011, 101). On this point, both Hume and Smith were echoing their fellow Scotsman, James Steuart, who claimed that 'a modern economy', meaning the rising commercial society of the late eighteenth century, 'is the most effective bridle ever was invented against the folly of despotism ... the sovereign finds himself so bound up by the laws of his political economy that every transgression of them runs him into new difficulties' (Steuart

1767, 322; cited by MacGilvray 2011, 94). The sovereign or government is best prevented from exercising arbitrary power by the laws of political economy itself, and thus to maintain economic vitality those with power will need to operate within the limits of these laws and thereby protect the liberties of those who would seek to engage in commercial transactions. This is the reasoning behind Hume and Smith's claim that freedom depends on commerce rather than commerce on freedom. Commerce can thus serve the classical republican ideal of assuring that arbitrary power does not interfere with the freedom to exercise one's virtue, for in this case it is the economy itself which serves as a check on arbitrary power. There is a key difference with the classical ideal, however, for in modern commercial societies the freedom that is protected by the laws of political economy is not the freedom to exercise one's civic virtue in order to perfect the state of which one is a part; rather, the freedom that is protected is more in line with the negative liberty to be left alone to do what one wants as long as it is not disallowed by the laws of one's society. The liberty at work here is clearly targeted in Adam Smith's famous line that 'It is not from the benevolence of the butcher, the brewer, or the baker that we expect our dinner, but from their regard to their own interest' (Smith 1976b, 19). In other words, the fact that an economy grows and prospers and we are able to 'expect our dinner' is not accounted for by a classical republican's sense of duty toward the state, or by any effort to further develop one's civic virtue, but simply by people's pursuit of 'their own interest', along with the invisible hand guiding the process through the laws of economics.

With Smith's argument for the invisible hand, however, we come upon another forced narrative. Rather than the forced narrative the classical republicans reject – the use of arbitrary power by those who *forcibly* interfere with our ability to realise our moral virtue, or the forced narrative of a predetermining essence or truth, whether of a Platonic Form or of a pre-existent closed society – we have instead the forced narrative of a depersonalised power. This depersonalised power can serve a good purpose, and for Smith, as MacGilvray points out, 'depersonalized commercial relationships' are indeed a way of undermining and attacking 'personalized forms of domination' (MacGilvray 2011, 109). The needs of commercial markets, for instance, keep in check the potential abuses of those who may otherwise exercise arbitrary power, hence the argument of both Smith and Hume, echoing Steuart's comments about bridling the 'folly of despotism', that our freedom depends on the pursuit of commerce. At the same time, however, a depersonalised power can be equally intolerable and force itself upon us in arbitrary, unpredictable ways. Smith was aware of the many negative effects that attend commercial society, a fact that is often overlooked, and thus he called for the exercise of political power to counter the worst of these effects.[1] When Smith's own caution and concerns are ignored, and the processes and effects of economic activity are depersonalised, those processes come to be viewed as something that is forced upon us like a natural phenomenon. An economic depression thus comes to be viewed like a natural disaster rather than as something that should be the subject of political intervention. Friedrich Hayek, among others, embraces this depersonalised view of economic processes, claiming that regardless of the economic consequences we suffer, 'so long as the intent of the act that harms me is not to make me serve another person's ends, its effect on my freedom is not different from that of any natural calamity – a fire or a flood that destroys my house or an accident that harms my health' (Hayek 2011, 204; cited by MacGilvray 2011, 172). When a boss fires an employee because they need to increase the firm's profit margins, or when the market crashes and wipes out the retirement funds of millions of people, these events are for Hayek depersonalised phenomena; thus, rather than being seen as rooted in the domination of one individual or group over another, their negative consequences are to be judged as equivalent to natural calamities. After such a calamity we may pick up the pieces and help those in need, but for Hayek we are not to look to any person or group as being to blame as a cause of the event, a cause that may then justify the deployment of forms of political power to prevent such calamities in the future. The economy, in short, should remain free from political interference.

In contrast to Hayek's embrace of the forced nature of economic processes, processes he claims will best provide for the needs and welfare of society when left alone, Ellen Wood criticises capitalism precisely for of its forced nature. According to Wood, the forced nature of capitalism is already apparent at the heart of most accounts of its origin; in her book, *The Origin of Capitalism*, she argues that most of these accounts view the emergence of capitalism as the long-awaited solution to a problem, or as a solution without a problem as we would put it. According to Wood, 'Since historians first began explaining the emergence of capitalism, there has scarcely existed an explanation that did not begin by assuming the very thing that needed to be explained' (Wood 2002, 3). Most efforts 'to explain capitalism's distinct drive to maximize profits', she argues, do so by presupposing that very drive, or 'the existence of a universal profit-maximizing rationality' (4). What these origin stories fail to recognise is that 'the dominant and distinctive characteristic of the capitalist market is not opportunity or choice [for profit-maximizing activity] but, on the contrary, *compulsion*' (7, emphasis added). Wood's understanding of the origin of capitalism is thus diametrically opposed to traditional accounts.

---

1. See Schliesser 2017 where this point is stressed.

Far from seeing that origin as involving a compulsion to enter the market, traditional accounts claim that 'capitalism emerged when the market was liberated from age-old constraints' (11). Implicit in these accounts, therefore, is a story of liberation and freedom rather than one of compulsion and forced bondage. What is thus missed, Wood argues, are the 'specific ways in which the market operates in capitalism ... its specific laws of motion that uniquely compel people to enter the market, to reinvest surpluses and to produce "efficiently" by improving labour productivity – the laws of competition, profit-maximization, and capital accumulation' (16).

Wood's account of the origin of capitalism is, by her own admission, one that sets out to elaborate more thoroughly the 'decisive break from the classic model' she claims came with Marx's theory of primitive accumulation. What is distinctive in Marx's account, according to Wood, is his understanding of capital as not simply 'wealth or profit but also as a social relation, and his emphasis on the transformation of social property relations as the real "primitive accumulation"' (Wood 2002, 31). In other words, what is most important in accounting for capitalism is not that there was a change in the role wealth and profit played in economic relations, although there was certainly an intensification of this role, but rather the idea that the 'point of departure' of capitalism was, as Marx put it in *Capital*, 'nothing other than the process which divorces the worker from the ownership of the conditions of his labour ... So-called primitive accumulation, therefore, is nothing else than the historical process of divorcing the producer from the means of production' (Marx 1990, 874–5). In particular, this historical process occurred in its 'classic form', according to Marx, only in England with the 'expropriation of the agricultural producer, of the peasant, from the soil' (876). It is precisely this 'expropriation of the agricultural producer' that Wood's account focuses on. As she puts it, for Marx, 'no amount of accumulation ... by itself constitutes capital, nor will it produce capitalism' (Wood 2002, 36). Capitalism thus did not arise after a particular level of wealth was achieved, a threshold that triggered a transformation in the way business was done, as Smith argues (according to Wood), but rather was the result of a transformation of social property relations that generated the capitalist 'laws of motion' (36). Where Wood's account of primitive accumulation differs from Marx's is that while Marx admits to leaving to 'one side ... the purely economic forces behind the agricultural revolution', focusing instead on 'the violent means employed' (Marx 1990, 875), Wood turns her attention to the economic forces that give rise to the capitalist 'laws of motion'.

Central to Wood's explanation of the origin of capitalism, and the primary reason why she thinks Marx was right to claim that the process of primitive accumulation began in the English countryside, is that English elites lacked, unlike their peers in France and Holland, the extra-economic means to extract surplus value from those who worked their land. Elites in France, for instance, could rely on monies gained from positions granted through royal patronage, or through politically granted powers to extract taxes from producers. In England, by contrast, such patronage and powers to tax were not widely available, and thus in response to the general decline of agricultural prices in the sixteenth century, landowners turned to economic processes to acquire surplus. In particular, they established a 'system of "competitive rents", in which landlords ... would effectively lease land to the highest bidder' (Wood 2002, 101). Competition for access to land, coupled with 'unfixed, variable rents responsive to market imperatives', meant that it was not 'the *opportunities* afforded by the market but rather its *imperatives* that drove petty commodity producers to accumulate' (102). Without a fixed lease, commodity producers needed to compete for land and this, in turn, compelled them to seek 'the improvement of productivity, and self-sustaining economic development' (102) so that they could gain access to land and provide the surplus necessary to maintain the lease. With the profits acquired, they were further compelled, in order to remain competitive and maintain their lease, to reinvest their profits in order to improve efficiency and profitability, with profits yet again being reinvested in order to stave off further competition. The result of this process is what Wood calls the capitalist 'laws of motion', laws that mandate endless accumulation and competition. With the emphasis placed on these 'laws', Wood's account does not stress, as most do, the force and violence of the enclosures, or the laws passed in support of these enclosures, as the primary reason why the agricultural worker was forcibly divorced 'from the ownership of the conditions of his labour', although these forces were certainly at work; Wood argues instead that the economic imperatives and the emergence of the capitalist laws of motion were what motivated the process of enclosures so as to maximise profitability. The enclosures were an effect, not a cause, of the capitalist 'laws of motion'.

It is important to clarify a couple of points. First, when Wood refers to the capitalist 'laws of motion', she uses scare quotes, and this is precisely to alert us to the contingency with which these processes emerged, a contingency that is now often taken for a necessity, a law of nature, *à la* Hayek. Marx was already critical of the tendency to view the processes of capitalism as being simply in accordance with the laws of nature, and by extension the will of God. Quoting a line from Virgil's *Aeneid* – '*Tantae molis erat*' (so great was the effort) – Marx refers in this context to the effort 'to unleash the "eternal natural laws" of the capitalist mode of production, to complete the process of separation between the workers and the conditions of their labour' (Marx 1990, 925) – that is, to complete the process of primitive accumulation. In a footnote to this passage, Marx points to Edmund Burke as evidence for the success of this great effort: 'This sycophant, who, in the pay of the English oligarchy', claimed (as Marx cites him), "The laws of commerce are the laws of Nature, and therefore the laws of God."'

The second point to stress is that the capitalist 'laws of motion' only work if they are also self-limiting. As Wood puts it, the history of capitalism 'exemplifies one of the founding contradictions of capitalism: the need to impose its imperatives as universally as possible, and the need to limit the damaging consequences that this universalization has for capital itself' (Wood 2002, 155). Wood cites the example of Ireland, where its entry into the market, having been compelled to follow the capitalist 'laws of motion', posed a threat to English wealth as it became increasingly competitive. England thus needed to restrict development in Ireland to prevent this from happening. This is precisely the point Deleuze and Guattari stress when they argue that 'The State, its police, and its army form a gigantic enterprise of antiproduction' (Deleuze and Guattari 1977, 235). That is, the state serves to provide the limits capitalism itself needs in order to stave off the tendency of capitalist production to break and transgress every limit, a transgression which would undermine the stability and viability of the political economy itself. This is what Deleuze and Guattari will refer to as the 'schizophrenic' tendency of capitalism, or, as they put it: 'schizophrenia is the exterior limit of capitalism itself or the conclusion of its deepest tendency, [and yet] ... capitalism only functions on condition that it inhibit this tendency, or that it push back or displace this limit, by substituting for it its own immanent relative limits, which it continually reproduces on a widened scale' (246). Deleuze and Guattari thus echo, as we will see below (§5.2.a), Karl Polanyi's arguments about the double movement of economic liberalism (or capitalism) – the movement that both undermines customs, traditions, families, etc., and defends society against this movement (see Polanyi 2001).

At this point it will be useful to return to our earlier discussion of the nature of a problem as being without limit, or as *apeiron*, in line with Plato's understanding of the always progressing nature of more and less (recall §2.2.a). As *apeiron* a problem is not to be confused or confounded with its solutions, solutions that are determinate and yet do not exhaust the nature of the problem. Capitalism, as Deleuze and Guattari understand it, is similarly *apeiron*, or a problem that is not exhausted by the immanent limits that serve as solutions to the problem that is capital. As we pursue a genetic inquiry into the determinate, immanent limits necessary to the functioning of capitalism itself, the question becomes one of determining how one should respond to such limits. Should we encourage the breaching of the limits and the contradictions that will undermine the stability of capitalist economies (an

101

argument advocated by accelerationists[2]), or should we enhance the powers of the state and allow it to place even stricter limits upon the capitalist 'laws of motion'? In the case of Ireland, used by Wood to exemplify 'one of the founding contradictions of capitalism', it becomes a matter of making sense of capital, and as such the two paradoxical de/differentiating tendencies lurk. On the one hand, should the English limit and restrict Irish farmers' access to markets, and do so through the powers of the English state, thus removing or dedifferentiating an emerging threat to their own ability to maximise profits? Or should the market be allowed to continue apace under the capitalist 'laws of motion' and the differentiating tendencies this involves? In its contemporary form, these alternatives are often presented as the choice between laissez-faire capitalism and state socialism, though both depend, as Wood, Deleuze and Guattari and others have shown, on the determinate limits necessary to capitalism itself.

What the contemporary debates regarding capitalism largely fail to recognise – and this marks the importance of Wood's book – is the fact that capitalism, whether shepherded by state power or left untouched, does not lead to the enhancement of freedom but rather to the expansion of the imperatives and compulsions associated with the capitalist 'laws of motion'. It is at this point, precisely, that a classical republican critique of capitalism could be made, and William Clare Roberts has done just this in his book *Marx's Inferno*. If the task of classical republicanism is to eliminate arbitrary power, then this is also a task one should take on in addressing capitalism. By being forced to enter the market, placing our labour power at its mercy, we are subjected to economic processes that disrupt one's ability to 'achieve one's ends'; as Roberts puts it, 'there is no way to *ensure* that one's labor power, or one's commodity in general, is marketable. That is precisely the problem' (Roberts 2017, 88). One is thus forced to market oneself, to place one's labour power, or one's commodity in general, on the market, and yet the results of doing so are *forced* upon one by impersonal market forces. One is thus not free under capitalism, according to classical republicanism as Roberts understands it, for 'it renders us systematically irresponsible for our economic life' (101). As a result of capitalism and its process of primitive accumulation, our life-activity or labour has thus been divorced from the very conditions of this life-activity. We must attain these conditions on the market, where we then are subject to its arbitrary, impersonal and unpredictable effects. All this is simply the result, on Roberts' reading of Marx, of the ongoing effects of primitive accumulation; Marx's critique of capitalism can thus be read, Roberts concludes, 'as radicalizing the republican tradition for which

---

2. For more on accelerationism, see Mackay 2014.

freedom as non-domination is the highest virtue of institutions' (231). By recognising the contingent nature of the capitalist 'laws of motion' – which were the result of strategies developed in response to specific historical conditions, or solutions to a problem – one can begin to ask if the consequences of economic processes should be taken, as Hayek, Burke and others take them, as instances of impersonal laws of nature. In short, the key question to ask is whether the freedom of free markets entails a confusion of *being forced* (by the contingent capitalist 'laws of motion') with *being free*. When one questions or problematises the liberty that has come to be identified with processes that force themselves upon us, then the problem that has not been exhausted by the solution that is capitalism may well create possibilities for transformation, for an undermining of the capitalist 'laws of motion'.

It is not necessary to begin this process, however, with the grand institutional and economic structures that one may want to undermine and overthrow. One can begin where one is, with the simplest of interactions, in a process of critical analysis and enquiry that may result in a problematisation of one's relations to self, others and the world. This is the approach I am calling a critical existentialism, an approach in line with what Deleuze and Hume would have us do. Our enquiries and critical analyses, therefore, should, as Hume argued, have 'a direct reference to action and society' (Hume 1999, 1.6). To do this, we can begin with expectations and habits that are ready to hand. What is the nature of this belief or behaviour, this habit or expectation? Is it legitimate or illegitimate, justified or arbitrary? This will be the key question for Hume. For Deleuze as well it is the recognition of the problem or Idea that is inseparable from solutions that will allow us to begin to unpack it and discern whether its solutions are legitimate or illegitimate, whether they are acceptable solutions or the kind that are forced upon us as solutions without a problem. This process of critical analysis can begin, as Deleuze makes clear, with our most mundane relations:

> We sometimes go on as though people can't express themselves. In fact, they're always expressing themselves. The sorriest couples are those where the woman can't be preoccupied or tired without the man saying 'What's wrong? Say something... ', or the man, without the woman saying ... , and so on. Radio and television have spread this spirit everywhere, and we're riddled with pointless talk, insane quantities of words and images. Stupidity's never blind or mute. So it's not a problem of getting people to express themselves but of providing little gaps of solitude and silence in which they might eventually find something to say. Repressive forces don't stop people expressing themselves but rather force them to express themselves. What a relief to have nothing to say, the right to say nothing, because only then is there a chance of framing the rare, and ever rarer, thing that might be worth saying. ('Mediators', in Deleuze 1995, 129)

103

Deleuze will offer a similarly mundane example in his 'Postscript on Control Societies' when he notes that 'If the stupidest TV game shows are so successful, it's because they're a perfect reflection of the way businesses are run … businesses are constantly introducing an inexorable rivalry presented as healthy competition, a wonderful motivation that sets individuals against one another and sets itself up in each of them, dividing each within himself' (Deleuze 1995, 179). A game shows thus takes the rivalry between businesses, the compulsion and necessity to compete on the market that comes with the capitalist 'laws of motion', and presents this as fun, as something we not only ought to do but should want to do, something we should incorporate into our relations with others and ourselves. We take on the division within ourselves, for instance, in the rivalry between our current self and the self that seeks self-improvement, the self that seeks to better itself through processes of 'continuing education and … continuous assessment' (179). Deleuze closes this essay with an important question, and one that gets to the heart of his problematising approach: noting that 'Many young people have a strange craving to be "motivated", they're always asking for special courses and continuing education', he then adds that 'it's their job to discover whose ends these serve, just as older people discovered, with considerable difficulty, who was benefiting from disciplines' (182). Those who were subjected to the disciplinary institutions Foucault discussed – factories, schools, etc. – came to recognise, 'with considerable difficulty', that it was not their ends being served and thus they began to organise, unionise and work towards different ends; so too Deleuze is arguing that, having transitioned from a disciplinary society to a control society, we have a similar need to discover, through difficult questioning, the ends that are being forced upon us.

2. Challenging Narratives

a) Good faith/bad faith

At his point we can return to the existential tradition, and to the strong parallels we can see between that tradition and classical republicanism if we view both in terms of a Deleuzean understanding of the problematic nature of making sense. Although we have already brought Nietzsche and Deleuze into this discussion, and highlighted some key differences between Nietzsche and classical republicanism (§3.1.a), there remain two key components that are seemingly essential to the republican project but that have been subject to severe criticisms from those identified with the existential tradition. To show that the parallel we find between classical republicanism and the existential

104

tradition is more than a glancing similarity, we will begin with why it seems inappropriate, on a first reading (or perhaps after many readings), to find anything substantial in the parallel.

The two important features of the republican project are, first, the predictability that is necessary if individuals are to achieve their ends, a predictability that is undermined by the presence of arbitrary power; and, second, the teleology connected with this predictability, or the goals connected to realising one's civic virtue and potential. Both assumptions come under heavy attack from both Nietzsche and Deleuze. In a letter to his friend Franz Overbeck, for instance, Nietzsche praises Spinoza, in whom he claims to have found 'a precursor', for, among other things, his denial of 'the freedom of the will, teleology, the moral world-order, the unegoístic, and evil' (Nietzsche 1954, 92). Nietzsche will also speak critically of the transformation, or deformation, of human beings into predictable, calculable beings. As he puts it in *On The Genealogy of Morals*, if human beings are to become the 'animal with the right to make promises', then they 'first of all have become calculable, regular, necessary [in order] to be able to stand security for [their] own future, which is what one who promises does!' (Nietzsche 1969, 57–8). In other places, Nietzsche will criticise contemporary moral theories for their 'collective drive toward timidity masquerading behind an intellectual front', with the goal being 'foremost that life be rid of all the dangers it once held and that each and every person should help toward this end with all one's might' (Nietzsche 2011, 127). This was the reason, again as mentioned above (§3.1.a), for Nietzsche's claim that refraining 'from injury, violence, and exploitation and placing one's will on a par with that of someone else', is nothing less than a 'will to the denial of life' (Nietzsche 1966, §259, 203). In short, a life that entails the enhancement of one's powers, an increase in joy in Spinoza's sense, is one that will engage in injury, violence and exploitation, along with which come the unpredictabilities and dangers of living. But these are precisely what contemporary moral theories seek to eliminate, exhorting that a predictable, calculable, secure existence is to be sought for 'with all one's might'. The result of such efforts, Nietzsche claims, is that we 'grate off all the rough and sharp edges from life ... turning humanity into sand ... Tiny, soft, round, endless grains of sand!' The 'democratic instincts of the modern soul', with its 'mediocritization and depreciation of humanity in value', are thus symptomatic, for Nietzsche, of a fundamental 'will to negate life' (§259, 203).

One also finds many of these claims in Deleuze's work, for he too criticises the notion of predictability and arguably values the unpredictable over the predictable. Referring to what he calls the 'crisis in contemporary literature', for instance, Deleuze claims that it is a result of the 'system of rapid turnover' tied to the emphasis placed on bestsellers (a result of the capitalist 'laws of motion'); but 'Fast turnover', he adds, 'necessarily means selling people what they expect: even what's "daring," "scandalous," strange, and so on falls into the market's predictable forms' (Deleuze 1995, 128). Deleuze argues that, in contrast to the sought for predictability of the bestseller – the endless stream of sequels in the *Star Wars* franchise for instance – 'The conditions of literary creation, which emerge only unpredictably, with a slow turnover and progressive recognition, are fragile.' There may be 'Future Becketts or Kafkas', he notes, but they will 'of course be unlike Beckett or Kafka' (128), and they will not arise predictably – in fact they may go unnoticed. If there is a value that Deleuze would call upon, therefore, predictability would not appear to be one of them.

How, if at all, are we to reconcile the classical republican critique of arbitrary power, and its reliance on the predictability necessary to exercise our virtue effectively, with Nietzsche's and Deleuze's critique of the problems they see arising from *forcing* human beings into predictable moulds or forced narratives? Should we even bother attempting to reconcile them? I believe we should, and the key to doing so is to begin by unpacking what is meant by being forced into predictable moulds, with the emphasis on the *forced* nature of the process. We can get an indication of how Deleuze understands this process by returning to the same essay in which he diagnoses the crisis in contemporary literature. In discussing the 'insane quantities of words and images' that bombard us each day on radio and television, and now on social media and the internet, Deleuze points out that 'Repressive forces don't stop people expressing themselves but rather *force* them to express themselves' (Deleuze 1995, 129, emphasis added). The flood of words and images, in other words, do not provide us with a smorgasbord from which we can freely choose the words, images, narratives, etc., that best suit us; to the contrary, for Deleuze this flood forces upon us a habit of avoiding silence, where words and images must fill the voids – no awkward silences! We even feel forced to ask our partners what's wrong, as Deleuze says a few lines earlier, if they are more quiet than usual. Freedom, therefore, or non-domination in the classical republican sense, is thus to be contrasted with the repressive powers that force us into continually expressing ourselves, and for Deleuze this freedom comes when we 'have nothing to say', for only when we have 'the right to say nothing ... is there a chance of framing the rare, and ever rarer, thing that might be worth saying' (129).

For Deleuze, therefore, there is clearly a value being asserted concerning this freedom and right to say nothing, the freedom from repressive forces that enables us to frame the 'thing that might be worth saying'. Taking these points into consideration, and in light of the arguments from the previous chapter, a Deleuzian ethic could be stated as follows: to live in good faith, or in accordance with one's virtue, is to embrace life as a problem, and this is *good* faith precisely because it is affirmative and embraces the problematic as such and the implications this entails. It is also a *faith* because one is embracing and affirming a reality that gives us no determinate reasons or hopes upon which to justify our affirmations. One cannot even say just what it is that is being affirmed. By contrast, to live in bad faith is to reject or negate the problematic, to live life as expected, or in accordance with rules, customs, etc., that serve as solutions to the problems of life, solutions to how, when, where and in what circumstances we should do what is expected of us, and solutions that precisely predetermine what this should be. Such solutions serve, moreover, as solutions without a problem, and thus we have a faith here as well, but now a faith in a solution, and a faith that it may indeed be a solution without a problem, or if not so in this case, then at least a faith that there is, somewhere, a possible salvation to be had in a final solution.

What then are the implications of embracing and affirming life as a problem? First and foremost, this affirmation is inseparable from an enhancement of the life processes that are irreducible to that which is already determinately given (recall our earlier discussion of Spinoza and joy [§1.2.a and §3.1.a]). Secondly, and relatedly, this enhancement of life processes is not to be confused with a quantitative enhancement, with an increase in one's own human capital, in Gary Becker's sense of that term (see Becker 1964). It is precisely the freedom from quantitative increase, from filling awkward silences with determinate words and images, that Deleuze encourages as a form of resistance to those powers that force us to express ourselves. Echoing his own call to affirm 'the right to say nothing, because only then is there a chance of framing the rare, and ever rarer, thing that might be worth saying', Deleuze's response to the crisis of literature is that while 'We may congratulate ourselves on the quantitative increase in books, and larger print runs ... young writers will end up moulded in a literary space that leaves them no possibility of creating anything' (Deleuze 1995, 128). The enhancement of life processes that comes with the affirmation of life as a problem is thus not a quantitative enhancement or increase; as we have been arguing, it is nothing less than the process of making sense, and as such it entails both the process of increased determination, a differentiating movement, and the move towards delirium, a dedifferentiating movement. Stated differently, making sense involves a tendency both towards the universal, towards a universal delirium that cannot be reduced to any determinate particular (the delirium that conditions Nietzsche's claim to be all the names in history), and a tendency towards the particular, to differentiations that can be explicated *ad infinitum*. To affirm life as a problem, as a process of making sense, is thus to embrace a process that is neither universal or particular, the universal and the particular being abstractions, but instead affirms the provisional, problematic nature of the determinate ways in which things are done, the determinate ways in which things make sense.

To clarify by way of contrast, the rejection or negation of the problematic, or bad faith as I have defined it, is characterised precisely by the fact that it does not affirm the provisional, problematic nature of the determinate ways in which things are done, and rejects any move that might problematise or reveal the problems that are inseparable from those determinate ways, thereby showing them up as simply solutions to problems they have not exhausted. Bad faith, moreover, is characterised not by the way it makes sense of things, but more importantly by the involuntary, knee-jerk rejection that occurs with encounters that do not make sense. One way to read Nietzsche's work is as an ongoing effort to diagnose these points of resistance, to provoke the knee-jerk reactions that reveal one's limitations, the solutions one takes to be solutions without a problem. When one reads through the chapter titles of *Ecce Homo*, for instance (Nietzsche 1969), titles such as 'Why I am so Wise', 'Why I am so Clever', 'Why I Write Such Good Books', 'Why I am Destiny', one's knee-jerk reaction may well be negative, an involuntary rejection – at least that is how many of my students react. But if this reaction occurs, then it is to be interpreted, for Nietzsche, as symptomatic of a set of values that takes being humble and self-effacing, among other things, as a way of making sense, unproblematically, of how one ought to live one's life. This set of values is what Nietzsche identifies as slave morality; hence the automatic, involuntary aversion to his chapter titles is the result of encountering values that cannot be affirmed by slave morality, values that determine the limits, from the perspective of that morality, of what makes sense of how things ought to be.

Restating Nietzsche's diagnostic, critical efforts in terms of good faith and bad faith, good faith entails affirming the problematic nature of one's own determinate values, or the inseparability of a problem from these values. When one encounters something that provokes an automatic rejection or negation, as we all do at some point or another, then a good faith response is to affirm the problematic nature of one's own values, rather than take them to be unproblematic, or as solutions without a problem, which is the bad faith response. To flesh out these points further, we will turn to four examples that will illustrate what I take to be involved in cases of *good* and *bad* faith. In the next section I will discuss conspiracy theories as an example of bad faith narratives, or as *forced* narratives, and contrast these with what a good faith narrative would entail. With this discussion in hand, we will then turn in the next chapter to the existential tradition, where the theme of good and bad faith is more pronounced. I will begin with Søren Kierkegaard, and in particular his short but influential *The Sickness unto Death*, in order to bring in some of the key elements that will continue to circulate throughout much of the work of the existential writers. This will provide us with further resources to differentiate between good and bad faith narratives, such that we can then set out to critically and productively confront the latter. We will then turn to Jean-Paul Sartre's discussion of bad faith to develop our discussion of the existential tradition, and finally to Camus' *The Rebel*, in which Camus calls upon what may be called a good faith rebellion in response to the shattering of the traditional political order that occurred in the wake of the French Revolution. These discussions will show how existential thought may contribute to a critical theory of contemporary society, or to what I call a critical existentialism.

b) Conspiracy narratives

On 14 December 2012, Adam Lanza took his mother's assault rifle from a storage chest, shot and killed his mother, and then drove to Sandy Hook Elementary School where he shot and killed twenty children, all between six and seven years of age, and six adult staff members. He then shot and killed himself as police began to enter the school. Not long after this event, the 'official' narrative account of what happened came to be challenged by some who offered an alternative account. Most prominent among these was Alex Jones, an American radio host and prominent conspiracy theorist, who claimed that the shooting was a 'giant hoax', a 'completely fake' event that was staged in order to sway public opinion towards stricter gun control legislation. Jones has since recanted, in part no doubt due to defamation lawsuits that were filed against him. He was not alone, however. James Fetzer, a former professor of philosophy of science at the University of Minnesota, Duluth, has promoted his own version of the Sandy Hook conspiracy theory, among others (he cofounded 'Scholars for 9/11 Truth' to further his 9/11 conspiracy theory, and has also supported alternative theories of the Kennedy assassination and the Holocaust). James Tracy, a former communications professor at Florida Atlantic University, has also claimed the Sandy Hook massacre was a 'false flag' operation designed to sway public opinion. Tracy would later harass parents of the children who were killed, insisting they prove their child was dead. He was successfully sued for harassment and fired from his tenured position.

The list of conspiracy theories could continue of course, since it is not a short list, but in focusing on the Sandy Hook case for the moment the point to be stressed is that the narratives conspiracy theorists put forward do attempt to make sense of a certain set of facts. The supposed 'smoking gun' in the Sandy Hook case, for instance, is a photograph of Barack Obama backstage at a Newtown vigil in honour of the victims with a young blond girl sitting on his lap. This girl, so the conspiracy narrative goes, is six-year-old Emilie Parker, one of the 'supposed' twenty children killed. This 'fact' and others are then quilted together to construct an alternative narrative. Fetzer put together several such accounts in his edited collection, *Nobody Died at Sandy Hook*, a book for which he and co-editor Mike Palacek recently lost a defamation case. In the case of the 9/11 attacks, the rapid collapse of the towers is often pointed to as the 'smoking gun' that proves that the attack was staged since, the theory goes, they could not have collapsed as quickly as they did without key structural weakening having taken place in advance of the attack (such as the reinforced steel frames of the buildings being cut). In both cases, however, these 'facts' have failed to stand up to further scrutiny. The girl on Obama's lap was the dead girl's sister, while the collapse of the twin towers is consistent with physics because of the incredibly high temperatures of the fires caused by the jet fuel.

Conspiracy theorists, however, do not hang their hat on just a single 'smoking gun' fact, but will attempt to build a narrative that draws a number of facts together to make sense of the event, and do so in a way that is at odds with the 'official' narrative. Two issues here are especially relevant to the distinction between good and bad faith that I am setting forth. First, in addition to the conspiracy narrative account, there is often a self-affirmation narrative that accompanies and further justifies accepting the conspiracy theory. As discussed earlier (§2.1.d), David Sherman and Geoffrey Cohen have shown that a narrative or 'self-system', as Claude Steele puts it, is one 'that essentially explains ourselves', and that it is crucial for this self-system to 'maintain a phenomenal experience of the self − self-conceptions and images − as adaptively and morally adequate, i.e., as competent, good, coherent, unitary, stable, capable of free choice, capable of controlling important outcomes, and so on' (Steele 1988, 262). This self-system is what gets put to the test after 'experiencing a self-threat'. Sherman and Cohen found that in response to such threats people 'may engage in any number of strategies to reaffirm self-integrity via social judgment ... [including] comparing the self with a clearly inferior other, gossiping negatively about a third party, or harshly judging a political ingroup member who fails to demonstrate as much fervor as one personally does' (Sherman and Cohen 2006, 203), among other strategies. The same strategies are deployed by conspiracy theorists whose narrative accounts invite criticism and ridicule, leading them no doubt to experience self-threat, to which they respond by citing the inferiority of the public at large, a public who naively accept the 'official' narrative, while the conspiracy theorists, in a proud moment of self-affirmation and defiance, claim that they have not been duped by the official narrative and have the courage to speak the truth as they see it. A consequence of this strategy, and this is the second key issue, is that many conspiracy theorists remain unperturbed by facts or evidence which debunk their narrative, since they refuse to relent on the self-affirmation narrative that paints them as better than those who accept the 'official' narrative. The self-affirmation narrative is thus not a space of reasons, in Wilfrid Sellars' sense of the term (developed further by Robert Brandom), a space where formal and informal rules of inference lead to and justify one's conclusions.

We can now begin to clarify the distinction between good and bad faith narratives as I have been setting it forth. Although the conspiracy theorist may well act from a narrative of self-affirmation, their conspiracy narratives quickly encounter determinate facts and evidence that they must reject or exclude from their account. If it is indeed true that nobody died at Sandy Hook, then the conspiracy theorist must reject the fact that there were so many funerals, so many grieving parents, plus many other facts that the 'official' narrative accounts for. The conspiracy narrative must thus limit itself to a small constellation of facts from which it spins its narrative, and reject those facts that may contest or challenge its account. It is for this reason that a conspiracy theory, understood as we have sketched it here, is to be thought of as an example of bad faith. This is because such narratives presuppose the truth of their account, a truth that is in essence presented as a solution without a problem. The 'alternative' narrative is assumed to be the proper account, and one that thereafter excludes any facts that may problematise it. When the knee-jerk reaction of rejection or denial kicks in, we see the tell-tale symptoms of bad faith, and yet it is disguised or hidden behind a veil of self-affirmation, but again a self-affirmation that rests on bad faith. Good faith, by contrast, embraces the problematic nature of narratives, or the inseparability of a problem from the narratives that make sense of our life and world. As such, these narratives may well be undone or undermined by changing circumstances, facts, etc. – in short, by problematisations – but they may also come to draw in more facts, more relationships and details, as part of the process of making sense. Both tendencies are affirmed when one embraces the problems inseparable from one's narratives, or when one is in good faith. We can now clarify this process further by turning to the existential tradition, for a common theme that appears in the otherwise varied writings and concerns of those most frequently associated with existentialism is an emphasis upon living authentically, or in good faith, and such a life embraces the difficulty of making sense of one's situation.

111

§4 Stop Making Sense

1. Existentialism Revisited

In this chapter we will begin to draw together a number of the themes and threads of earlier chapters, while preparing the way for our discussion of the political implications of the paradoxical process of making sense. In particular, our attention here will be on the de/differentiating tendencies of making sense, and on how these tendencies come to bear on the problem of making sense of one's life, a problem that has a pronounced resonance within the existential tradition. With Kierkegaard, especially, one cannot overstate the relevance of paradox to his understanding of the nature of human existence, though Sartre and Camus, as we will see, each in their own way continue to press important aspects of Kierkegaard's thought. We will then extend Kierkegaard's project, bringing in the work of Erving Goffman as well as Harold Garfinkel's ethnomethodological studies, in order to argue for a symptomatological approach to discerning and resisting the tendencies to rely on solutions without a problem. This the approach I have been calling critical existentialism, which we will develop further in the context of Adorno's critique of Heidegger's understanding of authenticity. Bringing the paradoxical de/differentiating tendencies of making sense into conversation with the existential focus on an authentic, meaningful life, and with an emphasis on Kierkegaard's arguments, we will be able to address Adorno's criticisms and show how we can, in new and important ways, answer Hume's call to pursue a philosophy that has 'a direct reference to action and society' (Hume 1999, 1.6).

a) Kierkegaard and infinite difference

In *The Sickness unto Death* (1849), Søren Kierkegaard identifies the sickness of the title as despair, and more precisely the despair that death does not bring about the end of what one is – namely, spirit. In a body that is sick and suffering, the sickness that ends with death also ends this person's suffering, and thus death will be, in this sense, a blessing. For Kierkegaard, however, there is a 'sickness of the soul [that] does not consume [the soul] as the sickness of the body consumes the body' (Kierkegaard 1980b, 20). Kierkegaard thus comes to Plato's conclusion from *The Republic* (X 608c–610) when he argues that 'If there were nothing eternal in a man, he could not despair at all; if despair could consume his self, then there would be no despair at all' (Kierkegaard 1980b, 21). In other words, for Kierkegaard despair is precisely the sickness that will not bring about the end, in death, of what one is by nature – namely, spirit. This despair is analogous, Kierkegaard notes, to the 'ambitious man whose slogan is "Either Caesar or nothing" [but who] does not get to be Caesar, [so] he despairs over it'. More importantly, as Kierkegaard adds, 'this also means something else: precisely because he did not get to be Caesar, he now cannot bear to be himself' (19). Since he failed to be Caesar, he now despairs over being who he is; similarly with those who fail to become who they are as spirit, they too now despair of being who they are. Kierkegaard thus comes to his key point: 'to be unaware of being defined as spirit is precisely what despair is' (25).

But what does it mean to be 'defined as spirit', to be 'unaware' that one is so defined, and for this to entail a despair at a death or end that will not come? To begin to clarify we can take the case of worldly loss – the loss of a loved one. Such a loss will cause grief and despair, and despair not only at the loss of the loved one but also at a reality that brings such suffering and sorrow. It is precisely here that cracks begin to appear in the manner in which one has been living one's life, cracks that let the light of spirit through. This may not occur, for as Kierkegaard recognises, the 'physician of souls will certainly agree with me that, on the whole, most men live without ever becoming conscious of being destined as spirit – hence all the so-called security, contentment with life, etc., which is simply despair' (Kierkegaard 1980b, 26). Worldly loss and despair, however, or a life overwhelmed with a grief brought on by tragedy, may mark a turning point where one's destiny as spirit comes to be revealed. What is significant here is not the actual loss, for as Kierkegaard says, 'to lose the things of this world is not to despair; yet this is what he talks about, and this is what he calls despairing' (51). The shattering of our security and contentment through tragedy, death and loss is thus not despair, even though it is all we tend to think or talk about when we come to despair. But this despair that is not a despair that can begin a process that may move one towards an overcoming of despair, and this is where the illuminating crack emerges. In particular, what may happen is that, with the worldly loss one suffers, 'the self infinitely magnifies the actual loss and then despairs over the earthly *in toto*'. However, Kierkegaard adds, 'as soon as this distinction (between despairing over the earthly and over something earthly) must be maintained essentially, there is also an essential advance in consciousness of the self' (60). What is going on here, according to Kierkegaard, and this is key, is that the actual loss, the determinate, particular loss one suffers and over which one despairs, comes to be magnified infinitely through the imagination to the point where it swallows the entirety of the world itself. One despairs over existence in general, for its mortal, fleeting nature inevitably brings with it a loss one cannot overcome. One then encounters, Kierkegaard claims, an essential distinction that is crucial to the awareness of a self that is no longer in despair: in short, as Kierkegaard puts it, 'the state of the self when despair is completely rooted out is this: in relating itself to itself and in willing to be itself, the self rests transparently in the power that established it' (14).

The nature of this power the self rests transparently in is expressed, Kierkegaard argues, precisely in the despair over the earthly, rather than *something* earthly; that is, what is expressed and revealed here is a self that is a relationship and synthesis of the infinite (the earthly) and the finite (something earthly). Kierkegaard is quite forthright in his assertion that 'The self is composed of infinitude and finitude. However, this synthesis is a relation, and a relation that, even though it is derived, relates itself to itself, which is freedom' (Kierkegaard 1980b, 29). The relation that is the self as a synthesis of infinitude and finitude is freedom because this is a self that relates to itself and becomes what it is not by virtue of something else but by its own nature. This lack of dependency on another to become what one is is just what Kierkegaard, along with Hegel and others, takes to be the defining characteristic of freedom. Although Kierkegaard recognises that this relationship of self to self, as a composition of infinitude and finitude, is derived, meaning it rests 'transparently in the power that established it' (that is, God), this power, as we will see, is at the very core of what one is as spirit; it is what is expressed in a meaningful existence, and it is thus integral to what one becomes when one becomes who one is. Before getting to the point where this relationship becomes clear, Kierkegaard first elaborates upon how infinitude and finitude are involved in the process whereby one becomes what one is:

> To become oneself is to become concrete. But to become concrete is neither to become finite nor to become infinite, for that which is to become concrete is indeed a synthesis. Consequently, the progress of the becoming must be an infinite moving away from itself in the infinitizing of the self, and an infinite coming back to itself in the finitizing process. (Kierkegaard 1980b, 30)

When one despairs over something earthly, the loss of a loved one for instance, and 'infinitely magnifies' this loss to the point where it becomes despair over the earthly *in toto*, then a step is taken towards becoming oneself as concrete, but only if the 'infinite moving away' that comes with despairing the earthly *in toto* is accompanied by an 'infinite coming back'. What this entails is that the imagination, which for Kierkegaard 'is the medium for the

114

process of infinitizing' (30), does not allow the self to vanish in an infinite world of delirious possibility. When the imagination goes unchecked, then 'possibility seems greater and greater to the self; more and more becomes possible because nothing becomes actual. Eventually everything seems possible, but this is exactly the point at which the abyss swallows up the self' (36). It is for this reason that to become oneself, to become concrete, the infinitising move must be limited by a finitising process, or the infinite possibilities generated by the imagination must be limited by necessity – 'just as finitude is the limiting aspect in relation to infinitude, so also necessity is the constraint in relation to possibility' (35). The reason for these constraints is that to become oneself as concrete means becoming a meaningful self, or a self whereby one's life and existence takes on significance. If the infinitising move of the imagination is not countered by the finitising move of necessity, then nothing becomes meaningful in life since everything is equally possible, nothing is actually existent, and thus everything can become the basis for providing the reason or purpose which renders life meaningful. Similarly, if everything is necessary, if there are no possibilities other than what is necessarily and actually predetermined and given, then for Kierkegaard 'everything has become trivial' (40) and the self one becomes lacks meaning and significance for it does not have the possibility or freedom necessary to differentiate between what is meaningful and meaningless, what is relevant and irrelevant. As Kierkegaard puts it, 'if there is nothing but necessity, man is essentially as inarticulate as the animals' (40–1). To live a meaningful existence, therefore, one must live both the infinitising and the finitising becomings (the de/differentiating movements as we have called them), one must express through one's life the absolute infinite/finite difference that constitutes one's concrete existence.

What is crucial therefore to the process of becoming oneself, to becoming concrete, is that one avoid pushing the infinitising process to its limit, to the complete, infinite abstraction from concrete actuality, from the world where one lives one's life, with the result that one becomes swallowed in a world of meaningless possibilities. But one must also avoid pushing the finitising process to its limit, to the point where one's life is reduced to that which is, to the actual, which is given and predetermined in accordance with necessity, and thus a life that is equally meaningless and trivial. For most people, however, this is just the move they find it easiest to make, for by living a life reduced to the necessities of the finite and actual, one does not risk the uncertainties and possibilities that come with becoming oneself, and thus one seeks 'with all one's might', as Nietzsche critically observed (and as cited earlier), to live such that 'life be rid of all the dangers' (Nietzsche 2011, 127). As Kierkegaard describes this most common scenario,

Surrounded by hordes of men, absorbed in all sorts of secular matters, more and more shrewd about the ways of the world – such a person forgets himself, forgets his name divinely understood, does not dare to believe in himself, finds it too hazardous to be himself and far easier to be like the others, to become a copy, a number, a mass man. (Kierkegaard 1980b, 33–4)

Yet another way of avoiding the hazards associated with becoming oneself, this time with respect to the move towards infinite possibility, where the 'abyss swallows up the self' (36), is to constrain the possible within the limits of the probable, within a mathematically calculable form that tames infinite possibility, a move that leaves us with the risk-free comforts of the probable. By doing this, however, one is unable to come into relationship with oneself, or 'become concrete', for 'to become concrete', as Kierkegaard argues, 'is neither to become infinite nor to become finite', and yet by becoming calculable and probable, 'a copy, a number, a mass man', one becomes finite. This is what the 'mass man' does: the 'philistine-bourgeois mentality', as Kierkegaard puts it, 'lacks every qualification of spirit and is completely wrapped up in probability within which possibility finds its small corner; therefore it lacks the possibility of becoming aware of God' (41); rather than embracing the infinitising move that allows one to become concrete, one instead 'leads possibility around imprisoned in the cage of probability' (42).

A symptom that one has indeed imprisoned possibility 'in the cage of probability', and hence a symptom of not relating oneself to oneself, is when one takes offence at what is involved in becoming concrete – namely, the process of bringing into relationship the infinite difference between infinite and finite, possibility and necessity. If one thinks in terms of probability rather than the infinitising process, then one will quickly take offence upon realising that affirming oneself involves an infinite difference that cannot be reduced to probability, cannot be imprisoned in a cage. This is precisely the point of Kierkegaard's example of 'a poor day laborer and the mightiest emperor who ever lived' (Kierkegaard 1980b, 84). Although one may be able to think this difference, the difficulty and possibility of offence arises when one attempts to think the relationship and synthesis of the difference in becoming who one is. As Kierkegaard develops the example, he notes that if the emperor were 'suddenly seized on the idea of sending for the day laborer', not only would the labourer be surprised by the improbability of this happening, having assumed the emperor never even 'knew he existed', but he would consider himself to be 'indescribably favored just to be permitted to see the emperor once, something he would relate to his children and grandchildren as the most important event in his life' (84). From the perspective of probabilities, the event of meeting the emperor would be a singular event, the most important, significant event in his life. However, if the emperor were to call upon the labourer and tell him that 'he wanted him for a son-in-law: what then?'; Kierkegaard claims that the labourer 'would be more or less puzzled, self-conscious, and embarrassed by it' (84). Such an event would not only be a highly improbable event, more importantly it would be so *infinitely* unlikely that the labourer could not possibly make sense of it, or if he did make sense of it he would do so by assuming that the emperor certainly did not mean to have him as his son-in-law but rather wanted to 'make a fool of him, make him a laughingstock of the whole city'. He would thus seek some 'external reality' or evidence he could be certain of, or that at least was highly probable, in order to determine whether 'the emperor was indeed in earnest about this, or whether he only wanted to pull the poor man's leg, make him unhappy for his whole life, and ultimately send him to a madhouse' (84). Imagine, Kierkegaard continues, that no such external reality is offered, that no evidence or facts can be provided with the certainty or probability the labourer wants, but instead what is needed is the internal reality of faith alone; then, if 'everything was left up to faith', the person who does not have 'sufficient humble courage to dare to believe it ... would be offended' (85).

To become oneself, therefore, to become concrete, entails an affirmation of and a belief and faith in an infinite difference that cannot be reduced to external probabilities and certainties, and yet is nothing less than the process and power one rests transparently in. This faith, however, is an offence to reason and thought precisely because the infinite difference cannot be reduced to, or be explained in terms of, any evidence or determinate facts with which one might calculate the probabilities associated with one's belief, or non-belief if the probabilities merit such scepticism. The result of this offence, for Kierkegaard, is sin, which he claims is, 'before God, or with the conception of God, in despair not to will to be oneself, or in despair to will to be oneself. Thus sin is intensified weakness or intensified defiance: sin is the intensification of despair' (Kierkegaard 1980b, 77). Since 'to be unaware of being defined as spirit is precisely what despair is' (25), sin intensifies this despair both when one refuses to affirm the infinite difference and relation one is, and when one lacks the strength and courage to do so. From Kierkegaard's perspective, moreover, the Christian church only makes this situation worse. 'Christendom's basic trouble', he claims, 'is really Christianity, that the teaching about God-man ... is profaned by being preached day in and day out, that the qualitative difference between God and man is pantheistically abolished' (117). In other words, by whitewashing the infinite difference between God and man, the church is a few short steps from taking up Spinoza's pantheistic claim that God is nature, or that there is no difference, much less an infinite one, that cannot be thought. Understood in this way, the God-man relation comes to be thought in conceptual terms, but for

Kierkegaard this misses the key point about becoming the individual we are; namely, 'an individual human being cannot be thought, but only the concept "man"' (119). It is thus the thought of becoming the concrete *individual* one is that provokes offence, but the preaching of the church removes any cause for offence by providing us with a God-man relation that can be thought, and thought with concepts that are in turn easy to act upon. By doing this, however, the church keeps us in despair, that is, keeps us unaware of ourselves as spirit resting in the power of absolute, infinite difference.

Returning to Kierkegaard's understanding of sin – that is, the despair at willing to be oneself – we can see now that sin itself is not to be thought of in conceptual terms, as a category or type that may include the particular individuals and actions that are instances of sin. To the contrary, since sin is despair at willing to become the concrete *individual* one is, sin itself cannot be thought in conceptual terms. Kierkegaard is forthright on this point, arguing that 'The category of sin is the category of individuality. Sin cannot be thought speculatively at all [for] speculatively, we are supposed to look away from the single individual; therefore, speculatively, we can speak only super-ficially about sin' (Kierkegaard 1980b, 119–20). What this superficiality about sin leaves us with is a concern for particular sins, for those actions we can identify as sins, and for the rules and codes of conduct people are expected to act in accordance with. The reason for this is simple: such actions can be identified and thought about conceptually, and thus thought of as rules-as-rails, which is precisely what the churches provide on Sunday mornings. For Kierkegaard, by contrast, what is crucial is to becoming concrete is that one becomes neither infinite nor finite but rather 'an infinite self-consistency' (107) that involves both tendencies, both the infinitising and finitising process. It is thus the state of sin that is more worrisome for Kierkegaard, for while this also involves a consistency of processes that underlie one's actions, it is a consistency that perpetuates the state of sin whereby one despairs at willing to become oneself. As Kierkegaard puts it, 'the state of sin is the sin; the particular sins are not the continuance of sin but the expression for the continuance of sin ... The state of sin is a worse sin than the particular sins; it is the sin' (106). This state of sin as the continuance of sin, however, is incapable of being thought conceptually, for it is precisely the consistency of the *concrete individual's* despair at willing, and thus when sin is thought it is to the determinate particulars that one turns, to that which can be thought of as falling under a concept, in this case the concept of sin as preached and promulgated on Sunday mornings. Most people, Kierkegaard claims, 'never experience putting everything together on one thing, never achieve the idea of an infinite self-consistency. That is why they are always talking among themselves about the particular, particular good deeds, particular sins' (107).

To overcome sin, which means overcoming our willing or not willing to be the individual we are, thus involves becoming an infinite self-consistency that, paradoxically, cannot be thought and provokes offence when we do attempt to think it. The same is true, as we have seen, for the state of sin, which only God can think. Kierkegaard claims, for instance, that 'God does not avail himself of an abridgment', such as a concept which merges, for the sake of simplicity, an indefinite number of particulars under its heading, for 'he comprehends actuality itself, all its particulars; for him the single individual does not lie beneath the concept' (Kierkegaard 1980b, 121). God, however, is infinitely different from the particular, finite individual, and yet God is the power that comprehends and embraces the individual, the power inseparable from the processes whereby we become concrete individuals. But to think this process of becoming concrete – to think the absolute, infinite difference between the power of God and the power of our finite existence, an infinite difference that conditions our individual, concrete being – may well provoke offence. In fact, it usually does, unless one has become desensitised to the offence by the teachings of the church, which provide the masses with user-friendly, easily understood versions of the relation between God and man. Despite these efforts of the church, however, Kierkegaard is quite clear in asserting that they fail: 'The existence of an infinite qualitative difference between God and man constitutes the possibility of offense, which cannot be removed' (127). Neither sin, despair, nor the contented life of a regular churchgoer, who is also in despair according to Kierkegaard, can remove the possibility of offence, since the infinite difference cannot be removed. This difference, in fact, is the very power our concrete individuality and existence rests in, and it is the person of faith, Kierkegaard claims, who lives the recognition of this reality. 'The person who does not take offense worships in faith.' 'But to worship', he adds, 'which is the expression of faith, is to express that the infinite, chasmic, qualitative abyss between them [God and man] is confirmed' (129). Rather than take offence and not will to be oneself, as the person in sin does, the person of faith wills to be themselves and in doing so expresses the infinite difference that cannot be thought but can only be lived in their concrete, individual existence; and to live in this way is precisely what makes life meaningful. It is the person of faith, therefore, who lives their existence without despair, who embraces the finite life they live, with all the loss and heartbreak this entails, and they do so with a faith that this existence rests in an infinite power that is meaningful and significant. The 'infinite, chasmic, qualitative abyss' that one's faith expresses is what makes sense of one's life, gives it a meaning and significance that is inseparable from one's concrete existence, but a meaning and significance that cannot be thought – it must be lived, and with infinite passion as Kierkegaard argues.

The faith that affirms and expresses this infinite difference is for Kierkegaard what overcomes despair and sin by embracing existence itself as the basis and means for our salvation – that is, salvation as a life free of sin and despair. The significance of Jesus emerges for Kierkegaard at just this point, for with Jesus the infinite difference is there for us to behold, not through thought and reason but through faith, and thus faith in a divine Christ is itself integral to a life free from sin and despair. Unsurprisingly, therefore, as Kierkegaard comes to the end of *The Sickness unto Death*, he reminds us of the infinite difference between God and man that is expressed through the incarnation that is Jesus:

> When God lets himself be born and become man, this is not an idle caprice, some fancy he hits upon just to be doing something, perhaps to put an end to the boredom that has brashly been said must be involved in being God – it is not in order to have an adventure. No, when God does this, then this fact is the earnestness of existence. (Kierkegaard 1980b, 130)

'To become oneself is to become concrete' (30), but this becoming is nothing less than the earnestness of existence, and an existence that cannot be reduced to, or is not to be confused with, the abstract determinate concepts and thoughts we use to understand existence. To become concrete is to exist earnestly, and the incarnation of God in man is precisely this earnestness of existence, an earnestness we become through faith when we become, in our concrete existence, the spiritual being we are.

b) Sartre on bad faith

To unpack this a bit further, let us now turn to Sartre's famous discussion of bad faith. The problem with which Sartre begins is to explain how one can lie to oneself. Unlike a normal lie, where the deceiver knows the truth they intend to withhold from the deceived, in bad faith, Sartre claims, 'it is from myself that I am hiding the truth' (Sartre 1956, 49). If we know the truth that we withhold from ourselves, then how can we be deceived regarding this truth? And if we are being deceived how can we simultaneously know the truth? After arguing that the psychoanalytic solution to this problem fails, Sartre turns to everyday examples to diagnose what is going on in cases of bad faith. The most common strategy for hiding the truth from oneself, he claims, is to take advantage of the fact that the nature of consciousness is simultaneously 'to be what it is not and not to be what it is' (70). That is, consciousness is nothing but what it is conscious of – Sartre here follows Husserl's understanding of the intentionality of consciousness whereby consciousness is always only consciousness of something (see Husserl 1983, 73) – and thus our consciousness *is what it is not*, namely our projects in the world, the some-things consciousness is a consciousness of, *and* at the same time consciousness *is not what it is*, or not to be confused with that which it is a consciousness of. In the case of the woman out on a date, Sartre's first example, she responds to the man who holds her hand – soon after telling her how attractive she is – by divorcing 'the body from the soul ... the hand rests inert between the warm hands of her companion – neither consenting nor resisting – a thing' (Sartre 1956, 56). This, according to Sartre, is a prototypically bad faith move; the woman is lying to herself, for she is hiding from herself the true nature of consciousness, including her body as part of her conscious projects, by reducing it to the status of a thing, and yet she retains this truth by being conscious of this thing, her inert hand, neither consenting or resisting.

The relationship between bad faith and our conscious projects in the world becomes even clearer with Sartre's famous second example, that of the café waiter. With the actions of the waiter – the movements that are 'a little too precise, a little too rapid', the 'eyes [which] express an interest a little too solicitous for the order' – we have, for Sartre, a person whose 'behavior seems to us a game ... He is playing at being a waiter in a café' (Sartre 1956, 59). Sartre acknowledges that there are socially defined roles one is expected to play if one is to gain and retain the approval of others. The 'public demands', for instance, 'the dance of the grocer ... [and thus a] grocer who dreams is offensive to the buyer because such a grocer is not wholly a grocer'. The same is true for the waiter: if they fail to play the role as expected they will likely invite public disapproval, and bad tips! As a human being, however, or as a conscious being-for-itself, 'the waiter in the café can not be immediately a café waiter in the sense that this inkwell is an inkwell, or the glass is a glass' (59). If I am a waiter in good faith, then I will recognise that I am playing a socially prescribed role, and thus will be a waiter 'only in the neutralized mode, as the actor is Hamlet, by mechanically making the typical gestures of my state and by aiming at myself as an imaginary café waiter through those gestures taken as an "analogue"' (60). For Sartre then, one should maintain a sense of the provisional, staged nature of one's actions, of the fact that they do not follow from any permanent, essential nature. The waiter who is in good faith is thus to take on the gestures, the fast movements, the eyes and expressiveness of a waiter as a role, and perform it with the translucency of consciousness that they are playing at being a waiter. The waiter slips into bad faith, however, when he becomes either conscious of himself as a waiter in the same sense that an inkwell is an inkwell – if he assumes, for instance, that he was destined to be a waiter – or if he is conscious of himself as *not being* a waiter 'in the sense', as Sartre puts it, 'in which this table is not an inkwell' (64). In both cases one is in bad faith, for rather than accepting the consciousness that is always only involved in projects, and the facticity that comes with the situations in which we are consciously engaged, one either reduces oneself and others to pure facticity, to being-in-itself, or appeals to a pure transcendence where we are none of these things, the result being that we 'leave facticity to find ourselves suddenly beyond the present and the factual condition of man' (56).

Extending and generalising Sartre's claim that the café waiter can only be a waiter by analogy, we could say that embodying the roles that are socially expected of us, or acquiring 'a feel for the game' as Bourdieu puts it (see Bourdieu 1990, 11, and *Inquiry* §9.11, where this is discussed in more detail), is an essential part of living the lives we live. For Sartre, the mistake of bad faith consists in turning away from our lives as conscious beings, and hence as engaged in a world of things, including the facticity of our own situation and the roles that are associated with this situation – the expectations of a father, mother, teacher, etc. Good faith for Sartre entails recognising the freedom or transcendence of consciousness in relation to these roles. This does not entail denying them – saying one is not a waiter, a father, etc., in the same sense that a table is not an inkwell – nor does it entail reducing oneself to being nothing but these roles, for in both cases we have bad faith. We are thus not to adopt a cynical attitude towards the roles we play in life, for a cynical detachment from our projects simply undermines the very fact that we are those projects. What we are to do, and this will be what Sartre focuses on in Part II of *Being and Nothingness*, is to live in the translucency of consciousness, or in the awareness that it is in our nature both to be what we are not – that is, the projects and socially mandated roles that we are – and to not be who we are – that is, the consciousness that is not our projects and roles.

c) Camus and metaphysical rebellion

If we are to take bad faith as living life in accordance with a solution to which there is no problem, or living a role as if it is who we are, like an inkwell is an inkwell, then we find in Camus' *The Rebel* a precise date for the emergence of this bad faith – 1789. More precisely, Camus argues that 'Seventeen eighty-nine is the starting-point of modern time', for with the French Revolution humanity 'overthrew the principle of divine right and … introduce[d] to the historical scene the forces of negation and rebellion' (Camus 2000, 64). Before the French Revolution, whether it be the 'Inca and the pariah', or those who endorsed the principle of divine right monarchy, 'the problem of revolt never arises, because for them it has been solved by tradition before they had time to raise it – the answer being that tradition is sacrosanct. If, in the sacrosanct world, the problem of revolt does not arise, it is because no real problems are to be found in it – all the answers having been given simultaneously' (8). It may seem that it is the sacrosanct tradition that characterises a world of bad faith, of living life in accordance with solutions for which there is no problem, and indeed Camus points out that 'no real problems are to be found' in the sacrosanct world. If this is indeed true, and it is debatable, then Camus' point is that prior to 1789 living in good faith, or as a rebel, was not truly possible, for one would have had no awareness of problems inseparable from solutions (to put it in the terms being used here).

Camus' historicisation of bad faith highlights a key difference between him and Sartre. Whereas for Sartre bad faith simply comes with being a conscious being, as one who simultaneously is what one is not and is not what one is, which presumably has been the case for as long as conscious human beings have existed, for Camus the possibility of living with a consciousness of life as a problem – and thus a life where one can challenge and rebel against answers and solutions that are forced upon one as if they were incontestable solutions without a problem – is of fairly recent origin. But we should be wary of taking Camus' historicising move too seriously, or at least of assuming that it excludes other aspects of life where the consciousness of life as a problem, i.e. good faith, may have been a key component of human experience well before 1789. There are a couple reasons for this caution. First, in the Introduction to *The Rebel* Camus states, in rather Sartrean terms, that 'Man is the only creature who refuses to be what he is' (Camus 2000, xii), implying that our tendency to rebel against the various ways in which we find ourselves living is not simply a historically recent phenomenon. Camus implies this even more strongly, and again in Sartrean terms, when he claims that 'There is not one human being who, above a certain elementary level of consciousness, does not exhaust himself in trying to find formulae or attitudes which will give his existence the unity it lacks' (207). This recalls Camus' arguments in the *Myth of Sisyphus*, where he claims (recall §1.1.a) – again in general terms that imply a universal human condition rather than a historically specific one – that there is a fundamental disparity between the purposelessness we find in the world and our desire to find in it a unity that gives life a meaning and purpose.

To reconcile Camus' claim regarding the 'universal' nature of human existence as one that involves seeking that which it is not – that is, a unity that gives life a meaning and purpose – with his claim that 1789 is the 'starting-point of modern times', we should note that for Camus what is unique to modern times is the 'metaphysical revolt' (Camus 2000, 14). What emerges in the wake of the revolutions of the late eighteenth century, therefore, is the 'metaphysical rebel', one who 'attacks a shattered world to make it whole' (11). We can thus distinguish between the existential rebel, who 'refuses to be what he is' – such as Sisyphus, who refuses to bow to the pressure of living life only if it has unity and purpose – and the metaphysical rebel, who is concerned with restoring unity and purpose to a 'shattered world'. What was shattered with modern times, according to Camus, was the sacrosanct, unproblematic nature of tradition, and most especially the manner in which this tradition helped to provide the unity and purpose human existence lacks. With modern times, therefore, we could say a new form of bad faith emerges. In addition to the Sartrean bad faith, where one takes oneself to be what one is not (a thing in itself), and Camus' version where one takes one's life to have a unity and purpose it lacks, we have a post-1789 version that we might call a philosophical or metaphysical bad faith. The reason for Camus' focus on this particular form of bad faith is that eliminating the divine-right justification for political power has led us to the point where those in power often admit 'with equanimity that murder has justification', because 'of the indifference to life which is the mark of nihilism' (x). (Camus wrote *The Rebel* just a few years after the Second World War, when the risks that come with this nihilism were palpable [I will return to this theme below, see §5.1.a].)

As Camus understands nihilism, at least in the context of *The Rebel*, it is characterised by 'the inability to believe … [and] its most serious symptom is not found in atheism, but in the inability to believe in what is, to see what is happening, and to live life as it is offered' (Camus 2000, 41). Since 1789, according to Camus, there have been two forms of metaphysical rebellion that have had significant political implications. In the first, the transcendence of God and divine right is replaced by the 'transcendence of principles', as he puts it. The Jacobin Saint-Just emerges as a key figure here, and in particular his willingness 'to go to his death for love of principle and despite all the realities of the situation … His principles cannot accept the condition of things' (80). Saint-Just goes to his death defending the principles of the revolution, oblivious to what was happening on the ground – the emerging factions, the reign of terror – and thus to the great distance that separated his principles, which were taken as solutions without a problem, from the realities he encountered on a daily basis. In the second form of metaphysical rebellion we have Hegel and, especially, Marx, who Camus claims went further than the Jacobins, for whereas they 'destroyed the transcendence of a personal god', the tradition begun by Hegel and carried forward by Marx initiated the 'contemporary atheism [that destroys] the transcendence of principles as well'. Marx thus throws Hegel's 'transcendence of reason' into 'the stream of history' (148). The problem with making this move, according to Camus, is that we likewise fail to see what is happening in life, or pay heed to life as it is offered, for our life as lived is simply caught up in historical processes over which we have no control.

This where good faith enters the scene for Camus. More precisely, he rejects the bad faith form of metaphysical rebellion, or nihilism, where one fails to see life as it is, including its problematic nature, and instead sees life as playing its predetermined role in accordance with unquestioned forces, whether the force of transcendent principle or the force of history. In both cases life becomes what it is not, an object, a determinate thing subject to powers that involve a solution without a problem and where the nihilist subsequently refuses, or is unable, to see the problematic nature inseparable from life. As Camus makes this point, he claims that 'rebellion, in man', or what we might call acting in good faith, 'is the refusal to be treated as an object and to be reduced to simple historical terms ... But man, by rebelling, imposes in his turn a limit to history and at this limit the promise of a value is born' (Camus 2000, 195). The form this rebellion takes is artistic creation, where 'instead of killing and dying in order to produce the being that we are not', the being that has the unity which gives life an unproblematic meaning, 'we have to live and let live in order to create what we are' (197). This creation of what we are, moreover, is not to be done in accordance with predetermining rules, whether these be transcendent principles or historical processes. For Camus, one who accepts life as it is given, and its problematic nature, will be prepared to 'renounce nihilism of formal principles and nihilism without principles' (216). The contemporary rebel 'cannot turn away from the world and from history without denying the very principle of his rebellion, nor can he choose eternal life without resigning himself, in one sense, to evil' (229). In other words, in being attentive to life as it is given, including the problems inseparable from it, one must be attuned to that which provokes thought, our knee-jerk negative reactions, and thus have a 'higher taste' for the problems that may allow us to challenge and rebel against things as they are. In doing this we cannot turn away from the world and from history, for it is precisely history and the world that provide us with that upon which we must exercise our higher taste for problems. Nor should our higher taste be exercised in the name of eternal principles that transcend this life, for in doing so we may come to feel justified in murder as a result of an indifference to life, an indifference that arises when we value eternal principles that are taken to be superior to whatever we might value or concern ourselves with in this mortal, fragile life.

2. Facts and Fictions

a) Finding one's way

To consider now the role eternal principles or narratives may play in helping one find one's way through life – even if, as Camus warned, this involves turning a blind eye to the evils one encounters in life – we can return to Kierkegaard. Kierkegaard was well aware of the problem one encounters in attempting to live the relationship between the determinate realities of daily life and that which is irreducible to any determinate reality – that is, the problem of living the infinite difference that we are as spirit. In one of the many instances where he recognises this, he states the problem as follows:

> is not God so unnoticeable, so secretly present in His works, that a man might very well live his entire life, be married, become known and respected as citizen, father, and captain of the hunt, without ever having discovered God in His works, and without ever having received any impression of the infinitude of the ethical, because he helped himself out by having recourse to the customs and traditions prevailing in the town where he happened to live? As a mother admonishes her child when it sets off for a party: 'Now be sure to behave yourself, and do as you see the other well-behaved children do', – so he might manage to live by conducting himself as he sees others do. He would never do anything first, and he would never have any opinion which he did not first know that others had; for this 'others' would be for him the first. Upon extraordinary occasions he would behave as when at a banquet a dish is served, and one does not know how it should be eaten: he would look around until he saw how the others did it, and so forth. Such a man might perhaps know many things, perhaps even know the System by rote; he might be an inhabitant of a Christian country, and bow his head whenever the name of God was mentioned; he would perhaps also see God in nature when in company with others who saw God; he would be a pleasant society man – and yet he would have been deceived by the direct nature of his relationship to the truth, to the ethical, and to God ... Essentially it is the God-relationship that makes a man a man, and yet he lacked this. No one would hesitate, however, to regard him as a real man (for the absence of inwardness is not directly apparent); in reality he would constitute a sort of marionette, very deceptively imitating everything human – even to the extent of having children by his wife. (Kierkegaard 1968, 218–19)

This passage distils a number of themes from Kierkegaard's work, themes we have already discussed regarding despair, understood by him as an un-awareness of 'being defined as spirit' (4.1.a). A life completely attuned to the customs, traditions and expectations of others may well be a life which brings security, acceptance and contentment, but in itself it is 'simply despair' according to Kierkegaard. This contentment continues to be despair, as we saw, because the true removal of despair requires a self that wilfully relates itself to itself, which entails affirming both infinitising and finitising processes, or the problem of infinite difference. On the one hand the self that is lost in the infinite possibilities that follow upon carrying the infinitising process to its end, and on the other hand the self that remains confined to the determinate, to the actualised traditions, customs, and necessities of one's time, are both selves that do not will to be themselves as a relationship of infinite difference – or the God-relationship as Kierkegaard puts it in the passage cited above. This God-relationship, moreover, is not a determinate relationship between a determinate, infinite God, and a determinate, finite self. It is, rather, a relationship that cannot be thought, despite Hegel's arguments to the contrary, and thus for Kierkegaard it is only a relationship that can be lived, with passion, in one's concrete individuality, a relationship that entails a leap of faith that cannot be justified by any determinate facts or reasons.

But what does it mean to live in faith, to live the God-relationship? Kierkegaard is clear what it does not mean – namely, it is not simply doing as others do, such as eating an unfamiliar banquet dish in the manner one observes others eating it, or more generally living one's life as others live their lives. Living in the God-relationship, however, does not mean that one cannot do as others do, get married, have children, etc. If, as Kierkegaard puts it, 'the absence of inwardness is not directly apparent', nor, it should be added, is the presence of inwardness directly apparent, precisely because the God-relationship is not to be confused with the determinate, actualised and apparent phenomena that would fill the pages of a descriptive account of one's life. But how then can one live without despair, live in faith, while married, etc., and do so without becoming 'a sort of marionette, very deceptively imitating everything human'? Put simply, one ought to live one's life as a fictional narrative, that is, a narrative irreducible to any determinate set of factual events, events that may constitute the determinate content of one's life.

To clarify what this entails, we can recall Spinoza's critique of Descartes – specifically, his claim that we cannot understand the essence of God, or anything for that matter, as Descartes attempts to do, by way of a determinate property (or *propria* [see 1.2.a]]) of the thing, but can do so only by understanding the power from which such properties follow. As we saw in the example of a circle, to define it as 'a figure in which the lines drawn from the center to the circumference are equal' does not truly define or 'explain the essence of the circle', its 'inmost essence', but describes 'only a property of it' (Spinoza 1985, 39; II/34). What we need instead, Spinoza claims, is 'a concept, or definition, of the thing such that when it is considered alone, without any others conjoined, all the thing's properties can be deduced from it'. For the circle, this concept or definition is precisely the process involved in generating a circle: 'it is the figure that is described by any line of which one end is fixed and the other movable' (39).

Returning now to our extension Kierkegaard's point, to live our life as a fictional narrative that is irreducible to any set of determinate facts is to live the life that is the power and condition for the determinate events and facts that come to be identified with one's life as lived, and as recorded and represented in autobiographical and biographical accounts. We can now further clarify Kierkegaard's claim that 'the state of the self when despair is completely rooted out [occurs when,] in relating itself to itself and in willing to be itself, the self rests transparently in the power that established it' (Kierkegaard 1980b, 14). This power is precisely the God-relationship, or the truth and inwardness that is not to be confused with the determinate properties and facts of one's life; it is rather the power that generates such facts, the power inseparable from the facts and that which they always presuppose, just as the circle for Spinoza presupposes the power that generates the circle, and just as for him everything in nature presupposes the power that is God's nature ('God's power is his essence itself' as Spinoza puts it [Spinoza 1985, 439; II/77]). For Kierkegaard, the relationship of the self to itself, as we saw, rests transparently in God when it relates to itself as both infinitising and finitising. Stated in terms of facts and fictions, to live our lives as infinitising is to live a fiction irreducible to the determinate facts and the situations in which we find ourselves living. Taken to an extreme – or to the nihilism Camus describes as 'the inability to believe in what is, to see what is happening, and to live life as it is offered' (Camus 2000, 41) – this tendency leads one to turn away from life as it is offered and towards an eternal set of values or principles that are taken to be superior to, and are not to be confused with, the facts that one encounters in one's life as actually lived. One can thus end up as Saint-Just did, going to one's 'death for love of principle and despite all the realities of the situation ... [for one's] principles cannot accept the condition of things' (80). To live our lives as finitising is to be concerned with the finite, determinate details and facts of our lives, with life as it is offered. When this tendency is taken to the nihilist extreme, one allows one's life to be entirely dictated by how things are, by the way things are done, or by how others do what they do, thus becoming the marionette Kierkegaard cautions us against. What is lacking in this tendency is any basis for critiquing the present, for challenging how things are done, since there is no basis beyond what is actually done for challenging how things are done. We thus have here the 'nihilism without principles' that Camus contrasts with the 'nihilism of formal principles' (216). The key for him, and for Kierkegaard on my reading, is that neither of these tendencies become actualised to the exclusion of the other, but rather enter into a relationship, a *problematic* relationship, one that is for Kierkegaard nothing less than the God-relationship. Our life as it rests in the God-relationship is our life as an existing concrete individual, such that it cannot be captured or subsumed under any categories or concepts of judgment.

To clarify the implications of entering into a problematic relationship that tends both towards the infinite and the finite, let us turn to the problem of finding one's way. Earlier we discussed the problem David Sudnow encountered in attempting to learn to play improvisational jazz on the keyboard (see 2.1.c). The problem there was to find one's way across the keyboard when that way has not been predetermined by an already written score. When Sudnow was struggling, or unsure where to go and looking to find his way, he would often resort to the scalar devices and jazz chords and runs his instructor gave him, cobbling them together in a way that didn't quite work. His instructor, by contrast, knew his way around the keyboard and played improvisational jazz with apparent ease. It was also obvious to Sudnow that his instructor was 'not simply using the few scalar devices' that he himself would fall back on, but 'was going many more places over the keyboard' (Sudnow 1978, 25). The scalar devices and jazz-sounding chords Sudnow was given did not exhaust the possibilities of playing improvisational jazz, much as solutions do not exhaust the problems they give voice to. When Sudnow did find his way and played aesthetically pleasing improvisational jazz, what he discovered was that he did not need to 'lunge', as he put it, or find a note or chord somewhere other than where his hands already were. Paradoxically, what he found was that 'choices could be made anywhere, that there was no need to lunge, that usable notes for any chord lay just at hand' (94). In other words, an indeterminate number of possibilities are always already inseparable from where one actually, determinately, is. Stated in Kierkegaard's terms, and in relation to a concrete, individual life, the ethical and religious value of a life is irreducible to abstract generalities and principles – such as certain codes of ethics or religious doctrine. This is why the story of Abraham and Isaac is so crucial for Kierkegaard, for in not acting in accordance with the moral doctrines one associates with Christianity, God, in a move Kierkegaard calls the transcendence of the ethical, exemplifies the reality of a religious value or truth that cannot be captured by abstract categories or rules (see *Fear and Trembling*, Kierkegaard 2006). God is thus not in a relationship of judgment to individuals, if by this one understands a judgment that subsumes the individual under an abstract category or type. For God, to repeat Kierkegaard's claim, 'the single individual does not lie beneath the concept' (Kierkegaard 1980b, 121). The individual has an ethical or religious value that can only be found where one finds oneself in an existence that entails both an infinitising movement (or dedifferentiating movement) that concepts and categories attempt, unsuccessfully, to capture by subsuming an indefinite number of particulars 'beneath the concept', and a finitising movement (differentiating movement) in that the ethical and religious value is to be found right where one is, with the determinate givens of life as it is offered. To recall Sudnow's point, in finding one's way around the keyboard while playing improvisational jazz, one is neither following a predetermined path, nor is what one is playing reducible to what is actually being played; rather, 'there is melodying' (Sudnow 1978, 146). Similarly for Kierkegaard, in finding one's way and living a life of meaning and value, one is neither following a predetermined path whereby one simply lives in accordance with the rules, customs and traditions of one's time, nor is one's life reducible to what one actually does with it, to the determinate facts and details that could fill the pages of a descriptive account; rather, there is existing going on, or, as Kierkegaard understands it, one is *becoming concrete*, or living the God-relationship. To live the God-relationship is thus to live a life that embraces both the infinitising and finitising tendencies of life, and to live this way without reducing life to the realisation of each tendency, whether to the abstract rules, will and judgment of God, on the one hand (a judgment frequently upheld and propagated by the church and theologians), or to a life that is simply lived in accord with how things are actually done, with the already established and determinate expectations of one's time and place, on the other hand.

Whether he was familiar with Kierkegaard's work or not, Fyodor Dostoyevsky certainly encountered many of the same problems Kierkegaard did in his attempt to give full meaning and value to one's individual existence. In his short novel *Notes from Underground*, a text that has come to be identified as a classic in the existential tradition, Dostoyevsky presents the anonymous narrator as one who is torn by the paradox of existence, or by the dual demands of becoming simultaneously infinite and finite. Early in the novel the narrator recognises how different he is from a man of action, from someone who has no trouble feeling justified in the actions they engage in. As the narrator describes such a person: 'a man of the nineteenth century is morally bound, above all things, to be a colorless being, since a man of character, a man of action, is a being who is essentially limited' (Dostoyevsky 1992, 5), and limited in particular by the truths that justify their actions, or by the walls that provide the unquestioned basis for doing what they do. The man of action will have no problem exacting revenge upon someone, being equally convinced of the truth that they were wronged and that taking revenge for this wrong is indeed the proper course of action. For a 'man of acute sensibility', by contrast, such as the anonymous narrator understands himself to be, such bedrock truths are never reached. As he states his situation, if he were 'to take revenge upon each and every person who offended me, I should never really be able to revenge myself upon such persons, for the reason that, in all probability, I should never be able finally to make up my mind to any given course of action, even if I had the power to carry it out' (8–9). As with the scepticism brought on by an infinite regress, the underground man never reaches a starting point from which to justify his actions, a starting point that is immune to further questioning. The man of action has such starting points, or so they believe, and thus 'For them a wall connotes something calming, something morally decisive, final, and even mystical' (9). They thus set about doing what they do, such as seeking revenge, in a completely un-perturbed manner. In particular, the wall consists of 'the laws of nature, of the deductions of learning, and the science of mathematics', and thus if we are told we 'are descended from an ape ... [or] that a single drop of [our] fat is of more essential value to [us] than the bodies of a hundred thousand men who resemble [us]', then we must 'just accept what they tell [us], and make up [our] mind to do nothing at all, since the formula that twice two make four is mathematics. To that find an objection if you can!' (11–12). For the underground man, by contrast, 'the laws of Nature ... [and] the formula that twice two make four do not meet with [his] acceptance'. 'I am not', he adds, 'going to accept that wall merely because I have run up against it, and have no means to knock it down' (12). And since he does not accept such walls, the underground man finds it difficult to live and act in the world with others.

This difficulty of living with others becomes an important theme as the novel progresses. From the awkward events surrounding the dinner party with former classmates to his encounter with Liza at a brothel and after, the underground man's inability to unquestioningly adhere to the usual rules of etiquette and decorum result in failed social encounters, the failures that ultimately led the anonymous narrator to an underground life removed from the world of others. The underground man did not completely fail to follow established rules and expectations, however, for in his encounters with Liza in particular he often modelled his discourses on what he had read in books. After a long monologue on the nature of love and family, for instance, Liza asked the narrator 'What made you say it all?' (Dostoyevsky 1992, 84). After asking her what she meant, she followed up with the comment, 'Well, one would almost think that you were speaking from a book' (85). In other words, rather than interacting in a spontaneous, 'real' way with Liza, his comments and observations came from elsewhere, from books. He was a marionette of books, to rephrase Kierkegaard. The underground man nonetheless refuses to identify himself with the usual lot of mankind, with the men of action for instance. In fact, in the final paragraph of the *Notes from Underground*, the narrator, addressing 'all my fellow men', claims that he has 'been more alive than you' for he has 'carried to a finish, in my life, what you have never even dared to carry half-way, although you have constantly mistaken your cowardice for prudence' (113). The problem with the underground man's bookish ways, his hiding behind the words and narratives of books and fictions rather than living meaningfully, as himself, is that he does not know what it would entail for his life to have the meaning that would justify his actions and interactions. Unlike the man of action who takes their actions to be fully real and justified, the underground man is conscious of living a bookish life, and it is precisely his awareness of living such a life, along with the problems it has brought, that led him to the only other alternative he thought possible – that is, a life underground. The conclusion this leads the underground man to is that, unlike the man of action who takes walls such as the laws of nature, customs, status, etc., to be unquestionable realities, he does not accept such walls, but at the price of not knowing what is real, and hence not knowing what justifies his actions or gives meaning and value to his life. The narrator thus ends his notes as follows:

> We do not even know where present-day reality is to be found, nor what it is called. Whenever we are left to our own devices, and deprived of our bookish rules, we at once grow confused, and lose our way – we know not what to do, nor what to observe, nor what to love, nor what to hate, nor what to respect, nor what to despise. We grow weary of being human beings at all – of possessing real, individual flesh and blood. We are ashamed of being human – we account it beneath our dignity. Rather, we aim at becoming personalities of a general, a fictitious type. Yes, all of us are still-born creatures, not children sprung of living fathers; and that fact is coming more and more to please us. Soon we shall have invented a way of being born of nothing but ideas! But enough of this: I intend to bring these 'Notes from Underground' to a close. (Dostoyevsky 1992, 113)

Dostoyevsky's observation that people would be confused and lose their way without 'bookish rules', and hence their motivation to become 'personalities of a general, a fictitious type' in order to know their way in the world, will find a strong concurring voice in Nietzsche. In the *Gay Science*, Nietzsche quite bluntly claims that all the 'common people' want 'when they want "knowledge" ... [is] this: something unfamiliar is to be traced back to something *familiar*'. And a few lines later he adds, 'Is it not the *instinct of fear* that bids us to know?' (Nietzsche 1974, §355, 214). Even the philosopher, Nietzsche claims, generally falls among the common people in desiring the familiar and identifying that with knowledge. For the 'philosopher who imagined the world to be "known" when he had reduced it to the "idea"', Nietzsche claims, 'wasn't it precisely because the "idea" was so familiar to him and he was so used to it?' (§355, 214). But the fear that motivates the desire to know, along with the desire to live a life in accordance with bookish rules, and hence the aspiration to be 'born of nothing but ideas', is not for Nietzsche to be confused with knowledge. In fact, while the 'familiar is what we are used to, … what we are used to is the most difficult to "know" – that is, to view as a problem, to see as strange, as distant, as "outside us"' (215). In other words, to restate it in the terms we have used throughout, what is familiar is simply a solution to a problem, and a solution without a problem is 'the most difficult to "know"' precisely because knowledge is a process, a process of learning we might say. To state it in yet another way, to know is to think, to think in an encounter with that which provokes thought, that which is viewed 'as a problem … as strange, as distant, as "outside us"', and thus the familiar is that which does not provoke thought and so is the most difficult to know.

Some clarification is in order at this point. One could argue that Nietzsche is conflating two separate processes – learning and knowing. If I know how to swim, for instance, I have a skill I can call upon if I find myself in the water. Someone who is learning to swim does not have this skill and thus their life could be at risk if they were to find themselves in deep water. For Bruno Latour this is the distinction between science in the making and ready-made science (see Latour 1987). The latter is what we find in the textbooks, which relay established knowledge such that, for example, the double helix structure of DNA is presented as one of many facts we should learn if we are going to 'know' biology. The former, science in the making, is the process that eventually led to the establishment of the facts regarding the structure of DNA, including the other competing theories and claims, and the debates that were active at the time while the research was still in process. This distinction is also critical to the very structure and functioning of universities, since at least the German university reforms of the early nineteenth century, where the university is seen to perform two key tasks – teaching and research. Teaching consists of presenting established knowledge to students, and the Master's degree, as traditionally understood, certifies that a student has sufficient knowledge of their discipline to serve in the role of teacher (such as teaching Scripture, Law, etc.). Research consists of discovering new knowledge, of contributing new facts to a discipline, and the PhD is given to those who contribute new knowledge to their field.[1] But these distinctions, from Nietzsche's perspective, tend to overlook a key metaphysical assumption that guides his thought. The implication of these distinctions is that the knowledge and skills gained by research or learning are as real as, if not more

---

1. For more on German university reform and the history of the PhD, see Östling 2018.

real than, the processes that led to this knowledge. For Nietzsche, by contrast, the stable facts one comes to know, often assuming them to correspond to the nature of reality, are in fact less real than the processual reality these facts simply limit, serving as an abbreviation or heuristic which enables us to feel at home and find our way in a world that is constantly changing. The facts that are familiar and 'known', therefore, do not lead us to knowledge of reality, but rather make it harder to think the reality that is problematic, strange and unfamiliar.

By understanding it as a process of encountering what is problematic, strange and unfamiliar, or as involving becomings that are irreducible to the facts that reduce becoming to that which *is* the case, Nietzsche aligns knowledge with a process of critical inquiry. More precisely, knowledge entails a fearless encounter with the strange and unfamiliar, a willingness to find in the familiar the problem that has not been exhausted by that which is familiar. In short, a life of knowledge as Nietzsche understands it will problematise the familiar, bringing out the unfamiliar that is inseparable from it and thus making possible something new. 'What is new, however', Nietzsche points out, 'is under all circumstances *evil*, being that which wants to conquer, to overthrow the old boundary stones and pieties; and only what is old is good!' (Nietzsche 1974, §4, 32). The old and familiar, the bookish rules and established customs, are the comforting walls that we take to be good and by which we justify our actions. Since the new challenges our established ways, our pieties, it is feared and taken to be evil. Despite the efforts of 'good men' to take 'old thoughts ... and make them bear fruit', Nietzsche recognises that the 'land is eventually exhausted, and the ploughshare of evil must come time and time again' (§4, 32). To know, therefore, is to be fearless and challenge the familiar and the old, encountering the problem that is inseparable from the old, and in the process provoking the thought and learning that affirms and embraces the problematic nature of reality.

Applying this critical thought-provoking method to the social norms and customs of one's time entails, for Nietzsche, determining whether the roles one finds oneself in, including the bookish expectations and rules that go with such roles, allow one to affirm the problematic nature of reality rather than encourage the acceptance of solutions without a problem. To clarify, let us look at roles and expectations as they are given, and given such that they can be the subject of empirical study. In his famous study of the roles we perform in relation to others, Erving Goffman's working premise is that 'When an individual enters the presence of others, they commonly seek to acquire information about him or to bring into play information about him already possessed', and this 'information about the individual helps to define the situations, enabling others to know in advance what he will expect

134

of them and what they may expect of him' (Goffman 1956, 1). In social contexts, therefore, we become 'sign-vehicles', as Goffman puts it, bearers of information which let others know which role we are performing so that they can respond accordingly. In a very real sense then, and as Dostoyevsky well knew, much of our social life is a matter of manifesting a predetermined role, of living by the book. As Goffman states his thesis:

> Society is organized on the principle that any individual who possesses certain social characteristics has a moral right to expect that others will value and treat him in a correspondingly appropriate way. Connected with this principle is a second, namely that an individual who implicitly or explicitly signifies that he has certain social characteristics ought to have this claim honored by others and ought in fact to be what he claims he is. (Goffman 1956, 6).

To take just one of the many examples he brings into his study, Goffman found a difference in behaviour between two friends at lunch, on the one hand, and an interaction between a person in a specialist occupation and their client, on the other. In the former, 'a reciprocal show of affection, respect, and concern for the other is maintained', whereas in the latter 'the specialist often maintains an image of disinterested involvement in the problem of the client, while the client responds with a show of respect for the competence and integrity of the specialist' (Goffman 1956, 4). If the expectations involved in these roles are not met – if the friend is quiet and disinterested, or the specialist is overly friendly – then 'the interaction itself may come to a confused and embarrassed halt' as a result of these 'disruptive events' (6).

Harold Garfinkel, drawing from Alfred Schutz's phenomenological approach and offering an even finer-grained account of everyday expectations than Goffman, has shown just how pervasive the social feedback of others is in maintaining the roles we play. In a series of intentional disruptions to everyday routines, Garfinkel shows that interactions are largely determined by the maintenance of routine rather than by a sharing of determinate meanings. For example, in a series of experiments where a commonplace remark was challenged in order to reveal the true, determinate meaning of the remark, Garfinkel showed how much of the routines of everyday interaction presuppose 'specifically vague' expressions that do not 'frame a clearly restricted set of possible determinations but ... include as their essentially intended and sanctioned features an accompanying "fringe" of determinations that are open' (Garfinkel 1967, 41); that is, these expressions are open to possibilities of interpretation that are presupposed so as to maintain the ongoing routines of everyday interactions. When the experimenter attempts to narrow down what is meant to something precise, to a determinate meaning, the disruption reveals the emotional reliance upon the vague meanings of everyday discourse.

135

The following is a typical example of what occurs between a subject (S) and an experimenter (E) during such a disruptive event:

> The subject was telling the experimenter, a member of the subject's car pool, about having a flat tire while going to work the previous day.
> (S) I had a flat tire.
> (E) What do you mean, you had a flat tire?
> She appeared momentarily stunned. Then she answered in a hostile way: 'What do you mean, "What do you mean?" A flat tire is a flat tire. That is what I meant. Nothing special. What a crazy question!' (Garfinkel 1967, 42)

In another example the emotions get even more aroused:

> The victim waved his hand cheerily
> (S) How are you?
> (E) How am I in regard to what? My health, my finances, my school work, my peace of mind, my ... ?
> (S) (Red in the face and suddenly out of control.) Look! I was just trying to be polite. Frankly, I don't give a damn how you are. (44)

Nietzsche's own symptomatological approach bears similarities to what Garfinkel's experimenters encountered when they disrupted the expectations of everyday routine. As we have seen, if one has a negative knee-jerk reaction to the chapter titles from *Ecce Homo* (see 4.1.a), then for Nietzsche this is symptomatic of the predominance of slave morality as a set of values that makes sense of and accounts for the judgments we make. For one whose values assert and affirm behaviours that manifest humility, Nietzsche's self-aggrandising chapter titles will certainly be at odds with these values, hence the negative knee-jerk reaction. Garfinkel's experiments showed, similarly, that people are inclined to react negatively to having their everyday expectations and routines disrupted. There is, however, a big difference between the disruptions that are at play here, and this point is key. Whereas Nietzsche's disruptions are used to diagnose the dominance of slave values and thereby open up the possibility of changing these values, or allow for the transvaluation of values that Nietzsche called for, Garfinkel and Goffman, by contrast, see their disruptions as evidence not for that which needs to be changed but for that which is to be maintained – our everyday routines, customs and social roles – if we are to avoid problematic social interactions and the unexpected results these may bring.

It is at this point that Nietzsche's approach, coupled with the existential figures who followed his lead, such as Camus, can provide us with a way to think critically about the social roles we may find ourselves performing, often without even being aware of doing so. Nietzsche's symptomatological approach, which reveals the limits that provoke negative reactions, is to be pursued such that what is revealed is one's narrative, or the consistency pre-supposed by that which is affirmed. This consistency is precisely the narrative, or outright fiction, which provides for the coherence of self, a self that is affirmed. Repeating Steele's claim (see 2.1.d), what is critical in such narratives is that they 'maintain a phenomenal experience of the self – self-conceptions and images – as adaptively and morally adequate, i.e., as competent, good, coherent, unitary, stable, capable of free choice, capable of controlling important outcomes, and so on' (Steele 1988, 262). What Nietzsche's diag-nostic approach reveals are precisely those encounters where the coherence and consistency of this 'phenomenal experience' comes under threat. For Goffman and Garfinkel as well, disruptive events that do not fit with our everyday expectations help us to recognise the roles we follow largely without question, roles the encounters they studied had problematised. As we will now see, in his extension of Nietzsche's project, along with his critical response to the existential concept of authenticity, Adorno provides an example of what we could call a critical existentialism, or an approach to developing a taste for the problems that are inseparable from the everyday routines and roles of daily life.

b) Adorno and critical existentialism

Adorno was well aware of the theory Goffman put forth in his *The Presenta-tion of Self in Everyday Life*, but rather than study and describe, as Goffman did, the various ways in which we maintain our everyday roles and routines in the face of contingencies, Adorno turns a critical eye towards these very roles, arguing that their automatic, unquestioning acceptance largely per-petuates the social structures Adorno seeks to transform. What Goffman's and Garfinkel's theories ultimately rationalise, as do other contemporaneous theories such as that found in Eric Berne's *Games People Play*, is a tendency that leaves us in a situation where, as Adorno puts it, the 'edge is removed from the living subject's protest against being condemned to play roles' (Adorno 1973, 71). Rather than critically examine the institutions and social structures that condemn and force us into particular roles, theorists such as Goffman, Berne et al. ultimately leave us with a quietism that maintains these institutions and social structures, along with the various roles one plays within them.

On this point, it would seem that Adorno would be very much in agreement with the existentialists. Sartre, for instance, as we saw earlier (§4.1.b), claims that those who aspire to be that which they are not, namely a being-in-itself, such as the waiter who desires to be a waiter, are living in bad faith. As conscious beings involved in projects in the world, we cannot be the beings that consciousness is consciousness of, for consciousness is what it is (i.e., conscious) only in the mode that it is not what it is consciousness of. Sartre thus sets out to highlight the freedom of consciousness that is inseparable from each and every one of our projects, a freedom that can thus serve as the basis for a critique of each and every role we may play. For example, according to Sartre, and Simone de Beauvoir who extends his arguments (see de Beauvoir 2011), women are not the fairer, weaker sex in the same way that an inkpot is an inkpot. The roles women play in our society are not founded on an essential nature whereby a girl is destined to pursue or not pursue certain possibilities in the same way that an acorn is destined to become an oak tree rather than a pine tree. These roles, rather, are expressions of human freedom as this freedom has become embodied in various social structures and institutions. A consequence of this Sartrean critique of the essentialism that underlies many of the gender roles in society is that these roles may well be undermined, transformed or 'relativised' (to borrow Horkheimer's term [2002, p. 207]).

The critique of everyday roles in society is even more pronounced in Heidegger. In a justly famous passage, Heidegger argues that by 'utilizing public means of transport and in making use of information services such as the newspaper, every Other is like the next' (Heidegger 1962, 164). Rather than becoming the unique individual we are, we come to fill pre-established roles and live in accordance with what Heidegger calls the 'real dictatorship of the "they"', which he claims occurs when we

> take pleasure and enjoy ourselves as they take pleasure; we read, see, and judge about literature and art as they see and judge; likewise we shrink back from the 'great mass' as they shrink back; we find 'shocking' what they find shocking. The 'they', which is nothing definite, and which all are, though not as the sum, prescribes the kind of Being of everydayness. (Heidegger 1962, 164)

It would thus seem that both Sartre and Heidegger agree with Adorno in urging us to question the everyday roles and routines we find ourselves forced to perform. Moreover, they would also seem to agree with Adorno's criticism of theorists such as Goffman and Berne, whose work appears to leave unchallenged the very roles and social structures Adorno, along with Sartre and Heidegger, set out to challenge. Despite these close parallels, which he recognises are there, Adorno argues that by and large the existentialists ultimately undermine their own critique by basing it on the concept of authenticity. This is the central claim of Adorno's book, *The Jargon of Authenticity*. In short, rather than challenging the 'dictatorship of the "they"', the existential focus on authenticity reinforces, rather than questions, the social structures that rely on this dictatorship. With Heidegger in his sights, Adorno argues that the mindless, meaningless chatter one engages in when thinking and speaking as the 'they' do, is in actuality 'forced on men by a social structure which negates them as subjects long before this is done by the newspaper companies' (Adorno 1973, 102). As Gillian Rose summarises Adorno's position, Heidegger's 'notion of authenticity implies a social condition in which relations to others and thus to oneself are simple and transparent. To advance such a position in a society in which social relations are not simple and transparent lends support to the mode of domination in that society' (Rose 1978, 95).

What Rose is referring to here is Adorno's interpretation of authenticity whereby the 'jargon [of authenticity] cures Dasein from the wound of meaninglessness' by abstracting it from any ontic identification, leaving it fully in possession of itself, or declaring 'that the person owns himself' (Adorno 1973, 114). For Adorno, this self-ownership becomes the 'unlosable element, which has no substratum but its own concept, [and hence] the tautological selfness of the self', or the transparency of self to self as Rose puts it, is that 'which the authentics possess and the inauthentics lack. The essence of Dasein, i.e., what is more than its mere existence, is nothing but its selfness: it is itself' (116). The authentic person is not to be attached to or identified with its relationships or projects in the world, for Dasein entails, in its essence, a fundamental non-relationship – namely, to one's own death – that cannot be reduced to any determinate fact. As we saw earlier (see 2.2.c), for Heidegger, 'Dying, which is essentially mine in such a way that no one can be my representative', has nonetheless fallen under the dictatorship of the 'they', or the world of everydayness that 'is constituted by the way things have been publicly interpreted, which expresses itself in idle talk' (Heidegger 1962, 296). To avoid the dictatorship of the 'they', therefore, one must reclaim the dying 'which is essentially mine', and embrace the relationship of one's 'Being towards death as a possibility', a possibility that 'is as far as possible from anything actual'. Since this possibility involves a reality that is 'as far as possible from anything actual', the relationship we embrace thus becomes our 'ownmost non-relational possibility' (307). That is, to live authentically is to live a life that embraces a 'non-relational possibility' that cannot be reduced to any determinate fact, or to any ontic reality as Heidegger puts it, for we cannot enter into any possible relationship with the determinate fact of our own death, and yet it is just this possibility which we are to courageously affirm if we are to live an authentic existence. The problem with Heidegger's position, however, and this is a point Rose will stress, is that death becomes for him the way in which to think and live a totality that cannot be thought or lived. Heidegger thus 'singles out his authentic death', Adorno claims, 'as something that is extremely real and at the same time beyond all facticity' (Adorno 1973, 148), and it is for this reason that 'death becomes the onto-logical foundation of totality', since death as non-relational-possibility serves as the 'unity of the whole content of real life' (146) that is irreducible to the factual, determinate content of this life. Adorno claims, however, that by making this move Heidegger in the end obscures factual and determinate social structures and ultimately reinforces and encourages the move away from the determinate reality, with all its relations and expectations, that the dictatorship of the 'they' thrives on. Adorno concludes from this that, 'In spite of its eager neutrality and distance from society, authenticity thus stands on the side of the conditions of production, which, contrary to reason, per-petuate want' (112).

In her book *The Melancholy Science*, Gillian Rose focuses on this claim of Adorno's that the conditions of production that perpetuate want are precisely what the jargon of authenticity presupposes and reinforces. As she puts it, 'Adorno construes Marx's theory of value so that it describes the process which structures social reality at the level of meaning, or, more accurately, at the level of illusion' (Rose 1978, 180). 'This process', she claims, 'is the production and exchange of commodities which entails "the reduction of the products to be exchanged to their equivalents, to something abstract", and that which is abstract, in this sense, is conceptual. This "conceptual entity" Adorno calls "illusion"' (180, citing Adorno et al. 1976, 80). Stated more precisely, when goods and services are exchanged on the market, the exchange value at which one is able to acquire these goods and services is both different from their use value and involves a fundamental illusion or 'systematic misrecognition', as Rose puts it. If I were to buy my wife a purse from Burberry, say a Mini Leather Two-handle Title Bag for $1,590.00, the abstract equivalence involved here is with all those other goods and services I could also get for $1,590.00, such as round-trip tickets from New Orleans to London, a month's mortgage payment, etc. The systematic misrecognition or illusion involved here, according to Rose's reading of Adorno, is, firstly, 'that (exchange) value is a property of the commodity' – 'exchange value appears to be a real attribute of commodities although it is not a real attribute' (28), and thus the price of the purse, for example, comes to be seen as appropriate given the nature and quality of the purse itself (the fine materials, handcrafted touches, etc.); secondly, and of even more interest to Adorno and Rose, the abstract nature and equality of exchange value 'masks real inequality' – the inequality between those who can and cannot buy a Burberry purse – and for this reason and others, as we will see, 'it amounts to a mode of domination

140

which turns men into the mass of individuals and (somehow) destroys the "individual" as such' (84). This is the heart of Adorno's critique of Heidegger, for by focusing on one's authentic relationship to death, to an essential mine-ness that is not to be confused with anything actual or determinate, Heidegger essentially presupposes the very abstractness that encourages the forms of production that mask 'real inequality' and 'turn men into the mass of individuals', and thus into individuals who live under the dictatorship of the 'they'.

In her extension of Adorno's critique, Rose argues that Heidegger's thought is 'dirempted by the dual character of modern legality – the simultaneous autonomy and heteronomy of the legal person separated from the law of the state – and would mend such diremption with pseudo-holistic phantasms of "race", "ethnicity", "community"' (Rose 1978, 453). As Rose puts it, Heidegger's 'oeuvre is haunted … by the unacknowledged but evident diremption which he refused from start to finish, from origin to origin, to think' (456). To clarify this point, Rose recalls the inequality the illusion of exchange value masks, claiming that the diremption Heidegger could not think is 'between the forms of legal equality and the actuality of systematic inequality' (457). The diremption that is not thought by Heidegger is thus a social divide between the *abstract* equality of legal subjects, including the freedom and security of contracts between them, and the determinate, *concrete* social inequalities these laws create, laws that are in turn enforced by the state, thus reinforcing and perpetuating these inequalities (for more on the role of laws, see below, §5.2.c).

Before turning to what is involved in thinking the evident diremption Heidegger could not think, it must first be noted that there is a Heideggerian response to the Adorno/Rose critique. Most notably, one must not confuse Heidegger's claim that Dasein belongs to itself and is 'in each case mine' with a Lockean argument for the primacy of the determinate individual, and hence for the classical liberalism that underpins the appeal to the legal equality of individuals. Heidegger, in fact, is pointedly arguing against just this view of individualism, and it was for this reason that Dasein as being-towards-death entails a non-relational possibility that is 'as far as possible from anything actual'. Adorno is very much aware of this point, noting that 'Every entity is more than it is – as we are reminded by Being, in contrast to entity' (Adorno 1973, 102). In other words, Being, including Dasein as a being-towards-death, is not to be confused with any determinate entity, for as Heidegger puts it, Being is the presencing of the presence of entities and not that presence itself. That said, Adorno will highlight Heidegger's emphasis on the relational understanding of Being, even if it is a non-relational possibility that entails a relationship to that which can in no way be determinate or actual (i.e., death), noting that for Heidegger 'There is no entity whose determination and self-determination does not require something else, something which the entity itself is not … It therefore points beyond itself' (102). Adorno will argue, however, that Heidegger pushes this point too far, in seeking 'to hold on to that which points beyond itself, and to leave behind, as rubble, that beyond which it points' (102). By leaving behind the determinate entities that always point beyond themselves, Heidegger in essence leaves behind thinking, which for Adorno entails identifying the determinate nature of that which is thought – 'To think is to identify' (5) as he puts it. To think is thus to identify and differentiate something determinate, the something that is being thought.

Adorno claims that, in his effort to avoid a relapse of thought into the determinate nature of things themselves, including the self or ego as determinate subjectivity, Heidegger appeals to an understanding of Being as a third possibility, as a relational reality that is to be confused neither with determinate subjectivity nor with determinate entities. He thereby evades the difference or diremption (to use Rose's term) of subject and object by 'usurping a standpoint beyond the difference of subject and object' (85); in other words, Being is not to be confused with determinate subjects or objects precisely because it is, according to Heidegger, the presencing, clearing or truth (as *aletheia*) which makes such determinate realities (beings) possible. But this very move undermines thinking itself, Adorno argues, for 'We cannot assume any position in which that separation of subject and object will directly vanish, for the separation is inherent in each thought; it is inherent in thinking itself' (85). It is for just this reason that Heidegger's philosophical approach leaves us in principle unable to think the 'evident diremption' that runs through life and society, since the separation or diremption of subject and object is inherent in thinking, and it is this diremption that is ruled out from the start by Heidegger.

We are now in a position to clarify the nature of thinking the 'evident diremption' that lies at the basis of thinking itself and of the socio-economic system that masks structural inequalities in the name of legal, political equality. On the one hand, thinking entails identifying and conceptualising things in terms of predicates that apply to things other than the particular that is given and being thought at the moment. This is what Adorno will refer to as 'the so-called "constitutive problem"' – namely, the problem of how, given that thought is constrained to take its 'departure from the particular' in its attempt to identify and differentiate that which is determinate, we are then able to arrive at 'the abstract legality of the totality itself', a totality that entails a 'coercive mechanism' which binds or forces a thought of a particular into a thought of a universal or conceptual type (47). Stated in the terms we have been developing throughout this work, the 'constitutive problem' is precisely the process involved in constructing the problems that make solutions possible. It is the problem of drawing elements, particulars, into a coherence or consistency that makes determinate rules possible, rules that tie (legally bind) determinate particulars and instances to a determinate universal or predicate. One way of understanding the manner in which elements are drawn together as a problem is as a narrative. Narratives, as we have argued, are to be understood as problems that make sense but not in a logical manner, or not in a space of reasons that involves a determinate relationship between propositions and the inferences that can be drawn from them (recall Ricoeur [see §2.1.c]). Moreover, narratives can make sense of determinate elements and facts without themselves being reducible to any particular set of facts, and narratives as problems always involve the possibility of incorporating or excluding other facts, or of generating even further facts in support of the sense-making narrative itself. It is in this sense that the process of thinking, which entails creating a coherence and consistency of determinate facts, is a process of fictioning, a fictioning that is inseparable from, but not to be confused with, the facts that may loom large in the narrative. It is in this sense also that thinking, as Adorno understands it, involves a tendency towards idealism, or the dedifferentiating tendency that moves from determinate and differentiated facts and particulars to concepts and categories that are inseparable from but irreducible to these facts.

At the same time, however, Adorno points out that our thinking in terms of concepts and categories continually reaches its limits, or encounters an objectivity that refuses to be thought and constrained by the concepts and categories thought employs. As Adorno puts it: to 'comprehend a thing itself … is nothing but to perceive the individual moment in its immanent connection with others' (25); that is, every determinate fact, every determinate thing that is thought, presupposes a relationship to other determinate facts which could be thought but are not yet constrained by or captured by the current thought. There is thus always more to be thought than is actually thought, or always a further reason that can be given, something more that can be said as the infinitist would argue, and it is this more, according to Adorno, that makes language possible. Adorno is clear on this point: 'No concept would be thinkable, indeed none would be possible without the "more" that makes a language of language' (106). And it is on just this point that he breaks most clearly with Hegel, and comes to his view of negative dialectics. Put simply, rather than arguing, as Hegel does, that the dialectic proceeds by progressively coming to recognise the *identity* of the subject in that which was taken to be non-identical to it, Adorno argues that the dialectic proceeds by continually encountering the *non-identity* of objective reality immanent to the concepts and categories that are subjectively used to think that which is. Immanent to the thoughts that identify that which is, therefore, is a contradiction or untruth, 'the untruth of identity', as Adorno puts it, which points to 'the fact that the concept does not exhaust the thing conceived' (5). This 'untruth of identity' is precisely the more that 'makes a language of language', that assures the relationship of thought and language to a reality that is other than these thoughts and words, a reality that is nonetheless immanent to these thoughts. As Adorno puts it, 'What is, is more than it is. This "more" is not imposed upon it but remains immanent to it, as that which has been pushed out of it. In that sense, the nonidentical would be the thing's own identity against its identifications' (161). To think, therefore, is to encounter a reality that resists the very effort to think it, a reality that invites further thoughts, a veritable regress of thinking. For this reason Adorno concludes that 'a cognition that is to bear fruit will throw itself to the object *à fond perdu*. The vertigo this causes is an *index veri*' (33). A thinking that bears fruit, in venturing away from the identity and stability of the thoughts with which it begins, thus risks losing its way in a vertigo of endless appeals to other thoughts, appeals from which there is no return to where one started – the trail of crumbs has been eaten by birds – and this risk is precisely the objective reality (the more) immanent to thought itself. This is to be contrasted with the fictioning tendency, the differentiating tendency that hones in on the determinate and the particular, constructing the consistency and coherence of determinate facts and elements necessary for learning, for thinking a determinate thought and/or rule. Adorno's 'thinking that bears fruit' leaves us instead with the dedifferentiating tendency that undermines the determinate and particular, opening up a vertigo of the possible, to recall Kierkegaard, a vertigo that threatens to undermine the consistency and coherence of one's fictions and narratives.

We are now in a position to clarify how, for Adorno, one is to engage in a critical thinking about one's daily encounters. First and foremost, neither the fictioning, differentiating tendency towards the determinate and particular, nor the dedifferentiating tendency towards a universal delirium and vertigo, are to be actualised to the exclusion of the other. This is how we read Adorno's claim that, 'In truth, the subject is never quite the subject, and the object never quite the object; and yet the two are not pieced out of any third that might transcend them' (175). In contrast to Heidegger's effort to understand the difference between subject and object on the basis of a third – Being (presencing) – Adorno argues that each entails the other. Paradoxically, there is no determinate, already identified reality that transcends the thoughts which identify reality, and every such thought entails more than is actually thought, a more (or problem in our terms) that may undermine the determinate identity of that which is thought. It is for this reason that what is thought, including the stories and narratives that make sense of things, are never fully actualised, never fully make sense of things once and for all, for they may well be undermined by the determinate more that becomes actualised, or by the problems that come to be solved in different ways. These determinate solutions, moreover, are themselves never fully determinate and actualised for they too make sense only by virtue of the narratives, fictions or problems that these determinate facts give voice to. The task of critique is thus not to construct the definitive narrative that makes sense of all possible scenarios, and of all the determinate facts these scenarios may entail; nor is it simply a matter of challenging narratives with determinate facts that may problematise and undermine them. Rather, the task of critique consists of pushing the narratives that currently make sense of facts to the point where they no longer make sense, where they stop making sense and the vertigo of possibility lurks.

Let us now return to the 'evident diremption' of the legal equality of individuals that masks and obscures the actual inequalities at work in our society. On the one hand, the fiction and narrative that we as individuals are all equal, free and bearers of universal rights, rights such as the right to free speech, the right to enter into contracts, etc., is a narrative that makes sense of many of the social and political institutions we encounter and interact with on a daily basis. The key to the critique of this narrative, however, is not simply to point to the facts that show the many ways in which inequalities run throughout the society – for example, growing income inequality, disparities in the accumulation of wealth, the bifurcation of opportunities based on education, socio-economic background, etc. Since a narrative, as a fiction, is irreducible to the facts it makes sense of, one cannot, by such a presentation of facts alone, force a rethinking of that narrative. Conspiracy narratives, as we saw, are extreme versions of narratives that, for those who use them to make sense of certain scenarios, are largely resistant to revision in light of recalcitrant facts. What is needed, in addition to a factual inquiry and analysis that reveals the limits of a narrative, or the facts that it does not capture and make sense of, is a narrative that creates joy, in Spinoza's sense, by problematising the established narrative in a way that enhances one's capacities and powers; and it can do this only if it is a narrative that makes sense of indeterminate facts, or, paradoxically, of the facts that one cannot make sense of. The difference here is that a narrative that is taken to be a solution without a problem is one with a limit at which facts stop making sense, at which point such facts may well provoke a negative knee-jerk reaction, whereas a joyful narrative is one that embraces the infinite and limitless (*apeiron* [see earlier, §2.2.a]), and hence that which stops making sense. The result is that rather than having a negative reaction on encountering the limits of one's narrative, or living the encounter with sadness as Spinoza understands it, one encounters and affirms those

145

limits as precisely the power (God for Spinoza) that cannot be contained by our narratives, the power that is inseparable from whatever determinate narratives come to be created. It was this power that was inseparable from the melodying that enabled Sudnow to play improvisational jazz, rather than play from already determined chords, scales and jazz-sounding runs. Similarly, the power that is inseparable from a joyful narrative is inseparable from a narrativising that creates narratives without a predetermining set of facts, and thus a narrativising that is not done in accordance with a rule.[2]

Let us return to the social diremption brought about by the production of exchange value. The abstract equivalence value that underlies the production of exchange commodities garners political and theoretical support and justification from the abstract legality and equality of subjects, subjects free to sell their labour, enter into contracts, etc. What we have here is precisely a narrative that is largely taken to be irreducible to actual, determinate facts. One can thus hold to this narrative which makes sense of who we are as human beings – we are all created equal with shared, universal rights – despite the actual determinate facts we encounter on a daily basis in our lives, the actual inequalities, the injustices, the preferential legal protections for those with means, etc. To engage in a critique of this narrative, it is not sufficient to point to the determinate facts that do not instantiate the narrative. A partisan of the narrative will simply point to instances where the rule is instantiated and offer an alternative narrative to account for the facts one cites, arguing perhaps that those who want to address the cited inequalities will do so by way of policies that undermine the basic legal rights and equality of subjects. What the critic should set out to do, therefore, is operate from the assumption that the narrative is not an already determinate and determined rule, a rule one can then use to arrive at the instances which support the rule or formulate the policies that will do so; rather, the narrative as a solution without a problem is only a tendency of the fictioning process, a tendency which also includes the dedifferentiating tendency that undermines narratives as solutions. In other words, just as Adorno argued that 'the subject is never

---

2. We could return at this point to the discussion of Wittgenstein with which we began (and we will below, see §5.2.d), though it would entail a detour from the critical existentialism we are developing, and the manner in which this theory can be deployed in thinking through politics. But in brief: the form of life that Wittgenstein appealed to in order to avoid a universal, Platonic form that serves as a rule-as-rail independent of the particular instances of following the rule, and to avoid the rule by opinion or consensus in each and every particular case, can be understood as narrativising. Narrativising is not a third, à la Heidegger on Adorno's reading of him, but rather the two (universals and convention) are themselves abstractions from the narrativising process. There is thus no two to which there is added a third; there is only a one, a narrativising process, or God as absolutely infinite substance as Spinoza would put it.

quite the subject, and the object never quite the object' (175), similarly the universal, abstract legal equality of subjects is a tendency that never quite becomes actual, and the determinate facts of life also reflect a tendency that never quite becomes actual. The partisans of the legal rights of subjects to work, enter into contracts, etc., may well recognise this tendency as a tendency, arguing that we ought to hold out legal equality and freedom as an ideal to strive towards even if it is not yet actualised. This would be better, they might argue, than attempting to correct actual wrongs, the already present and determinate inequalities and injustices of today, for by doing this one ultimately undermines the legal equality and freedom of subjects. The key to a critical existentialism, however, as understood here, is to recognise that the abstract narratives and rules which justify and account for the determinate facts that instantiate and express these narratives and rules are both inseparably involved in a process that expresses the dual, de/differentiating tendencies of making sense. What the critical analysis of these tendencies entails, therefore, is the affirmation of both of them as tendencies, and thus an affirmation of the narrative and the facts as both being expressive of the dual tendencies of life. When one encounters a determinate fact or situation that provokes a negative knee-jerk reaction, we have a breakdown in the process, a point where the dual tendencies become bifurcated. At this point one can either reject the determinate facts or situations that one encounters – for example, reject Nietzsche's chapter titles and the narrative that would embrace such facts (e.g., master morality on Nietzsche's account) – or one can affirm the problematic nature that both determinate narratives and facts serve as solutions to. Thus, rather than rejecting the determinate as such, whether the facts or the narrative, one instead embraces and affirms the problem inseparable from them, and in doing so embraces the tendency towards undermining that may disrupt and alter both our narratives and the facts that we are capable of making sense of. When things stop making sense, moreover, one encounters the 'infinite enjoyment of existing', to use Spinoza's phrase, and it is this infinite enjoyment that is the problematic reality that allows for the possibility of expanding determinate facts and relations and the narratives which make sense of these facts and relations. Rather than rejecting the determinate facts of inequality and injustice, therefore, or rejecting the narrative of equality and rights, a critical existentialism will push the tendencies of both to the point where they stop making sense, since it is at this point that a rethinking of the facts and narratives that make sense of our lives becomes possible and may enable us to transform the lives we live.

To illustrate the sense in which the critique sketched here can be termed a critical existentialism, we can turn to the dispute that ended the friendship between Sartre and Camus. It erupted with the publication of Camus' *The*

147

Rebel and the scathing review that Francis Jeanson wrote of it in *Les Temps Modernes*, the journal Sartre founded, and thus the review was clearly published with his blessing. At issue, in short, was Camus' critical stance towards the communists, and in particular Stalin's regime, the implication being that Sartre's continued adherence to Stalinism exemplified the nihilism Camus challenged in *The Rebel* (recall §4.1.c). As noted earlier, Camus understands nihilism to be the 'inability to believe in what is, to see what is happening, and to live life as it is offered' (Camus 2000, 41); thus, by refusing to see what was happening in the camps Stalin established in the Soviet Union, and his mass murder of his own citizens, Sartre is seen by Camus as falling into nihilism. The criticism is that Sartre holds to the Stalinist narrative that sees communism as the best alternative to the capitalist system and the oppressive conditions it subjects workers to, and he holds to this narrative regardless of what the determinate facts may be, facts one ought to be attentive to if one is going to 'live life as it is offered', and hence live a life that challenges or refuses to endorse narratives that turn a blind eye to the sufferings and injustices those narratives tacitly promote.

Camus claims that Sartre has the 'relative right to ignore the fact of concentration camps in the Soviet Union as long as you [Sartre] do not address the questions raised by revolutionary ideology in general, and Marxism in particular' (Sprintzen and van den Hoven 2004, 141). In other words, from Camus' perspective, Sartre can ignore the camps only if he does not promote or discuss the ideologies (that is, the narratives) which support the very regime that implemented the camps. Since Sartre did support the narrative that communism is the best alternative to capitalism, Camus argues that he ought to have taken into consideration the connection between this narrative and its horrific consequences, that is, he ought to have taken note of the dangerous, murderous consequences of its inherent nihilism. In his response to Camus, Sartre argues that he did indeed address the horrors of the camps, that an issue of *Les Temps Modernes* dedicated 'an editorial to the camps as well as several articles', and that while he finds 'these camps inadmissible ... equally inadmissible is the use that the "so-called bourgeois press" makes of them every day' (142). For Sartre, therefore, the camps are indeed to be rejected, but this does not mean, as he understands Camus to be saying, that one ought to give up the communist ideology that is nominally associated with the regime that has carried out a genocide on its own people.[3]

---

3. There has been some debate among scholars regarding whether Stalin's regime intentionally committed genocide in Ukraine, in what is called the Holodomor genocide question. Robert Davies and Stephen Wheatcroft, for instance, do not believe that Stalin's policies were implemented with the intention to kill people, and thus they should not be classified

Sartre counters that one of the consequences of Camus' philosophical position regarding the absurdity of our existence, or the fact for him that there is no ultimate meaning that can be discerned despite our efforts to do just that, is that Camus is preternaturally predisposed simply to defend the status quo, to accept things as they are. Citing a sentence from Camus' *Letters to a German Friend* where he addresses 'a Nazi soldier [and says]: "For years now, you have tried to make me enter History"', Sartre concludes that Camus 'view[s] History with distrust', and '"since he believes himself *outside* [History], it's only normal that he poses conditions before entering *into it*"'. In particular, Camus acts like a 'little girl who tests the water with her toe', wondering whether it is too hot; in Camus' case it is a matter of asking, '"Has it [History] a meaning?"' (Sprintzen and van den Hoven 2004, 157). The result of this attitude, Sartre concludes, is that Camus is inclined to accept things as they are, and he leaves himself with no real basis for bringing about change. Camus, in short, embodies the attitude of Meursault from *The Stranger*, who, in response to his boss's question as to whether he 'wasn't interested in a change of life', claims to have said 'that people never change their lives, that in any case one life was as good as another and that I wasn't dissatisfied with mine here at all' (Camus 1989, 41). Such an attitude is telling, for Sartre, who argues that, although Camus sought to bring about change in 1941, this was forced upon him in order to prevent 'Hitlerian madness from destroying a world where solitary exaltation was still possible for some, and you [Camus] agreed to pay the price for your future exaltations. Today it's different. It's no longer a matter of *defending the status quo*, but of changing it' (Sprintzen and van den Hoven 2004, 157; emphasis in original). Since Camus sees himself as outside History, a History lacking in the meaning and purpose that might help one to find one's way through the complexities of life in the present, he remains quiescent with the status quo. For Sartre, by contrast, one cannot help but draw from History, and the question of whether or not it has a meaning is one that itself has 'no meaning', 'because History, apart from the men who make it, is only an abstract and static concept, of which it can neither be said that it has an end, or that it doesn't have one. And the problem is not to *know* its end, but to *give* one to it' (157).

Understood in the context of our arguments regarding the nature of problems and their dual de/differentiating tendencies, we can begin to clarify the nature of this dispute. In particular, with this understanding of the nature

---

as genocide (Davies and Wheatcroft 2009); on the other hand, Norman Naimark argues for what is the consensus view that the policies were indeed intentional and do count as genocide (in Naimark 2010). Both Camus and Sartre accept the consensus view, albeit Sartre somewhat hesitantly according to Camus.

of problems we can place Sartre's criticism into the context of Camus' point, cited earlier, that a contemporary rebel 'cannot turn away from the world and from history without denying the very principle of his rebellion, nor can he choose eternal life without resigning himself, in one sense, to evil' (Camus 2000, 229). Sartre is indeed right to claim that to change the world we need to throw ourselves into historical events and do so with a sense of meaning and purpose that we give to these events. This meaning, however, is a narrativising that tends towards the eternal, to use Camus' phrase, or the dedifferentiating of the determinate facts of history. There is thus the risk of nihilism that comes with giving meaning to history, for the narratives that guide our actions and give our projects meaning and purpose may also blind us to life as it is actually given, and lead us to ignore the evils that are done for the sake of the projects our narratives have justified. It was precisely for this reason that Camus argued we 'cannot turn away from the world and from history', but must enter history with caution, aware of the tendencies our narratives may lead to and yet embracing both the narratives that make sense of our projects as well as the determinate facts of 'life as it is offered'. We are thus not to be fearful of history, like the girl afraid the water may be too hot to enter, but must continue to discern whether our narratives are working with the facts. Does our narrative make sense of the determinate facts, or does it force us to reject them and turn away from them because they do not make sense? What is key to critical existentialism, therefore, is determining whether a given narrative works – that is, whether it makes sense of the facts while affirming the undermining tendencies that may transform the narrative, allowing solutions to become problematised, rather than excluding, in knee-jerk fashion, the facts that stop making sense while remaining committed to a narrative that is removed from life as it is offered. The critical target of critical existentialism will be just these instances of turning away from life as it is offered, when the narrative that make sense of one's life allows for evil, as exemplified for Camus by Saint-Just, as well as by Sartre's accommodation of the camps in Stalin's Soviet Union. It was no wonder that Sartre was quick to reply to *The Rebel* in forceful terms, first by way of Jeanson and later in his own words. Although it is certainly true that Sartre was aware of the evils done in the name of Marxist communism, and did indeed speak out against them, it also appears that he was not as sensitive as Camus to the problematic nature of making sense, to the fact that one must remain attentive to those places and circumstances where things stop making sense.

We are now in a better position to differentiate the critical theory that Adorno, Horkheimer and others in the Frankfurt School are associated with and the critical existentialism being set forth here. There is much that is of mutual concern, such as the harmful role illusions play in our lives as individuals and as societies – the illusion of exchange value for Adorno, for instance, and the illusion of solutions without problems in our case. Heidegger, as we saw, was unable to dispel the illusion of exchange value, and in the end ultimately reinforced it by stressing the importance of having an authentic relationship to one's death, a non-relationship that is 'essentially mine' and is in no way to be confused with any determinate, ontic realities. To dispel the illusions that follow from the production of exchange value, Adorno argues, we need to think the 'evident diremption' that Heidegger was unable to think, and this precisely because thinking entails the thought of something determinate, in this case the relationship between a determinate social structure, what Horkheimer calls 'the historically given commodity economy on which modern history rests' (Horkheimer 2002, 227), and the individuals who suffer gross inequalities and squalid conditions within that economy. One of the central tasks of critical theory, therefore, is to challenge this illusion so that the inequalities and injustices can be overcome and we can have, as Horkheimer put it, 'a truly united and rational society', a society where the individual 'could come into his own' (115–16). By stressing the nature of problems that are not exhausted by the solutions they make possible, critical existentialism does not seek – as Heidegger's understanding of Dasein as being-towards-death does according to Adorno – a foundation that is 'beyond all facticity' (Adorno 1973, 148); to the contrary, problems are only determinate and identifiable with the solutions they make possible, they are not separate and distinct from the solutions that give voice to them. At the same time, however, although a critical existentialism shares with critical theory the effort to challenge illusions, one such illusion would be to assume that the problem is one of attaining a 'truly united and rational society ... [where an individual] could come into his own'. Rather than embracing the problematic nature inseparable from solutions, this tends towards the forced narrative whereby the theoretical problem of addressing the inequalities brought on by the production of exchange value already anticipates the solution that will eliminate the problem. Although having much sympathy for the goals of critical theory, the task of critical existentialism involves pursuing its critical project while recognising the tendency for authentic, good faith narratives to become forced, bad faith narratives. As we turn now to the concluding chapter, we will begin to lay out the nature of this task.

§5 Towards a Critical Existentialism

1. A Sense of Place

In this final chapter we will extend and apply the critical existentialism that we began to develop in the previous chapter. We will begin by returning to Camus' concerns regarding nihilism, and to the justification of murder this nihilism leads to (recall §4.1.c). As we further develop these arguments, we will take up the theme of justified murder by turning to the conception of political power as Locke defines it – that is, as 'a Right of making Laws with Penalties of Death' (Locke 1988, §3) – and then explore the distinction Locke makes between political power and conjugal power. With this distinction, what becomes important is the justification of political power, or the question of what justifies state-sanctioned murder. In the later sections, we will see that the difficulties which follow upon making the distinction between conjugal and political power reflect the de/differentiating tendencies of the problem of making sense of life. Camus sought to maintain a delicate balance in relation to the problematic nature of life, resisting the nihilistic tendency, as he saw it, to assume that one or other of these tendencies is ever fully actualised and determinative, and determinative to the point of justifying murder. Along the way, as we explore the issues involved in attempting to maintain this balance, we will bring in work from studies in wayfinding, especially the work of Tim Ingold and J.J. Gibson, to show just how prevalent the tendency is to rely upon what Ingold calls the 'cartographic illusion', or the tendency to think that a map, in this case, simply represents a reality that is always already there. Bringing Adorno back into the discussion we will show how the cartographic illusion is yet another instance of the illusion of a solution without a problem, an illusion that is also common within political discourse. This will then set the stage for the closing sections, in which we will deploy a critical existentialism in order to challenge these illusions and encourage a rethinking of the key political ideas of freedom, law and progress.

a) Justified murder

In his defence of monarchical power, the seventeenth-century political theorist Sir Robert Filmer does not hesitate to equate a monarch's power and authority with the power of the father, and hence with the unquestioned authority he assumes the father has over the members of his family. In the first chapter of his *Patriarcha*, titled, appropriately enough, 'That the first Kings were Fathers of Families' (Filmer 1680, 1), Filmer forthrightly claims that Adam's power and authority were given to him by God, and likewise to 'the succeeding Patriarchs [who] had, by Right of Father-hood, Royal Authority over their Children'. From this Filmer concludes: 'I see not then how the Children of Adam, or of any man else can be free from subjection to their Parents: And this subjection of Children being the Fountain of all Regal Authority ... It follows, that Civil Power ... is by Divine Institution' (12). For Locke, however, the subjection of children to paternal authority is only temporary, and it 'terminates with the minority of the Child' (Locke 1988, §67). A father's power over his children ends when they, 'being by Nature as free as himself', attain the 'Age of Discretion', wherein one 'is presumed to know how far that Law ['whether Natural or Civil' as Locke says] is to be his Guide, and how far he may make use of his Freedom'; and the 'Age of Discretion', or the age of majority, occurs at 'the Age of one and twenty years, and in some cases sooner' (§59). Where Filmer goes wrong, as Locke sees it, is in assuming that the *obedience* one owes to the will of one's parents is equivalent to the *honour* one owes them. The former ends with the 'Age of Discretion' while the latter remains a duty for the rest of one's life.

For Locke, however, there are further limits to the power a father has over his family. In particular, he does not have the power of death, and it is just this power that distinguishes political power from conjugal power. Locke defines political power as follows:

> To be a Right of making Laws with Penalties of Death, and consequently all less Penalties, for the regulating and preserving of Property, and of employing the force of the Community, in the Execution of such Laws, and in the defence of the Common-wealth from Foreign Injury, and all this only for the Publick Good. (Locke 1988, §3).

The right to carry out penalties of death brings us to a motivating concern at work in Locke's critique of arbitrary power, a concern that will play itself out repeatedly with respect to political power – the concern with making sense of the arbitrariness of death. One looks among a range of reasons and justifications to make sense of death and its often arbitrary nature – those unexpected deaths, which may include one's own, that everyone has either encountered or knows is possible. One option is simply to accept the random nature of death, whether it be the result of God's arbitrary decision that one's time is up, a matter of being in the wrong place at the wrong time, or a matter of having an unlucky genetic predisposition to particular diseases and cancers. Another option is to claim that there is a reason that accounts for a death, why a particular person died when they did, though this may be a reason that we cannot understand. God may have a reason for deciding one's time is up, but it will be a reason 'which surpasses all understanding' (Philippians 4:7); there may be a reason for this death, but given the finite nature of our understanding we simply cannot grasp all that would be necessary to understand it. Finally, we can believe there is a non-arbitrary reason for one's death, a reason that justifies and accounts for it, and moreover this is a reason and justification one can understand.

A consequence of Locke's critique of Filmer's arguments in defence of a monarch's paternal power over their subjects, along with his subsequent distinction between conjugal and political power, is that with the right to carry out penalties which include penalties of death, the latter penalties must be justified rather than arbitrary. Unlike the power of a parent whose will is sufficient to justify their actions – a parent's 'because I said so' justification – the political power to carry out the punishment of death is a power that presupposes the 'Age of Discretion', or the consent of those who may be subject to the power that takes their life. As a result, the political power 'of making Laws with Penalties of Death' needs to be justified, and any death carried out by those who exercise political power needs to have a reason that people can understand and to which they can give their consent, so that those in 'a state of Reason' (Locke 1988, §59) can recognise that it has been done in accordance with the law and 'for the Publick Good'. It is precisely at this point, however, that the problem of making sense, or making sense as a problem, becomes integral to the various ways in which political power is carried out. As Camus came to recognise with respect to events subsequent to the French Revolution, and especially the events surrounding the rise of Nazism and the Second World War, appeals to the public good can easily obscure the brutal reality of what is in the end simply murder. As Camus laments, if 'in our time [one] admits with equanimity that murder has justification, this is because of the indifference to life which is the mark of nihilism' (Camus 2000, x). This nihilism, as we have seen, is to be found in an 'inability to believe in what is, to see what is happening, and to live life as it is offered' (41). For the sake of the public good, therefore, one may follow principles to their bitter, deadly end, as happened with the Jacobin Saint-Just, who succumbed to nihilism and, as Camus puts it, accepted 'death for love of principles and despite all the realities of the situation … the condition of things' (80). In other words, Saint-Just turned a blind eye to the many murders carried out under the reign of terror, believing they were fully justified and necessary in order to follow the principles of the revolution, and thus do that which was truly best for the public good. By failing to recognise 'the realities of the situation … the

154

condition of things', however, Saint-Just's revolution failed and he himself was eventually led to the guillotine.

For Camus, then, and building on the discussion from the previous chapter, the challenge is precisely to make sense of life and justify the actions that may well involve the necessity of death. The problem with making sense, however, as we have been arguing throughout, is that it involves both de/differentiating tendencies. For instance, in making sense of the right of political power to make laws 'with Penalties of Death', the process of making sense entails both a tendency towards that which is not to be confused with anything actual and a tendency towards increasingly differentiating *that* which makes sense. The nihilism of Saint-Just affirms the first tendency to the exclusion of the latter. By following principles he takes to be necessary to the full realisation of the public good, Saint-Just ignores 'the realities of the situation' and thus does not take account of how his principles make sense of that which is actually happening. Sartre's commitment to Stalin's communism could have been charged with similarly ignoring the 'realities of the situation' – in this case the camps and the murder of millions of Stalin's own citizens. Sartre, as we saw, claims to have been well aware of the existence of the camps and other problems within Stalin's regime, and yet his commitment to communism persists and he challenges Camus for not having the principles necessary to bring about change. In particular, Sartre set out to resist the capitalist exploitation of workers and map a way towards a goal that entailed, from his perspective, aligning with the *principles* of communism, even if this meant having at one time supported a Stalinist regime that *murdered* millions. It was for this reason, as we saw, that Sartre claimed Camus was inclined to defend the status quo rather than bring about the changes that he felt were necessary – hence Sartre's charge that Camus was to be classified as a bourgeois thinker rather than a true radical. In short, from Sartre's perspective, Camus was focused on *that* which makes sense to the exclusion of the *principles* that make sense of and justify political power.

As we saw earlier, however, although Camus admits that we 'cannot turn away from the world and from history', he is still conscious of the important role principles play in making sense of and justifying political power. Stated in the terms we have used here, for Camus we are to be alert to those determinate instances where the narratives that make sense of political power, and narratives that are irreducible to *that* which makes sense, stop making sense. Furthermore, the determinate instances that most tend to disrupt the capacity for narratives to make sense of political power are precisely those circumstances where political power exercises its right to carry out 'Penalties of Death'. As Sartre himself noted, Camus did not hesitate to resist the 'Hitlerian madness' (Sprintzen and van den Hoven 2004, 157) and the political power

155

Hitler wielded to inflict wanton violence and murder, which he did for the 'public good' as he and the National Socialists understood this. Camus thus did not succumb to the 'indifference to life which is the mark of nihilism' (Camus 2000, x). Sartre's challenge, however, still stands – namely, that one should not simply 'see what is happening' (41), even and most especially if what is happening is suffering and death, but must also adopt principles and a narrative that make sense of what is happening and provide a basis for differentiating between proper and improper exercises of political power. If nihilism for Camus consists of an indifference to life that leads one to admit 'with equanimity that murder has justification', then what principles, if any, can both entail an affirmation of life rather than indifference and lead one to accept the deaths that come with the exercise of political power?

At this point we can return to Locke, for his understanding of the limits of both conjugal and political power will continue to resonate throughout the modern era. Stated briefly, for Locke it is natural law that limits the exercise of both conjugal and political power – or, more precisely, allows us to differentiate between proper and improper exercises of power – and it is natural law that calls upon individuals to do what is necessary for the sake of self-preservation. Actions done from this necessity fall outside of any other conventional agreement we may enter into. For example, if someone kills another person in self-defence, fearing their own life would be taken if they did not use lethal force to save themselves, then the conventional, civil laws do not apply – natural law trumps civil law in such circumstances. The same is true for the state, or the commonwealth as Locke puts it, where political power is justified in using lethal force to eliminate those who would threaten the self-preservation of the state. It is thus the self-preservation of the state which justifies the 'Penalties of Death' for acts of treason and other capital crimes, or in the killings that occur during war, and today even, though controversially, in the use of drone strikes to pre-emptively kill perceived threats to national security.

It is at this point that Sartre's commitment to communism becomes espe-cially relevant. Stated simply, Sartre could well turn Locke's critique of Filmer back on Locke, for where Filmer confuses conjugal power with political power, Locke can be seen to conflate the self-preservation of our embodied life with the self-preservation of the life of the state. More to Sartre's point, and as will be detailed below, the self-preservation of the state in its modern form is integrally tied to the self-preservation and growth of capital, and this self-preservation and growth of capital is at odds with the self-preservation, freedom and thriving of our embodied lives. Locke, however, was well aware of the difference between embodied life and the life of the state, as indeed was Aristotle before him. Locke, for instance, famously argues that 'Every

Man has a Property in his own Person. This no Body has any Right to but himself'; to which he adds that 'The Labour of his Body, and the Work of his Hands, we may say, are properly his' (Locke 1988, §27). There is a limit, however, to the property one can accumulate through one's labour. As Locke puts it, we can take from nature, which was given by God to all in common, 'As much as any one can make use of to any advantage of life before it spoils; so much he may by his labour fix a Property in. Whatever is beyond this, is more than his share, and belongs to others' (§31). With the advent of money, however, this proviso does not apply, for as Locke notes, 'Gold and Silver ... may be hoarded up without injury to any one, these metals not spoileing or decaying in the hands of the possesser'. The result, Locke admits, is that 'Men have agreed to disproportionate and unequal Possession of the Earth', given that the value placed in gold and silver coin is 'only from the consent of Men' (§50). The self-preservation and growth of money wealth, therefore, and the needs attendant upon this growth (e.g., payment of interest on debt), are thus distinct for Locke from the self-preservation of our embodied self.

On this point Locke echoes Aristotle. In his *Politics*, Aristotle distinguishes between two uses of money. In the first, one uses money in exchange for that which one needs in order to maintain the household, and in the second one uses money to purchase things that one will then turn around and sell for a profit. As Aristotle puts it, 'Every piece of property has a double use ... one is the proper use of the article in question, the other is not. For example, a shoe may be used either to put on your foot or to offer in exchange' (Aristotle 1984, 1257a5). In the first use Aristotle claims there is a natural limit to the use of a piece of property – namely, the use that is necessary 'to re-establish nature's own equilibrium of self-sufficiency' (1257a28), or the self-preservation and maintenance of the household (οἰκονομία). In the second use of property, however, and as Locke will echo, the use of money in exchange for more money is a process in which Aristotle claims 'there is indeed no limit to the amount of riches to be got from this mode of acquiring goods' (1257b10). But the two modes of acquisition are frequently confused and conflated. 'The reason', Aristotle claims, 'why some people get this notion into their heads', namely that they need unlimited wealth, 'may be that they are eager for life but not for the good life; so, desire for life being unlimited, they desire also an unlimited amount of what enables it to go on' (1257b40). In other words, if the desire for life itself is unlimited, then in our terms there is no determinate manner in which life itself is to be desired and lived – life is a problem, as we have been arguing – and yet this desire is not to be confused and conflated with the determinate things that facilitate the self-preservation and well-being of life. Life as lived, in short, entails living within appropriate limits, the limits necessary for self-sufficiency according to

Aristotle, even though the nature of, and desire for, life is irreducible to the limits that serve life. For the life of money, by contrast, limits are always to be surpassed, and hence the life of money is only well-served when it grows beyond already established limits.

In the *Grundrisse*, Marx will largely restate Aristotle's distinction between natural and unnatural modes of acquisition with his distinction between use value and exchange value. This distinction, moreover, is crucially understood by Marx in terms of the relationship these different values have relative to *determinate* limits. As Marx argues, with echoes of both Locke and Aristotle:

> as representative of the general form of wealth – money – capital is the endless and limitless drive to go beyond its limiting barrier. Every boundary is and has to be a barrier for it. Else it would cease to be capital – money as self-reproductive. If ever it perceived a certain boundary not as a barrier, but became comfortable within it as a boundary, it would itself have declined from exchange value to use value, from the general form of wealth to a specific, substantial mode of the same. Capital as such creates a specific surplus value because it cannot create an infinite one all at once; but it is the constant movement to create more of the same. (Marx 1993, 334)

For Marx, therefore, as for Locke and Aristotle, money has the potential to become problematic as it continuously seeks to transgress already established limits and barriers in its endless pursuit of producing and reproducing 'more of the same'. There is a crucial difference, however, which returns us to Sartre's challenge to Camus – for Marx, the limits capital endlessly seeks 'to go beyond' are precisely the limits capital needs since it 'cannot create an infinite all at once'. These limits are thus immanent to the process of capital accumulation itself, and are in fact necessary to the process according to Marx; for both Aristotle and Locke, by contrast, these limits are imposed from outside, either, for Locke, by a political power that has by virtue of the consent of the governed the right to legislate and control the distribution and limits of property acquisition, or similarly for Aristotle by a deliberative body that reasons in accordance with virtue and recognises the limits within which a polity can function at equilibrium and self-sufficiency. Marx also recognises the importance of, and need for, an intervention external to the processes of capital accumulation that will limit and allay its worst excesses, but these limits are to be distinguished from the limits capital itself needs to continue its endless growth and self-reproduction. The risk for Marx, therefore, is that one confuses the limits capital needs for its continued growth and expansion with the limits that would truly transform, in Marx's terms, exchange value into use value.

We can now return to Sartre's critique of Camus. While Camus was alert to the tendency principles have to lead one to ignore what is happening on the ground, to the point of justifying murder, Sartre is alert to the need to challenge the status quo of the state, with the state being largely a vehicle for the self-reproduction of capital. Stated differently, far from truly limiting the nature of capital accumulation such that exchange value becomes use value, the legislative powers of modern states have provided the conditions and limits capital needs for its self-reproduction. What needs to be done, therefore, and this is central to both Sartre's Marxist critique and to critical existentialism, is to challenge the limits necessary for the self-reproduction of capital in order to affirm the freedom of a life that is irreducible to any determinate limits (life as problem, as *apeiron*). Camus, as we have seen, recognised the problematic nature of existence, and hence the tendencies to move both towards principles that are outside history (dedifferentiating tendency) and towards that which is offered to life as it is unfolding (differentiating tendency). In accusing Camus of being inclined to defend the status quo rather than challenge it, or by casting Camus as bourgeois, Sartre is in effect highlighting the need to challenge the limits the status quo maintains and which ultimately support the processes of capital accumulation and the degradation of human labour and life-activity that goes with these processes.

In these terms then, the task of critical existentialism assumes that, rather than taking barriers to be necessary for the limitless self-reproduction of capital, and thus risk confusing and conflating the limits that promote rather than undo capitalist accumulation, we ought instead to embrace the limitless, the *apeiron*, for the sake of the problematic Idea that is life, or embrace the processes necessary to and inseparable from life. We can clarify this point by noting the difference Marx stresses between how animals and humans create. In the *Economic and Philosophic Manuscripts*, Marx recognises that animals produce: 'They build themselves nests, dwellings, like the bees, beavers, ants, etc.', but, he adds, 'an animal only produces what it immediately needs for itself or its young. It produces one-sidedly, while man produces universally' (Marx 1988, 77). Clarifying what it means for humans to produce universally, Marx claims that while animals produce 'only under the dominion of immediate physical need ... [a human being] produces even when he is free from physical need and only truly produces in freedom therefrom. An animal produces only itself, while man reproduces the whole of nature' (77). To state this in the terms of the critical existentialism we are setting forth, humans produce universally because their productive creativity is a response to a problem, and this entails a process (dedifferentiation) that is irreducible to each of the determinate solutions that come to actualise and express the nature of the problem. Humans produce universally, therefore, not because they possess a determinate universal Idea which they then proceed to instantiate in each of their productions, by the rule-book so to speak; rather, the universal as problem is precisely that which each and every determinate identity presupposes. A production is universal in that every determinate human production presupposes a problem that the determinate production actualises in its determinate way, but the problem is not itself a determinate problem or Idea. Thus, unlike the animals who do set out, according to Marx, to produce that which is necessary to preserve their *determinate* identity, humans only produce universally on the basis of their indeterminate identity, an identity that then becomes a problem which prompts and motivates a productive life-activity that is not predetermined by any identity. Understood in this way, arbitrary power undermines the freedom of life-activity not simply, as was the case for Locke, because this power could at any moment, and without any appeal to a higher standard or law, terminate this life, but rather because this power attempts to predetermine the various ways in which one may engage in one's life-activity. This is an arbitrary power since, rather than allowing and affirming a life-activity that produces universally – where this production is a solution to a problem that remains inseparable from its solutions and thus assures their problematisation and transformation – it instead forces a life-activity to produce in accordance with determinate expectations, roles and narratives that are offered as solutions without a problem, and thus this power arbitrarily eliminates the problematic nature of life itself.

We can now see the significance of what Marx claims is unique about capitalism. In short, whereas Locke claims of the individual labourer that 'The Labour of his Body, and the Work of his Hands, we may say, are properly his' (Locke 1988, §27), Marx argues that capitalism is built upon the alienation of this labour, or the fact that it is the last thing the labourer possesses, and hence in order to live they are forced to sell their labour in exchange for a wage. The human capacity to produce universally is thus no longer that of responding to the problematic nature of one's determinate, embodied life, but rather becomes, under the wage-labour system of capitalism, increasingly predetermined by processes that determine the nature of one's life-activity, and a life-activity that is now geared towards the end of preserving one's determinate identity (putting food on the table) rather than allowing for that identity to become the problem that motivates a creative, free life-activity.

In rethinking the role of capitalism in modern society, then, what is key is precisely the immanent limits to the process of capital accumulation. Although they may be taken to be limits that check the excesses of the capitalist system of wage labour, in the end they may sustain the very system that predetermines the nature of one's life-activity. A critical existentialism, by contrast, will point to the limits necessary for a creative life-activity in order to challenge the status quo, and will attempt to transform the determinate limits that facilitate capitalist accumulation into determinate limits that become the problem to which our creative life-activity responds – responds by developing a taste for the systemic limits and the 'consistence and uniformity' that are necessary for learning (recall §1.3.c). In the context of rethinking law, freedom and progress, therefore, a critical existentialism will consist, in short, of engaging in thinking through life as it is lived along the following lines. With respect to Locke, for instance, the focus would be on the fact that civil law presupposes a limit that is immune to the processes of consent that justify political power – namely, natural law. Moreover, conjugal power also becomes a limit immanent to the processes of capitalist accumulation; that is, the family has become, as Melinda Cooper has shown (see §5.2.a), a limit to capitalism itself, but one that is necessary for the endless process of capitalist self-reproduction. Understood in this way, therefore, the private reserve of the family, a reserve outside the reach of contractual market exchange, is not a check on the growth of market exchange but is rather an instance of an immanent limit necessary to the growth of capital itself. Deleuze and Guattari make much the same point when they claim that capitalism involves 'an awesome schizophrenic accumulation of energy or charge' (Deleuze and Guattari 1977, 34), and it is precisely this schizophrenic energy that is, they argue, 'the exterior limit of capitalism itself or the conclusion of its deepest tendency, but ... capitalism only functions on condition that it inhibit this tendency, or that it push back or displace this limit, by substituting for it its own immanent relative limits, which it continually reproduces on a widened scale' (246). The family is one instance of the immanent limits capital needs. An existential critique of law, therefore, will seek both to identify these relative immanent limits, limits necessary for the functioning and growth of capitalism, and attempt to problematise them, not so that they will further the growth and self-reproduction of capital but rather in order to problematise human life-activity so that one may produce, as Marx put it, universally, or without limits (as *apeiron*).

This brings us to a second idea crucial to the thinking of modern society, including liberalism as Russell understood it (recall the Introduction) – namely, freedom. Developing Marx's theme that one only produces in freedom, or produces universally, on the basis of having already satisfied the needs tied to maintaining one's determinate identity, we can begin to rethink the implications of individual liberty. Stated simply, freedom is not to be understood solely in terms of the freedom to do what is necessary in order to maintain one's determinate self-identity; more importantly, freedom, as Marx understood it, entails producing universally, which in our terms involves living in response to a problem, and thus living in a way that is irreducible to any predetermining template. What such a living may consist of or look like will be discussed below, but before turning to this theme, we should first note that a related idea that is also integral to the self-conception of modern society – progress and prosperity – is also related to the problematic nature of life, but twists it towards furthering the endless growth and accumulation of capital. In particular, the eighteenth-century emphasis upon improvement served to encourage the growth of capital while simultaneously excluding forms of life-activity that do not produce in line with the expectations and needs of self-reproducing capital.

To begin to clarify these points further, we can return to Camus' claim that nihilism involves an 'inability to believe in what is … to live life as it is offered'. I will argue that the key to rethinking law, freedom and progress, and critically evaluating their place within many of the institutions of modern society, is to get lost politically, or get to the point where one cannot place their political direction or goal in the context of 'what is happening'. Problematizing one's determinate identity in order to foster the freedom associated with producing universally will thus result in a state where one has lost one's way, but it is in cases such as this that one is then able to produce universally. In other words, when one has lost one's sense of direction, one's sense of place, such as when lost in a fog for instance, then a consequence is that there are no significant focal points associated with the place where one is and what is happening, and hence the problem is precisely to develop a sense of place and direction and thereby pursue the goals this place makes possible. In living a life as a problem, similarly, there is the necessity of constructing a consistency and uniformity of relations in one's life such that one acquires a sense of what is happening and is thereby able to pursue life goals. In circumstances where boundaries are there simply to be transgressed in order to enable the endless growth of capital, we have a determinate solution to life that provides the problem, or life, with its solution and goal – the goal being to go beyond this barrier! Thus, rather than life as a problem which is inseparable from the determinate goals it makes possible, we have an always determinate barrier which defines in advance the solution to the problem of going beyond this barrier. Stated differently, a critical existentialism sets out to restore the possibility of getting lost, of losing one's sense of direction. When this occurs, two key reactions stand out: one can double down on one's already determined goal and simply navigate the best way there; or one can encounter 'life as it is offered' as a problem, and work to make sense of, and find one's way in, life such that solutions become possible, solutions that further life itself and enable one to create universally – that is, to live solutions that do not arbitrarily extinguish the nature of life as a problem.

b) Wayfinding

When Deleuze comes to name the nature of the encounter with 'life as it is offered', or the encounter with the nature of a problem, he claims that learning is the appropriate name for such an encounter: 'Learning', as we have seen, 'is the appropriate name for the subjective acts carried out when one is confronted with the objecticity [*objectité*] of a problem (Idea), whereas knowledge designates only the generality of concepts or the calm possession of a rule enabling solutions' (Deleuze 1994, 164). Stated differently, learning entails making sense of a problem, or finding one's way and sense of direction in the face of a problem, while knowledge designates the possession of a map whereby one can easily determine the route to take from where one is to where one wants to go. The close linkage we are making between making sense and finding one's way is intentional, and far from arbitrary, as is evident in French where the word *sens* is used for both meaning and direction. Moreover, both processes – making sense and finding one's way – involve the double movement of de/differentiation. Just as in learning to swim, returning to Deleuze's example, where one must both dedifferentiate existing habits and movements of the body – unlearn so to speak – in order to increasingly differentiate between the determinate movements and relations that are and are not relevant to acquiring the know-how of swimming, so too making sense involves dedifferentiating the context of utterance or circumstance that is meaningful so that one can differentiate and iterate other determinate instances of meaning; and so too, finally, as we will now see, in finding one's way and sense of direction one must both dedifferentiate from one's determinate location, and from the determinate sights visible from that location, in order to increasingly differentiate locations other than the current one.

With this understanding of finding one's way, we can come to a better understanding of one of the central debates regarding wayfinding. This is the debate over whether acquiring a sense of direction – a wayfinding ability – involves route knowledge or survey knowledge; or, stated another way, the question is over the role, if any, cognitive maps play in processes of wayfinding. The term cognitive map was first used by Edward Tolman (Tolman 1948). In an experiment with rats, Tolman constructed an elaborate apparatus that would lead the rats to food, though in a series of detours that initially led away from the food. Tolman then later placed the rats in a different apparatus, this time with a series of short-cuts that led to the food in addition to the initial detoured path. Among the series of short-cut paths, one led straight to the food, and Tolman's experiments showed that nearly all the rats took this more direct path to the food rather than the detoured path, even though they had never taken it before. The conclusion Tolman draws is that the rats had acquired a cognitive map of the food's location and used this map to navigate among the short-cuts to determine the more direct route to the food, even though they had not taken this route before. In a more recent example in support of cognitive maps, Kirill Istomin and Mark Dwyer (2009) construct a scenario where a person is taken from a hotel to a conference venue, with the hotel at the top right of a V-shaped configuration of streets and the conference venue at the bottom point of the V, and then later led from the conference venue to a restaurant at the top left of the V. The question Istomin and Dwyer ask is whether this person, on the following day for instance, could find their way directly from the hotel to the restaurant by taking the street that runs across the top of the V. They argue that the person could, but only because they have a cognitive map of where the restaurant is relative to the hotel, much as the rat has a cognitive map of the location of the food relative to where they are. For theorists such as Tim Ingold, however, there are no such cognitive maps, and wayfinding is made possible by a series of journeys through routes, routes that create a collage that allows one to find one's way. For Istomin and Dwyer, 'from the viewpoint of Ingold's theory, the man would be unable to select the unknown route' (2009, 32). Since the direct route from the hotel to the restaurant had never been traversed, the person attending the conference would not, on Ingold's theory according to Istomin and Dwyer, think to consider this route.

Despite Istomin and Dwyer's critique of Ingold, his position has a number of proponents who are not moved by these criticisms. Ingold, for instance, states his position quite forcefully, saying with respect to a cognitive map that 'there is no such map, and that the belief in its existence is a consequence of the mistaken attribution to native people of a sense of what it means to know one's whereabouts that effectively treats them as strangers in their own country' (Ingold 2000, 219). In other words, whereas one who is new to a territory may bring a map and use this to 'know one's whereabouts', this is not how natives acquire their sense of direction and wayfinding ability. For Ingold, the maps we use to orient ourselves within and navigate around a territory are an abstraction from the processes involved in wayfinding, and it is a mistake to project this abstraction onto the actual processes involved in coming to 'know one's whereabouts'. For Ingold, what is crucial to wayfinding is the process of moving from place to place, and 'places exist', he claims, 'not in space but as nodes in a matrix of movement. I shall call this matrix a "region"' (219). Wayfinding is thus, Ingold concludes, a process that 'more closely resembles storytelling than map-using. To use a map is to navigate by means of it: that is, to plot a course from one location to another in space. Wayfinding, by contrast, is a matter of moving from one place to another in a region' (219). To navigate is to have an already determinate representation or map of a territory, to determine one's location on this map, and then to determine or plot the course to the destination one wants to arrive at. Wayfinding, by contrast, involves a process of moving from place to place during which one continually updates one's trajectory based on the differential of that which has changed and that which has remained invariant.

On this latter point, Ingold follows Harry Heft's adaptation of Gibson's ecological theory of perception. Developing Gibson's claim that there is 'a kind of essential structure [that] underlies the superficial structure of an array when the point of observation moves' (Gibson 2014, 73), Heft argues that in wayfinding this becomes manifest as the distinction between '*perspective information* corresponding to the perceiver's own movements, and *invariant information* corresponding to persisting properties of environmental features' (Heft 1996, 110). As one moves through a place, the invariant information emerges in relation to the changing perspectives that come with one's movement. Wayfinding thus develops, according to Heft, through a process of encountering vistas and transitions. The vistas are the invariant structures that persist through our movements – the street ahead that remains invariant as we pass the buildings and storefronts on the street – and the transitions occur when the vistas themselves change – such as, for instance, when we turn off the road and see the hills in the distance that were previously hidden behind the buildings. Heft claims that, through a history of moving around from place to place, we come to know an invariant relative to the changing perspectives. As he puts it, 'it is justifiable to say that one can perceive the overall layout or configuration of the environment because this invariant structure can be detected or revealed as information in the context of changing perspective structure' (126). In other words, wayfinding entails a differential of the variable and changing, on the one hand, and the invariant and unchanging on the other. There is thus no pure movement, no movement that does not already presuppose the invariant structure relative to which the movement is recognised as movement; and similarly there is no pure invariant structure, or an unchanging structure that is not susceptible to revision, to discoveries along the way that alter the sense of what is invariant and unchanging relative to what is changing. Stated in our terms, wayfinding entails the double movement of making sense, the movement of dedifferentiation, or that which is unchanging and invariant relative to the differentiated perspectives one encounters along one's way, and the movement of differentiation, the differentiation of that which changes relative to the invariant. Ingold refers to this process of wayfinding as mapping, and he contrasts it to navigation, which is map-using (Ingold 2000, 231). In mapping, Ingold claims, one finds one's way through a process of orienting oneself with respect to invariant structures, but these invariant structures are not maps, representations of an already completed

165

and determinate space, since they are themselves inseparable from the process of wayfinding. Cognitive maps, and the maps one uses in navigating, are abstractions from this process of wayfinding. It is this abstraction that results in what Ingold calls the 'cartographic illusion', or 'the illusion [whereby] ... the form of the map arises, in mapmaking, as a direct transcription of the layout of the world' (234).

Returning now to Istomin and Dwyer's critique of Ingold, we can see that it can be reread in light of our understanding of the de/differentiating tendencies of making sense and as a result we can give credit to their arguments while also recognising the key points that Heft and Ingold make. In particular, a key claim in Istomin and Dwyer's argument is that 'the practical-mastery theory with its explicit denial of nonindexical cognitive representations', or more precisely Ingold's claim that there are no cognitive maps, 'cannot account for the whole range of wayfinding abilities that humans demonstrate' (Istomin and Dwyer 2009, 31). We saw earlier, for instance, that on Istomin and Dwyer's account Ingold cannot explain how the conference attendee would be able to find their way directly from the hotel to the restaurant if they had never actually taken that direct route. We can now see how, based on the variable/invariant differential of wayfinding, the attendee could indeed find their way. During their earlier trips from the hotel to the conference venue, and then from the venue to the restaurant, an invariant structure emerged as one of the tendencies that make sense of where one is, and it is this invariant structure that enables the conference attendee to find their way directly from the hotel to the restaurant. This invariant structure, as we have argued, is not an always already predetermined and predetermining space that a map merely represents, but is rather an emergent structure that is inseparable from the changing, variable differentiations that attend one's movements from place to place. Istomin and Dwyer are thus correct to conclude that 'Human wayfinding is based on both mental maps and the temporally ordered sequences of vistas and linkages' (36). This conclusion, however, is to be understood in terms of the double movement of making sense, otherwise the 'cartographic illusion' emerges when, as Ingold argues, we take a map to be an already complete and determinate representation of an always already available and determinate space.

To restate Ingold's distinction between mapping and mapmaking, and more importantly the problem he has with the 'cartographic illusion' associated with mapmaking, we could say that whereas mapping always entails the possibility of getting lost, mapmaking does not because maps are presented as solutions without a problem. With a map, the goal is already determined and mapped, along with where one is located on the map, and thus one can simply plot a course to get to where one wants to go without getting lost. Mapping, by contrast, is to be understood as an encounter with a problem, the problem of making sense of a place, and as such it entails both the possibility of doubling down on already established forms of wayfinding – established routes, etc. – and the possibility of getting lost amidst the vast array of focal points within the environment that cannot be placed, that do not come to form the consistence and uniformity necessary to develop a sense of where one is, a sense of place and direction. As we return again to Adorno's critical theory we will see that here too what is important is the possibility of becoming lost, of losing oneself in modern society, and it is this possibility that will serve as the basis for a critique of the illusions associated with key components of modern society – namely, law, freedom and progress.

c) ... à fond perdu

As we saw earlier, Adorno was also aware of the tendency to illusions, and he directed his critical analysis in particular towards the illusion that comes with the production of exchange value. As Gillian Rose summarised the illusion, in essence it boils down to the exchange value of a commodity being taken to be an actual property of this commodity, or as she puts it, 'exchange value appears to be a real attribute of commodities although it is not a real attribute' (Rose 1978, 28). Challenging this illusion, however, does not consist for Adorno in simply pointing out that exchange value is not an actual property of the commodity, or that exchange value is fundamentally different from use value. Although Adorno will claim that such statements are true, and will state them himself on occasion, one cannot then take refuge in some straightforward thinking that identifies an object stripped of illusion, enabling one thereby to discern the true nature and value of the thing itself. In fact, for Adorno the very effort to think and identify brings with it the very tendency to undermine precisely that which comes to be thought and identified. As we saw, Adorno claims that 'Every entity is more than it is' (Adorno 1973, 102), and thus to 'comprehend a thing itself ... is nothing but to perceive the individual moment in its immanent connection with others' (25); that is, to think and come to identify the nature of any determinate thing (recall Adorno's claim that 'to think is to identify' [5]) involves delving into the immanent connections this thing has with that which is more than it. This was why Adorno claimed that 'a cognition that is to bear fruit will throw itself to the object à fond perdu' (33), and thus will risk losing the very identity of that which it has attempted to think. If one sets out in an effort to think something, to identify the true, non-illusory nature of something – to distinguish use value from exchange value for instance – and if this thought

167

'bears fruit', then the identity of that which is thought becomes lost (hence the phrase, *à fond perdu*) in the vertigo of immanent relations, in an infinite regress of the more to be thought.

To state Adorno's point in the terms we have been developing here: in attempting to make sense of the thing, one follows both the movement of differentiation, following the infinite regress of immanent connections, and the movement of dedifferentiation by undermining the very identity of the thing one has attempted to think. The resulting vertigo that comes with 'a cognition that is to bear fruit', Adorno concludes, ought to lead to a 'changed philosophy', a philosophy that no longer believes it can possess the infinite in thought but is rather a 'changed philosophy [that] itself would be infinite in the sense of scorning solidification in a body of enumerable theorems' (Adorno 1973, 13). The attempt to solidify the infinite through 'a body of enumerable theorems' expresses the differentiating movement of making sense, a movement towards what Adorno claims is the demand of 'traditional thinking' whereby there is a 'frame of reference in which all things have their place. Not too much importance is attached to the intelligibility of the frame – it may even be laid down in dogmatic axioms – if only each reflection can be localized, and if unframed thoughts are kept out' (32–3). Whether we are dealing with narratives, maps, facts or thinking, they are each part of the tendency to delimit, frame and find a place for that which is being differentiated, and differentiated *ad infinitum*. At the same time, however, and as with wayfinding, this movement also entails the dedifferentiating tendency whereby one can get lost, or encounter the nature of a problem that is not to be confused and conflated with anything determinate. Finding one's way and making sense of things, therefore, entails bringing the paradoxical de/differentiation tendencies into a consistence and uniformity that allows for the possibility of something new, of establishing one's territory, or, finally, the possibility of learning.

With the concept of learning (as discussed earlier [see §1.3.c]), we can return to the theme of discerning the difference between the limits necessary to the endless growth and self-reproduction of capital and the limits necessary to affirming life as a problem, or as we would now put it, learning. With Deleuze's example of learning to swim, we have already noted that the double tendencies of de/differentiation are involved, an unlearning (dedifferentiation) of differentiated habits and bodily relations *and* an increased differentiation of elements relevant to the nature of the problem that is learning to swim; however, if one is to acquire the skill of learning to swim then the differentiated elements *relevant* to that skill need to be brought into a system of mutual, reciprocal relations with one another (what Deleuze and Guattari [1987] will call a plane of consistency). If the elements are not brought into a systemic set of relations, if they continue to exceed the limits necessary to construct the consistence and uniformity that enable learning, then learning will not be possible. One may become overwhelmed by the many elements one encounters when in the water, unable to separate the relevant from the irrelevant, and if that is the case then one will fail to learn to swim.

With Deleuze's claim that learning 'is the appropriate name for the subjective acts carried out when one is confronted with the objectivity [*objectité*] of a problem (Idea), whereas knowledge designates only the generality of concepts or the calm possession of a rule enabling solutions' (Deleuze 1994, 164), we can now better distinguish between the limits necessary to learning and the illusory limits necessary for the endless growth and reproduction of exchange value. If we take the case of knowledge, 'or the calm possession of a rule enabling solutions' as Deleuze puts it, then this rule can enable solutions precisely because it predetermines the path to them, and thus a problem has no independent reality and is instead subservient to the solution that has been enabled by the rule. For example, if we were to instruct someone who wants to learn to drive a stick shift car, we could perhaps offer, as a guide or set of rules, the following nine-step sequence:[1]

1. Press the clutch all the way to the floor board with your left foot (the gear shifter must be in the neutral position).
2. **Turn the ignition key**. If you are certain that the car is in neutral, you can remove your foot from the clutch.
3. **Press the brake**, or the center pedal, with your right foot.
4. **Position the gear shifter** so that the transmission is in the first gear.
5. **Remove your right foot from the brake pedal**. If you are on a flat surface, the vehicle should move very little.
6. **Slowly begin to place less pressure on the clutch** with your left foot. Depending on the vehicle, you may feel it begin to slowly roll forward.
7. As you gently release the clutch, **begin to press the accelerator** very delicately with your right foot.
8. Once you have released the clutch completely, you should now only be pressing the accelerator with your right foot. Congratulations – you're driving in first gear. Continue to build speed until you feel that you need to shift into second gear.
9. To switch to second gear, take your right foot off of the accelerator while simultaneously activating the clutch with your left foot. Move the gear shifter into second gear. Release the clutch as you begin to apply the accelerator again. Repeat this process to continue to build speed.

---

1. From the website: https://driving-tests.org/beginner-drivers/how-to-drive-a-stick-shift.

Stated in this form – and they could very well be stated even more simply, or more elaborately – the rules already presuppose that one has identified the key elements of the encounter that are relevant to learning to drive a stick shift. The clutch, gear stick, neutral position, brake, accelerator, whether one is on a flat surface, etc., must all be identified if one is then to follow the sequence of bringing these elements together in the sequence set out by the rules. Anyone who has learned to drive a stick shift car, however, will know that it is much more complicated than simply following these rules. The actual process of coordinating the elements in a fluid motion without stalling the car, or starting the car on an incline, addressing the idiosyncrasies that come with different cars, etc., all add difficulties to the learning process that elude the simplicity of these steps. This is the sense in which rules are derivative of the learning process; in other words, the learning that occurs when one is 'confronted with the objecticity of a problem' becomes the basis for the rules which abstract from this process. The illusory nature of the rules is thus not that they have no basis in the reality of the process or problem that is learning; rather, as with the cartographic illusion Ingold discusses, the illusion comes in when the rules are taken to exist independently of the process of learning, with learning taken to be merely the means to realise an already predetermined end or goal by way of following the rules and getting it right. The illusion, in other words, is to think of rules as being solutions without a problem, where the problem is simply the problem of realising an already predetermined and established solution. Rather than these rules being the effect or expression of the problems these solutions give voice to, the illusion is to think that problems are the effects of solutions, mere shadows of the solutions they facilitate.

Adorno's critique of capitalism and the processes tied to the production of exchange value can now be restated in light of what we have argued regarding the illusory nature of solutions without problems. As we saw earlier, Adorno develops Marx's argument from the *Grundrisse* that if ever the growth of money 'perceived a certain boundary not as a barrier, but became comfortable within it as a boundary, it would itself have declined from exchange value to use value' (Marx 1993, 334). We can now add to Adorno's claim that 'in advanced capitalist society an illusion of pure use-value … has been substituted for pure exchange-value. This exchange-value has deceptively taken over the function of use-value' (cited by Rose 1978, 63). In particular, we can bring to bear the distinction between the limits necessary for learning and the limits necessary for the endless growth of capital. More precisely, use value can be understood in terms of the relevant elements that come to construct the limits (plane of consistency) necessary to learning, while exchange value provides the already determined limits which prefigure the process whereby these limits come to be the barriers that are transgressed. Such limits may include, among many other things, the interest rate on debt, a rate that pre-determines the minimal amount of growth one must seek in order to pay the interest; the rate of shareholder value relative to one's corporate peers; and profit margins which corporations can then seek to increase, through monopolising growth, or allow to decline but increase overall profits through economies of scale, etc. In each case, a determinate, quantitative limit or set of limits establishes the standard or rules that enable the various attempts to solve the problem of maximising growth and profits. Where this becomes illusory, or the 'illusion of pure use-value' as Adorno puts it, is when a deter-minate exchange value is thought to be nothing less than the use-value of the commodity, where in reality the 'exchange-value has deceptively taken over the function of use-value'.

For Ingold the cartographic illusion arises when one takes a cognitive map to be a reality independent of the wayfinding, route-exploring processes that give rise to mapping as an emergent property of these processes; similarly, for Adorno, the illusion occurs when an abstract equivalent is taken to be a real property of the commodity when it is an emergent property of actual life practices. Stated differently, exchange values, maps, nine-step guides to driving a stick shift car, etc., are among the many things that are incor-porated into processes of making sense of one's world. The illusion arises when the process of making sense is taken to be predetermined by an already determinate map, exchange value, rule, etc., when the nature of these deter-minates ultimately presupposes the nature of a problem that is inseparable from processes of learning and making sense. One may take up a map, a price, a rule, etc., in attempting to make sense and learn in the confrontation with a problem, but the problem remains inseparable from that which is learned, including the maps, rules and exchange values that may then come to be confused (this is the illusion) with the process of making sense.

These illusions become more pressing when we see how they have come to play a role in perpetuating socio-economic inequalities. To see the way in which maps, for instance, can play a determinative role in shaping socio-economic realities, or in reinforcing racial biases, is rather straightfor-ward – namely, rather than accept the cartographic illusion and assume that a map is simply a representation of an already existing socio-economic space, a map can and should instead be seen as inseparable from processes of making sense of a socio-economic space. In his book, *Rethinking the Power of Maps*, Denis Wood offers a theory of maps that avoids the cartographic illusion and accounts for the manner in which maps express and enact power relations. At the basis of Wood's theory is the notion that 'maps are systems of proposi-tions', where for Wood 'a proposition is nothing more than a statement that affirms (or denies) the existence of something' (Wood 2010, 34). The manner in which a map affirms or denies something, moreover, consists for Wood of the signs of which 'maps are necessarily composed ... [and] where signs are unions of signifieds (the subject of the proposition, say the state) and signifiers (the marks put down on the paper, say the lines supposed to be the borders). The signifieds and the signifier are united by a code' (36). And a code, finally, is for Wood an 'assignment scheme (or rule) that couples items or elements from a conveyed system (the signified) to a conveying system (the signifier)' (78). Stated in the terms we have been using here, a code or assignment scheme is simply the process of making sense, the narrativising process (or melodying for Sudnow), which allows for the possibility of the distinction between, and hence the relationship between, the signifiers and signifieds of a map, much as making sense allows for the possibility of the distinction and relationship between knowledge (a rule, universal, principle, etc.) and that which is done in accordance with it (actions, etc.), a narrative and the events the narrative represents (or, finally, the musical score and playing the score). Codes, therefore, make sense of a map but are not to be reduced to the map itself, to either the signifier or signified, or to a supposed reality the map represents.

2016 Presidential Election Results by County[2]

---

2. This and the following map were created by Mark Newman, University of Michigan, at http://www-personal.umich.edu/~mejn/election/2016.

To clarify, let us take as an example the accompanying map of the 2016 presidential election. In Wood's terms, this map is a proposition that affirms (or denies) something, and does so through signs, which in this case consist of a union of signifieds (the results of the 2016 presidential election by county) and signifiers (a standard map projection of the United States with counties coloured red for counties carried by the Republican candidate [Trump] and blue for those carried by the Democratic candidate [Clinton]). What this map affirms or denies, however, is integrally tied to the code that allows us to make sense of this map. In particular, the code in this case is precisely the assignment scheme that brings the signifier and signified together with the result that the map appears to be dominated by Republican victories. It is not surprising that Donald Trump brings this map out to show how widespread his support is throughout the country. The illusion, however, is to assume that this map represents the reality as it is, independent of the processes (or codes) whereby one makes sense of reality. As has been argued throughout this book, the nature of a problem and making sense does not predetermine the solutions that give voice to this problem, or that which makes sense, and a given solution does not foreclose the possibility of other solutions, unless of course one remains beholden to the illusion that the given solution is a solution without a problem. In the case of Trump's favoured map, a different code could well have been used to make sense of the election results.

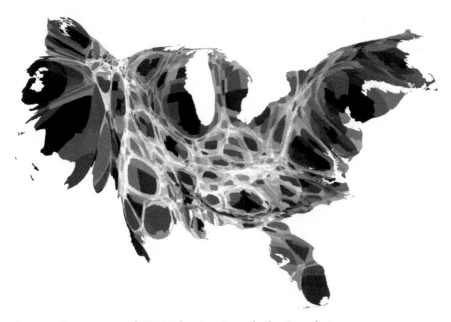

County Cartogram of 2016 Election Results by Population

In our alternative 'County Cartogram' map, for instance, the code that unites signifier and signified works by representing both the population sizes and vote counts of each county. Counties are thus enlarged or shrunk, relative to one another, depending on their population, and the election results are shaded from red to blue to reflect the majorities with which the candidates won the county. In contrast to Trump's favoured map, this one shows a more equal distribution of the electorate. It could be argued that this map more accurately represents the reality of the 2016 election, but we must be careful not to reify the reality this map is taken to represent. As many political scientists and commentators will remind us, the actual vote count represents only a slice of the population that is eligible to vote, nor does the map represent the interests of all residents in the country – of imprisoned felons (as well as most felons who have served their time) and non-citizen immigrants for instance. To recall our earlier discussion of conspiracy theories, however, the point we stressed there was that a conspiracy theory represents a reality as a solution without a problem, predetermining in advance what can or cannot be included in its narrative account. With respect to the two maps discussed here, it would be hyperbole to claim the first is a conspiracy theory and the second not, since they both code the election results; the difference between them, however, is that the first map includes less information than the second, and thus it excludes from its coding more of the ways in which it is possible to make sense of the election results. The second map also excludes elements as well, as we noted, but it does undermine the claims of those who would use the first map to support a particular political narrative – namely, that the United States is a conservative, republican nation with the exception of pockets of liberals in the large cities on the coasts.

This brings us back to the difference between the limits necessary for learning and those necessary for the growth of capital. A similar distinction was made in our discussion of conspiracy theories between narratives that predetermine what can or cannot be included and those which affirm the problem that is at the heart of making sense. Understood in this way maps can either affirm the problematic nature at the heart of mapping, and hence affirm the provisional nature of the map – a good faith map – or they can represent reality as a fait accompli – a bad faith map. Stated in Adorno's terms, a map may accept and perhaps even prompt a further thinking of the relations between elements, of the immanent connections that may, when thought through, undermine the original identity as represented by the map (à fond perdu); or a map may cut off the thought of those immanent connections beyond that which is given and reduce thought to that which is framed and represented by the map. When used for political purposes, the latter type of map can be used to reinforce and perpetuate existing inequalities and

prejudices. If we take the redlining maps the Home Owners' Loan Corpora-
tion (HOLC) used from the 1930s to the early 1950s, for example, they
reinforced and perpetuated the existing segregation of urban neighbourhoods
by designating primarily minority neighbourhoods as being at high risk of
loan default, and represented such neighbourhoods in red (as in the accompanying redlining map from Atlanta). Since the express purpose of such maps
was to highlight areas where loans would be at greater risk of default, those
living in redlined neighbourhoods were often denied access to home loans
and capital investment. Moreover, most of the neighbourhoods the HOLC
graded as high risk are still, more than eighty years later, predominantly
minority and of low to moderate income.

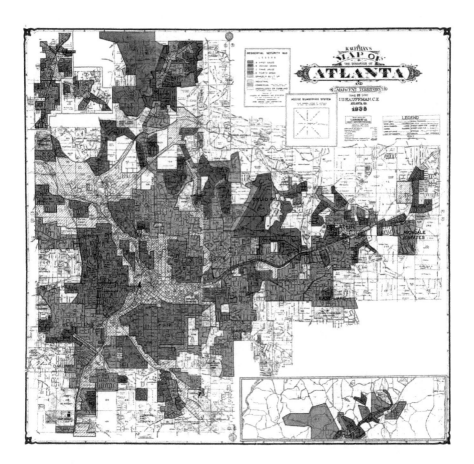

1938 HOLC Map for Atlanta[3]

---

3. This map is from the National Community Reinvestment Coalition website, at https://
ncrc.org/holc.

Rather than assume, however, that these maps represent actual risks which fully justify the practices of lending institutions, a critical existentialism would affirm the problem inseparable from the maps in order to force a thinking that may reveal alternative solutions to the problem, solutions other than those that were actually implemented. For instance, we can take as a case in point the role the family plays in the HOLC maps. On the surface the redlining maps simply highlight the relative degree of risk associated with the areas represented on the map. If we push the analysis, however, and ask why the redlined areas consist of predominantly black neighbourhoods, we can begin to see that what is at stake here is not simply an economic mapping but an expression of political power. As was discussed earlier, a founding principle of political power in the liberal tradition since Locke is that it differs from conjugal power. As Locke argues, conjugal power ends with the age of reason, with the age when a child becomes an adult who can make decisions for themselves, and it is here that political power acquires its legitimacy when these adults grant their consent to those who govern them. Political power thus presupposes conjugal relations – the families that raise children to adulthood. As the source of those who, by giving their consent, give legitimacy to political power, the family is the condition for differentiating between arbitrary and non-arbitrary exercises of power. Within the family, the father, and for Locke this meant the white, property-holding father, is able to maintain arbitrary power over his children, within the limits of natural law. The family thus serves as an independent source of political legitimacy, and for Locke (and much of modern society) a source that continues to limit the extent and reach of political power. Minorities, however, and especially black minorities, have often been excluded from the traditional relationship between conjugal and political power, and by extension from the endless growth of capital that political power facilitates. The HOLC redlining maps are a symptom of this more pervasive tendency. Stated in the terms developed here, and to be developed more fully below, the family can be understood to be a problem that is given voice and expressed in the various political solutions. Inseparable from the political, therefore, is the family – or household management (οίκονομία [from which we get the word 'economy'] as Aristotle discusses this (in *Politics* 1253b) – and thus politics is always already political economy. The family, as the social, as οίκονομία, can be the basis, as Marx argued, for a life-activity that produces universally (as *apeiron*), or it can be understood to be the already determinate limit that defines the agenda and goals for political power, the solution to every problem – the solution without a problem – and as such the family can also become the cartographic illusion one uses to identify and navigate one's way through the political landscape. From the time of Locke, as we shall see, discussions of political power have grappled with such illusions. It is to this that we now turn.

2. Pure Market Illusions

a) A family affair

In thinking through the implications of the claim that the family, or οἰκονομία, is a problem that is given voice and expressed in various political solutions, we can return to our earlier theme of confronting and thinking the nature of problems. Stated simply, the nature of a problem could be thought in terms of two abstractions, which are abstractions because they are thought of as separate from the processual reality that is the nature of a problem. At one end is the problem as a differentiating means to a determinate end or solution, or to one of many possible solutions. Learning to drive a stick shift car, for instance, or discovering the solution to a math problem, or tying one's shoes, or finding the best way to hike to the peak of a mountain, can all be taken to be determinate goals, where the problem is one of determining the means relevant to actualising the goal in each case. There may be more than one way to achieve the goal – hence the cliché that 'there's more than one path to the top of the mountain' – but the problem in these cases is sub-servient to the realisation of a solution that determines the very nature of the problem itself. At the dedifferentiating end of the continuum, the nature of a problem is not to be confused with a determinate solution, or a solution that predetermines the very nature of the problem itself such that the problem becomes simply a means to actualising the solution; to the contrary, the determinate solutions are made possible by the nature of the problem these solutions express without eliminating the nature of the problem. In other words, the solutions which express and give voice to the nature of a problem do not exhaust the problem which remains inseparable from the solutions themselves. Solutions are thus provisional and forever open to becoming problematised and transformed into yet other solutions. In contrast to the cliché of there being more than one path to the top of the mountain, where the top is the already identified and determinate solution to the problem, the nature of problems at the other end of the continuum is precisely what gives rise to the determinate solutions themselves, and these solutions are not predetermined. These two ends of the continuum, however, are ab-stractions. There is no determinate solution that completely predetermines the nature of a problem, and that does so such that the problem vanishes with the solution. Similarly, there is no pure problem that is completely

177

independent of determinate solutions. We can refer to these two abstractions as the illusions of pure solutions and pure problems, but this is simply another version of taking the de/differentiating tendencies of making sense as tendencies that have goals distinct from and transcendent to the tendencies themselves, the tendency to the abstract and universal rule on the one hand, and the tendency to the concrete and particular on the other.

Moving now to the political implications of these two illusions, we can begin, as Aristotle does, with the concern for the household maintenance of the family (οίκονομία).[4] The family, on the account offered here, is a problem that is given voice by the various forms of political power, forms that serve as solutions to the problem. Understood in this way, the family as problem can be taken to be either subservient to the determinate goals and solutions embodied in the various forms of political power, or it can be taken to be the reality that is not to be confused with any of the various forms of political power. If taken in either way, and thus as abstractions that are realised and independent from one another, then, as with the illusions of pure solutions and pure problems, we have in this case what we could call the illusions of pure politics and pure sociality. In the case of pure politics, the social is the problem that comes to be solved through the determinate nature and will of the sovereign, such as the monarch for Hobbes or the will and consent of the governed for Locke, a will instantiated and codified in the law (to be discussed below in §5.2.c). For both Hobbes and Locke, for instance, these solutions are already predetermined by the determinate law of nature that commands us and gives us the right as individuals living in a problematic relation with others (namely, in a state of war) to do that which is necessary for our *self*-preservation. The political solution to this problem is also made possible by the determinate faculty of reason that both enables us to grasp the law of nature and to consent to giving up some of our individual rights to political power for the sake of peace, security and the common good. The political solution, however, does not exhaust the nature of the social, or οίκονομία, as problem, as the illusion of pure politics would have it, and thus political solutions, as history bears frequent evidence to, will presuppose their own problematisation. At the same time, the problematic reality of the social is not an independent reality to be thought of as distinct from the solutions it makes possible. There is no pure state of nature, no utopian social gathering of noble savages distinct from the various forms of political power, nor, as the illusion of pure sociality would have it, does the social provide the basis for the solution to all our problems and the standard by which such solutions are to be judged.

---

4. See Aristotle's *Politics* 1252a (Book 1, ch. 1), and 1259b (Book 1, ch. 13).

To clarify the role these two illusions have played in political thought generally, and in particular in the theoretical underpinnings of modern liberalism as Russell understands it (recall the Introduction), we can focus on the role of the family in society and politics. On the one hand, the family can be seen as the problem which anticipates the political solution that resolves the problem (illusion of pure politics); on the other hand, the family can be seen as that which is distinct from and irreducible to the various forms of political power that emerge (illusion of pure sociality). As we saw, the problem of self-preservation – or more exactly the problem of self-preservation in a social context where all individuals have the same right to seek self-preservation (and hence the state of war for Hobbes) – is a problem that comes to be solved for Locke by the consent of rational adults; that is, by those who are no longer minors dependent upon their parents. This solution to the social as problem, to the problem of the state of war, is thus already predetermined by the very nature of rational, self-directed individuals, and the problem ideally vanishes with the emergence of a political power that is legitimised by the consent of such rational individuals (illusion of pure politics). On the other hand, the family is often held to be a reality that refuses to be absorbed by the political power it prepares the way for, a reality that falls outside the purview of important aspects of political power and yet provides the ideal model, in many key ways, for political action (illusion of pure sociality). The interaction and debates that arise from these two illusions will become manifest in various ways as various political systems take hold, such as in determining where the line is to be drawn between family and politics, where the affairs of the family are to be left untouched by those who wield political power, or where political power can or cannot act in defence of the family.

In his book, *The Great Transformation*, Karl Polanyi highlighted key aspects of modern society that resonate with the dual illusions we claim are natural by-products of the dual de/differentiating tendencies of making sense. In light of our earlier discussion of Ellen Wood's claims regarding the capitalist 'laws of motion' (Wood 2002, 16; recall §3.1.b), we can see that the compulsion of competitive markets to endlessly pursue growth and the self-reproduction of capital leads to the differentiation of markets and commodities, and in the process dedifferentiates the identity of many already established systems, including the family and other traditional social forms. This latter point is precisely what Polanyi stresses, and it is integral to his argument regarding the double movement that occurs with the rise of capitalism and its dependency on markets. As Polanyi puts it, with respect to 'Social history in the nineteenth century':

> While on the one hand markets spread all over the face of the globe and the amount of goods involved grew to unbelievable dimensions, on the other

hand a network of measures and policies was integrated into powerful institutions designed to check the action of the market relative to labor, land, and money ... a deep-seated movement sprang itself into being to resist the pernicious effects of a market-controlled economy. Society protected itself against the perils inherent in a self-regulating market system. (Polanyi 2001, 79–80)

Polanyi argues that for the apologists of self-regulating markets – such as Herbert Spencer, William Graham Sumner, Ludwig von Mises and Walter Lippman – the inevitable road to social progress 'was stopped by the realistic self-protection of society', though this was only realistic by Polanyi's lights, since the apologists claimed that such protective measures were 'a mistake due to impatience, greed, and shortsightedness, but for which the market would have resolved its difficulties' (148). Had society simply allowed self-regulating markets to progress unimpeded, the concerns that motivated its self-protective efforts would have been addressed by the markets themselves. For Polanyi, the 'question as to which of these two views' – self-regulating markets or self-protecting society – 'is correct is perhaps the most important problem of recent social history' (148). From Polanyi's perspective, however, 'Our own interpretation of the double movement ... is borne out by the evidence' (156). As he points out, 'the behavior of liberals themselves proved that the maintenance of freedom of trade – in our terms, of a self-regulating market – far from excluding intervention, in effect, demanded such action, and that liberals themselves regularly called for compulsory action on the part of the state' (157). Stated in the terms we used earlier, the very growth and self-reproduction of capital requires its own immanent limits, and thus self-regulating markets looked to political power in order to provide these limits, such as when England limited the development of Irish agriculture in the seventeenth century (recall §3.1.b), among many other instances (discussed below, §5.2.c). To state this process yet again, but this time in terms of the illusions of pure sociality and pure politics: the illusion of pure sociality appeals to a family that falls outside the realm of economic exchange, a realm not subservient to a self-regulating market, and it is this pure sociality that seeks protection; the illusion of pure politics appeals to a family that warrants and facilitates the measures taken by political power to further and protect the developing property holdings and contracts of consenting individuals.

This last point has been developed at length by Melinda Cooper in her book, *Family Values*. In turning to this book now we can further clarify the distinction between the limits necessary for the endless growth and reproduction of capital *and* the limits necessary for learning, or for producing universally in Marx's sense. Put simply, whereas the limit that learning requires is the consistency and uniformity of relations necessary to make possible the emergence of a new skill and the rule-type knowledge that comes with this, the limit necessary for the endless growth of capital is already determinate and known, being the limit that directs the flows of capital to already determined locations and places. It was precisely the protection of the flow of capital wealth to already determined places, and the reliance upon the state for providing such protection, that Polanyi stressed in defence of his concept of the double movement of recent social history. In contrast to the limits necessary for the endless growth of capital, and for what Marx called an economy of exchange value, there are the use values that emerge through social processes themselves rather than predetermining such processes. Such social processes do not remain untouched by or uninvolved in the determinate expectations and processes of economic and political power – hence avoiding the illusion of pure sociality – and yet a critical existentialism which problematises established political and economic relations by way of the limits necessary for the learning that is inseparable from social processes may well reveal the limits and determinate biases that serve to legitimate political power – hence avoiding the illusion of pure politics. Restating this point in terms of Polanyi's notion of double movement, the social and the political, the non-economic and the economic (or, better, political economy), both express the dual tendencies of making sense, and hence the processes associated with making sense of capital, especially given the social nature of capital (following Marx's theory of primitive accumulation [recall 3.1.b]). This will be precisely Melinda Cooper's point as well, and her reading of Polanyi looms large in her book, where a central theme is 'that what Polanyi calls the "double movement" would be better understood as fully internal to the dynamic of capital' (Cooper 2017, 15). More precisely, and turning her attention to the family, Cooper argues that 'The Polanyian social democrat shares the conservative's nostalgia for community, land, and family, but seeks to transform these institutions into conduits for state-based forms of social protection' (15). The need for social protection, however, is according to Cooper a need immanent to the processes of capitalism itself, to its double tendency of making sense, and not a need that calls upon protections external to capitalist processes, or the protections that Polanyi calls for. This is not to say that external protections are unnecessary, but since, as Cooper argues, the family becomes both that which needs to be protected from the effects of capitalism while also being that which facilitates the growth of capital itself, one may well confuse and confound external protections *against* capitalism with the very limits necessary for the endless accumulation of capital itself.

The historical background for Cooper's argument, to state it briefly, is that more people began to enter the workforce in the 1960s, especially blacks and women, just as economic growth was slowing and it was becoming increasingly difficult for a single wage-earner to support a family (what Cooper refers to as the Fordist family wage); the result was a perceived crisis concerning the proper role of the welfare state. Of noted relevance to this, according to Cooper, was the controversy surrounding the undue influence of one particular welfare program – namely, the Aid to Families with Dependent Children (AFDC) program, which gave aid to children who either lacked a mother or father in the home. Although it received only a tiny percentage of federal funds dedicated to social safety nets, the AFDC program served as a lightning rod that ultimately brought neoliberal conservatives and social, largely religious conservatives together in an alliance that would come to dominate conservative politics during the final decades of the twentieth century. The reason for the alliance, Cooper argues, was that both neoliberals and social conservatives saw the AFDC program as posing a threat to the flow of the wealth of society to the proper place – that is, to the family, meaning the nuclear family. This was why 'neoliberals and neoconservatives converged on the necessity of reinstating the family as the foundation of social and economic order' (Cooper 2017, 49). According to Cooper, this alliance drew from traditional poor laws, such as the 1601 Elizabethan Act for the Relief of the Poor, an act that 'introduced new filial obligation rules obliging adult children to care for their aging and impoverished parents … [and] making both parents liable for the support of illegitimate children and outlining criminal charges for illicit sex acts' (73). By reviving the role the family played in traditional poor laws such as this, the neoliberal-social conservative alliance adopted the notion that the family is its own domain independent of contractual exchange relations, and as a result is able to take on the costs and welfare of its own so that the state no longer has to. The family, in other words, by taking on the welfare of its own, becomes the limit capitalist growth needs, the limit that is beyond the grasp of market forces.

In response to Polanyi's argument that there needs to be a movement to counter the movement of capitalism itself, and the tendency of capitalism to undermine traditional social structures, Cooper points out that the very move to protect 'family values' in its current form has simply furthered the needs of capitalist growth, including the destructive tendencies Polanyi sought to minimise. On the one hand, the family does indeed tend towards the stable, invariant system outside market exchanges, and it tends towards the continual growth and reproduction of capital by offloading onto itself the hindrances to market processes. Understood in this way, the family entails both the dedifferentiating tendency insofar as it is not to be confused with the increasing differentiations that come with the growth of capital, and the de-differentiating tendency insofar as it provides the immanent limits that enable the growth and proliferation of markets. The family, in short, is nothing less than a process of making sense, a process whereby the problems of the family, of household maintenance or οἰκονομία, and thus not simply the nuclear family, come to be expressed and given voice by way of a number of political and economic structures and institutions. Neither tendency is ever fully actualised, as is the nature of problematic Ideas (see *Inquiry*), and every solution is provisional and never exhausts the problem it gives voice to. The family also provides us with a way of thinking through the nature of progress that is also often thought to be one of the defining characteristics of modern society. It is to this that we now turn.

b) Hume and improvement

To introduce the importance of the idea of progress to modern society, let us first say a little more about the family, and in particular the role it plays in the emerging split between the economy and politics. Stated simply, on the one hand, the family can be seen in the manner of Locke as the basis for political power in that it serves as an incubator of rational individuals, individuals who at the 'Age of Discretion' give their consent to those who govern, a consent based on the contractual agreement that those who govern will protect individuals' property rights, and hence their freedom to pursue their economic self-interest. On the other hand, the family can be seen as the basis and justification for economic activity, as that which determines the manner and purpose of economic activity, a basis we have seen already with Aristotle's stress on the importance of οἰκονομία. As the previous section showed, throughout the modern era, but especially so in recent decades, there has been a tension between the family as the determinate condition which facilitates the growth of capital (the limits necessary to the growth of capital, or exchange value), and the family as serving to limit the growth of capital to the interests and concerns of the social, of οἰκονομία, or the limits that are necessary for use value, as Marx claimed (as well as for learning, as argued for here). This latter point is key, and for Polanyi it is a central pillar of his argument. As he puts it:

> The outstanding discovery of recent historical and anthropological research is that man's economy, as a rule, is submerged in his social relationships. He does not act so as to safeguard his individual interest in the possession of material goods; he acts so as to safeguard his social standing, his social claims, his social assets. He values material goods only in so far as they serve this end. (Polanyi 2001, 48)

The double movement that is central to Polanyi's argument is a consequence of the emergence of economic processes that act independently of social processes, or act as if they were or ought to be independent of social processes. In response to the emergence of markets which follow, as Ellen Wood pointed out, their own 'laws of motion', Polanyi argues that 'a deep-seated movement sprang itself into being to resist the pernicious effects of a market-controlled economy. Society protected itself against the perils inherent in a self-regulating market system' (80). Locke's thought is also instrumental in the emerging split between economics and politics, or in the undermining and diremption of *political economy* by way of the illusion of pure politics. In taking the family to be an incubator of rational, self-guiding individuals, or *Homo economicus* as it has come to be known more recently, we have an argument for thinking that rational processes operate independently of social ties, or that social ties are to be understood in light of this rationality. The emergence of rational choice theory in the work of Gary Becker, among others, typifies this move. Moreover, despite the differences between Locke and Hobbes regarding the state of nature – for Locke one recognises wrongs being done in the state of nature, for Hobbes this only occurs after the social contract – they will each appeal to the primacy of rational self-interest in their account of the emergence of political power. *Homo economicus*, therefore, can be understood to operate autonomously and distinctly from the social animal that is engaged in household maintenance (οἰκονομία). However, before turning to the emergence of the divide between society and economics that has come to dominate modern society, in this section we will first stress the importance of the notion of improvement during this period. The concept of improvement emerged as a key component in the ongoing efforts to account for and make sense of the problem of the social, which included, among other things, accounting for the economic changes that were occurring at the time. One solution, as we saw, tended towards the illusion of pure politics, and it is with this move that the split between economics and politics becomes pronounced.

We can begin with Adam Smith and David Hume. Although both can be accurately placed in the tradition of classical liberalism, the liberalism one finds in Smith and Hume is one that paves the way for affirming the problematic nature of life, or for political economy as making sense of life. For both Smith and Hume, the social and the political are two tendencies of life itself, two movements that are never fully realised, never fully abstracted to the exclusion of their contrasting movement'. The tendency to the political, with the political understood (from Hobbes through Locke) as actions in accordance with rational self-interest, involves a move away from the social, a dedifferentiation of social ties, including family ties and any other concerns we may have for the welfare of others. This also leads to an understanding of economic processes in the same sense, and thus sets the stage for the separation of economics from politics, with politics focused on protecting the social or public good. This separation is apparent in Adam Smith's famous remark that 'It is not from the benevolence of the butcher, the brewer, or the baker that we expect our dinner, but from their regard to their own interest. We address ourselves, not to their humanity but to their self-love, and never talk to them of our own necessities but of their advantages' (Smith 1976b, I.ii, 26–7). The misuse of this quotation, however, is almost equal to its fame, for despite claiming that it is primarily self-interest that provides for the needs of others rather than any altruistic benevolence or concern, Smith will later appeal to the role of government in protecting society against the ravages workers suffer as a result of the manufacturing process and the division of labour. Recognising that 'any particular branch of trade or manufactures, is always in some respects different from, and even opposite to, that of the public', Smith proposes that as a result 'any new law or regulation of commerce which comes from this order [that is, from the 'branch of trade or manufactures'], ought always to be listened to with great precaution, and ought never be adopted till after having been long and carefully examined, not only with the most scrupulous, but with the most suspicious attention' (I.xi., 267). Smith's expression of concern for the effects of trade and manufacturing on the public, or what is in essence his own version of what will be Polanyi's double movement argument, is not novel or anomalous, moreover, but rather extends the arguments of his earlier book, *Theory of Moral Sentiments*, where it is admitted, in the very first line, that 'How selfish soever man may be supposed, there are evidently some principles in his nature which interest him in the fortune of others, and render their happiness necessary to him, though he derives nothing from it except the pleasure of seeing it' (Smith 1976a, I.i.I.1; 9).

Hume can also be seen to be taking up a defence of political economy, in our sense, a defence that resists taking up the Lockean move towards rational individualism. This is evident in Hume's critique of Hobbes' state of nature theory, where Hume argues that if a state of nature 'could ever exist' – a state where each individual is out for themselves and where every other individual has as an equal chance to get the scarce resources necessary for survival – then this is a state that 'may justly be doubted. Men are necessarily born in a family-society, at least, and are trained up by their parents to some rule of conduct and behaviour' (Hume 1999, 25). Hume also challenges what he takes to be the standard philosophical view which connects rationality with the ability to recognise the distinction of right from wrong. At the beginning of his *Enquiry Concerning the Principles of Morals*, he notes the 'controversy started of late' regarding whether the 'general foundation of MORALS', the distinction between right and wrong, is 'derived from REASON, or from

SENTIMENT' (13). Hume's stake in the controversy is clear: it is sentiment that serves as the foundation of morals. 'Extinguish all the warm feelings and prepossessions in favour of virtue', Hume argues, 'and all disgust or aversion to vice: Render men totally indifferent towards these distinctions; and morality is no longer a practical study, nor has any tendency to regulate our lives and actions' (15). In contrast to the Lockean model, therefore, where the family is seen to be primarily the place where we are under the command of parents until attaining the age of reason, for Hume the family is the place where we learn to be sociable – it is the model for our sociability – and where we come, hopefully, to have an interest and 'prepossession in favour of virtue'. Reason, as Hume makes clear, merely tells us what is the case, or how we might set about attaining what we are interested in, but reason itself is not the foundation of our interests or of what ought to be the case (see Hume 1999, 82).

Given Hume's claim that we all begin our lives 'in a family-society, at least', it is not surprising that he will go on to stress the social virtues, or precisely those actions that benefit society. In accounting for the social virtue of benevolence, for instance, a virtue that is praised even in instances where one's own self-interest is not involved (a point Smith recognised as well, as we saw above), Hume argues that 'a part, at least, of its merit arises from its tendency to promote the interests of our species, and bestow happiness on human society', and thus the 'social virtues are never regarded without their beneficial tendencies, nor viewed as barren and unfruitful'; this leads Hume to the conclusion that 'The happiness of mankind, the order of society, the harmony of families, the mutual support of friends, are always considered as the result of their gentle dominion over the breasts of men' (Hume 1999, 20). The role of the family, moreover, and of the friends we encounter and interact with, are key to this process whereby the 'gentle dominion' of the social virtues comes to take hold in our lives. On this point Hume is following his intellectual mentors, Francis Hutcheson and the Third Earl of Shaftesbury (who was also an influence on Hutcheson), for it was Shaftesbury himself who highlights the importance of the politeness he takes to be integral to the intellectual communities of his day – the coffee shop culture in London, the various improvement societies in Edinburgh, such as the Select Society of which Hume and Smith were both members, and the salons of France. For Shaftesbury, 'All Politeness is owing to Liberty', namely the liberty to free, open discussion, and it is through this discussion that 'We polish one another, and rub off our Corners and rough Sides by a sort of amicable Collision. To restrain this, is inevitably to bring a Rust upon Mens Understandings' (Anthony 2001, 41). Through frank and open discussion with others with whom we may disagree, an emphasis on politeness in this process, or on an 'amicable Collision' between differing views as Shaftesbury puts it, can lead to an advance and improvement of one's understanding of important matters. This process of improving through an 'amicable Collision' of ideas, what John Stuart Mill will later call the marketplace of ideas (see Mill 1991, 34), will loom large in Hutcheson's work, as well as in Hume's and Smith's, who will each follow in Hutcheson's footsteps.

With the notion of improvement, we come to one of the key ideas of modern society, and of liberalism as Russell understood it – the notion that free thought and inquiry, a freedom best exemplified in the processes of scientific enquiry, will lead to discoveries that will allow for social progress and prosperity. Discoveries that may lead to the improvement of society were just what the members of the Select Society of Edinburgh, for instance, hoped their polite conversations would lead to, or at least encourage. The topics discussed and debated at the Society's weekly meetings ranged from whether Milton is a better poet than Virgil, to whether 'intoxicating liquors' ought to be forbidden, and even to whether, to recall Wood's argument, 'the Tenure of Land Estates, by Entail in perpetuity, [is] preferable, for the good of families and the improvement of a Country, to the more unlimited exercise of property and power of alienation'.[5] (As we saw earlier, Wood argued that variable tenure on land, with competitive leasing, was instrumental to the emergence of the capitalist 'laws of motion' that forced farmers continually to enhance and improve their productivity so as to meet the demands of the market and pay rent while maintaining a profit [recall §3.1.b]). Gatherings such as the Select Society, therefore, were a perfect instance of the polite culture Shaftesbury encouraged (as did Addison and Steele[6]).

Hume's writings on economics and trade also exemplify a concern for what will most benefit society. In his essay 'Of the Jealousy of Trade', for example, Hume extends Shaftesbury's understanding of polite societies to the economic relations among nations. Just as Shaftesbury sees a benefit to all who participate in a polite social gathering, especially where sharply contrasting views may be shared in an 'amicable Collision', so too for Hume it is to every nation's interest to trade freely with others, even though these other nations may have their own contrasting interests. Hume, and then more forcefully Smith, will then adopt this Shaftesbury model as a premise in

---

5. Minute Book of the Select Society, National Library of Scotland (Adv.MS.23.1.1), folio 147, 17 March 1761; Milton or Virgil, folio 151, 8 January 1760. Not all saw the 'Tenure of Land Estates' in the same way, as evidenced by this question, 'Whether the Modern Method of improvement, by making large Farms be not ruinous to the Country?' (folio 147).

6. Joseph Addison and Richard Steele published *The Spectator*, a daily publication, from 1711 to 1712, which popularised the coffee house culture, and Addison and Steele were often fixtures in the more popular coffee houses of the day.

arguments challenging the mercantile model which assumes that any money (gold) that goes to another nation when you buy something they produce (wine from France for instance) will allow this nation to become wealthier at your expense. For Hume, by contrast, trade is not a zero-sum game and all nations benefit from free trade. How this works, according to Hume, is through an 'amicable Collision' of emulation and imitation of the skills and techniques of other nations. As one acquires these skills to produce what was once imported, one can then become a producer or exporter of these very same goods (in a phenomenon Jane Jacobs refers to as import replacement [see Jacobs 1969, 144–9]). It is through emulating and imitating trading partners who have better skills than ourselves that we acquire these skills. As Hume puts it, 'Every improvement, which we have since made, has arisen from our imitation of foreigners; and we ought so far to esteem it happy that they had previously made advances in arts and ingenuity' (Hume 1985, 328). The improvement in our understanding that comes, for Shaftesbury, from encounters with others who may think differently than ourselves, becomes, for Hume, the improvement that comes to all societies when they engage in free trade.

The stress Hume places on improvement, however, is not unproblematic. As Polanyi argues, the belief in progress and improvement becomes a matter of faith in modern society, and a faith that ultimately comes to validate and justify the separation of economic processes from political processes, or that 'must make us blind to the role of government in economic life' (Polanyi 2001, 39). That is, economic processes themselves, the 'amicable Collision[s]' of free trade, are taken to be the engine that drives social progress, and as a result government, so this faith assumes and argues, must not get in the way of progress. As Polanyi will repeatedly argue, however, there is no such thing as a pure self-regulating market that brings about progress that does not, at key points, rely upon the powers of the state and the laws this state enforces. The blind faith in improvement and progress will thus become the faith in self-regulating markets, and a faith that requires the powers of the state to provide the limits these markets need, markets that are now taken to be what facilitates the improvement that will lead to the prosperity of society as a whole. In Hume, this faith in improvement and progress is most on display in his call for institutions, and in particular legal institutions, to provide the security and stability necessary if the improvements of society are to take hold. As he puts it, if we have a good 'system of laws to regulate the administration of public affairs to the latest posterity', then the result is that we would become 'so little dependen[t] … on the humors and education of particular men, that one part of the same republic may be wisely conducted, and another weakly, by the very same men, merely on account of the difference of the forms and institutions, by which these parts are regulated' (Hume 1985, 24). As long as the legal institutions that are in place are good, then according to Hume it matters little who comes to fill the various roles a government needs to be filled, for the 'system of laws' will largely assure that they act for the best of society as a whole. As a determinate set of 'rules-as-rails', however, the laws Hume places his faith in are themselves conditioned by the problematic nature of existence, by problematic Ideas, and as such they presuppose the de/differentiating tendencies of making sense that harbour the potential to undermine the determinate nature of these laws. How problematic Ideas, or the problem of making sense, can both condition and undermine the rules-as-rails nature of the system of laws Hume called for, as well as the capitalist 'laws of motion' these same laws support and extend, will be the subject of the next section.

c) '...but it is legal'

A guiding theme in Katharina Pistor's recent book, *The Code of Capital*, is that the faith in laws as exhibited by Hume, for instance, is in no small part responsible for many of the negative effects of capital accumulation – growing inequality, depletion of resources, climate change, etc. In fact, Pistor argues that most of the existing critiques of capitalism ignore this key feature – namely, the role law plays in creating capital itself, and in the self-reproduction of capital. As Pistor puts it, 'Whereas Marxists see law primarily as an instrument for exercising power, for rational choice theorists, law operates both as a constraint on and as an expression of power, and the balance between the two is struck through bargaining'; and yet both approaches to understanding law, she argues, 'ignore the central role of law in the making of capital and its protection as private wealth' (Pistor 2019, 208). Pistor's arguments highlighting this role of law can be seen as following in the spirit of Foucault's effort to pursue a history of thought rather than a history of ideas. As Foucault states the difference: a 'history of ideas involves the analysis of a notion from its birth, through its development, and in the setting of other ideas which constitute its context'. A 'history of thought', by contrast, 'is the analysis of the way an unproblematic field of experience, or a set of practices, which were accepted without question, which were familiar and "silent", out of discussion, becomes a problem, raises discussion and debate, incites new reactions, and induces a crisis in the previously silent behavior, habits, practices, and institutions' (Foucault 2001, 74). Pistor's work on the relationship between law and capital is a work in history of thought, taken in Foucault's sense. In particular, Pistor argues that two assumptions regarding law and capital go largely unquestioned. First, 'Law is taken as a given, as exogeneous to the assets that are the harbingers of wealth' (Pistor 2019, 222); in other words, law, and the political, legislative and juridical practices that go into the making of law, are assumed to be separate from the wealth created through economic activity – an assumption that underlies the split of the economy from politics that is a feature of modern society, especially in contemporary neoliberalism. Secondly, Pistor argues that 'enormous deference is given to the claim that one's actions are "legal", that they are based on rights' (222). If one's actions are challenged, if one's wealth-creating activity is questioned, then one can simply claim one's actions are legal and hence are not subject to being doubted or interfered with. Since the legitimacy of law tends to be accepted without question, and law is thought to be a separate matter from the creation of wealth, the result for Pistor is that we are by habit predisposed to 'ignore the central role of law in the making of capital and its protection as private wealth' (208).

As Pistor makes clear throughout her book, wealth is much more than the possession of assets, whether they be financial assets, stocks or property, among others. In the case of property, for instance, the owner ideally wants added protections and benefits to enable them to shield their property from confiscation, to borrow against their property in order to procure cash, and so on. Although one may attempt to establish and maintain such privileges by force – and indeed this was, as Pistor notes, a common approach throughout the Middle Ages – a more reliable way to do so is through law, relying on the force of the state to impose and enforce one's legal claims. This is where lawyers become integral to the process of wealth creation. As Pistor puts it, 'Clients crave something that only the best lawyers can deliver: strong priority rights for the assets of their choice, durability over and above the life expectancy of competing assets, the option to convert financial assets into cash at will, and all of the above with legal force against the world' (Pistor 2019, 161). In the case of bankruptcy, for example, a lawyer will craft – or code, to use Pistor's phrase – the priority rights of who has privileged access to the remaining assets: certain creditors will be first in line while others will end up with nothing, and one's place in the line is determined by legal coding. A property-holder also benefits from legal coding that can protect their land or other assets from seizure in case of bankruptcy, and a good lawyer, Pistor notes, will be able through their coding efforts to give an asset the legal status that assures such protections.

Legal coding is thus key to the process of creating and protecting capital wealth. Pistor states the point quite bluntly: 'capital is made from two ingredients: an asset, and the legal code' (Pistor 2019, 2). A legal code, however, draws upon established laws, and these laws become the basis upon which the coding connects the law to an asset, much as the coding of a map, as we saw (see §5.1.c), connects the signifiers and markings on a map to the physical attributes and locations being mapped (signifieds). In the case of the legal coding of capital, the 'most important' laws 'are contract law, property rights, collateral law, trust, corporate, and bankruptcy law. These are the modules from which capital is coded' (3). In other words, a lawyer will take established bankruptcy law, for instance, in order to code the priority rights and protections associated with a certain class of assets, and the legitimacy of the resulting legal codes relies upon the laws, as signifiers, from which the codes were drawn, codes that then create capital assets (signifieds). As Pistor points out, lawyers do 'need to make sure that their coding efforts will be recognized and enforced by some state' (180); however, a legal code that is challenged in court may be struck down as not being in accordance with the law. Pistor offers a number of examples of this throughout her book, including the successful legal challenge to the way mortgages were coded as mortgage-backed securities – a challenge that came, unfortunately perhaps for the economy, well after the financial crisis brought on by the collapse of Lehman Brothers. Given the risk posed by bringing one's legal codings to court, it is not surprising, Pistor notes, that 'many lawyers will go to great lengths to avoid giving a court an opportunity to render a negative ruling on the legal coding they have employed for the benefit of hundreds, if not thousands, of clients'. The legal coding of lawyers is thus dependent upon 'the authority of state law', Pistor argues, 'but they [lawyers] avoid the courts, the law's traditional guardians, for fear that they might interfere with their coding work' (180).

Given the assumption that a lawyer's legal coding of assets will success-fully withstand a challenge in the courts, the assets that are thereby coded presuppose the force and power of the state to protect and enforce one's claims. If the resulting distribution of wealth entails great and increasing social inequalities, the assumption that the wealth is held legally goes a long way towards blunting the force of any criticism. This deference given to the legal nature of wealth is one of the two assumptions Pistor challenges, in a Foucauldian manner, the other being that legal processes are separate from economic ones. We can now see that the process of wealth creation is intimately tied to the processes of legal coding, and to codes that in turn rely on the state enforcement of law. Due to the fact that capital wealth is largely taken to be legal, and hence backed by the full authority and power of a state, most people are resigned to accepting the wealth inequalities of society. As Pistor puts it, 'Law's empire has less need for troops; it relies instead on the normative authority of the law, and its most powerful battle cry is "but it is legal"' (Pistor 2019, 8). The dominance of the law's normative authority is also reflected in the fact that rising profits and stock market values have become 'the standard measures for adjudicating success or failure of elected governments – in itself an indicator of the enormous cognitive sway capital has over polities' (20). Backed by the normative sway of the 'but it is legal' claim, the creation of wealth, along with its unequal distribution, has been largely rendered immune to criticism because the law, it is assumed, is an equal, impartial arbiter open to all.

This is precisely the assumption Pistor sets out to challenge. The law is not open and equal to all, but is available to those who can pay for lawyers with the skills needed to craft the legal codes that create and protect certain assets over and against the claims of others. This process of legal coding is not a market process, and thus the distribution of wealth it gives rise to is not the result of the type of market price system Hayek argued for, but rather is the result of privilege. Pistor is clear on this point: 'the legal code of capital does not follow the rules of competition; instead, it operates according to the logic of power and privilege' (Pistor 2019, 118). The law is thus not an impartial bystander separate from economic processes, but the very tool used by those who carve out wealth, and it has long been this way. With respect to the settlers 'in the "new world"', for example, Pistor notes that 'they claimed that no one before them could possibly claim prior title, because only the settlers had discovered the land and improved it', and since improvement and discovery were legally recognised, their claims were enforced and the indigenous peoples 'were expelled from their land without due process or just compensation, because their claims were not recognized in law' (125). In a twist to our earlier discussion of improvement (§5.2.b), and the Humean faith in improvement, we can see yet another way in which this faith has played a key role in the exercise and growth of power and privilege, in this case the power of the colonists as well as those who sought (as we saw earlier in Wood's discussion of primitive accumulation) to improve the land by enclosing it and displacing those who had long lived there. The normative status and defence of the law have thus fuelled, according to Pistor, the creation and growth of capital wealth, but they have at the same time created risks that threaten the prosperity and welfare of society – the very improvements that led to Hume's early optimism in relation to the economic liberalism of his day. In other words, the economic liberalism Hume helped to usher in involves its own undoing, or entails the dedifferentiating tendencies of making sense that may well lead to the undermining of the determinate ways economics and politics present themselves as solutions without a problem. Developing a taste for the problematic Ideas inseparable from these solutions is the task of critical existentialism. How it might carry out this task and problematise some of the key ideas – i.e., freedom, law and progress – that inform the self-conception of modern society, including the liberal and neoliberal traditions, is the issue to which we will now turn.

d) Critical existentialism

As I have emphasised throughout this book, the various forms in which our political life has come to be identified and categorised are to be understood as inseparable from a process of making sense that allows for the possibility of identifying one's territory (see 2.1.b), sense of place (see 5.1.b), and even one's political identity as an integral component to one's sense of self-worth (see 2.1.d). These same processes of making sense are inseparable from some of the important ways in which we have come to think about the liberal tradition in politics. Following Bertrand Russell's lead, although we could have followed the lead of others, we have focused our attention on three characteristic traits of liberalism – freedom, law and progress. Although these traits are not exclusive to liberalism, and the debates regarding the nature of liberalism itself are wide-ranging, we have taken them as a starting point to clarify the relationship between the problematic nature of life as making sense and the determinate identities and narratives that enable people to make sense of their lives, including of their political situation. This approach can be seen quite clearly, as I have been arguing, among the existential philosophers, and thus the critical existentialism being developed here will attempt to under-stand freedom, law and progress in light of the problematic Ideas that are inseparable from processes of making sense.

Placing freedom, law and progress in the context of processes of making sense will enable us to avoid not only the inevitability of these identities – the assumption that they reflect an essential nature or truth that was revealed and discovered with the rise of modern society – but also a historicism that would account for these identities in terms of other determinate identities, in this case the contingencies of circumstance, contingencies that could have been different. By arguing that a determinate identity is inseparable from a problematic Idea it expresses or gives voice to, and thus is not a solution without a problem, we avoid a historicist reductionism to the contingency of determinate facts and events. Moreover, since a determinate identity always presupposes the nature of the problematic Idea that conditions it, the identi-ties that emerge are not predetermined, meaning they are not prefigured or foreseen by that which conditions them; nor are they simply contingent, presupposing other determinate facts that could have been different than they were. To the contrary, these identities are fated, for a problem, as Deleuze puts it, 'always has the solution it deserves', or gets the identity it is fated to since this identity is precisely the solution a problem deserves 'in propor-tion to its own truth or falsity – in other words, in proportion to its sense' (Deleuze 1994, 159 [see earlier, 1.1.c]). To clarify this point and then relate it to the themes of freedom, law and progress, let us return to Kierkegaard.

Freedom

In our earlier discussion of Kierkegaard we saw that despair is what occurs when we are 'unaware of being defined as spirit' (Kierkegaard 1980b, 25, and see 4.1.a). Spirit is understood by Kierkegaard to be that which supports our nature as synthesis, as a synthesis of psyche and body, but more importantly as the synthesis of becoming concrete whereby 'to become concrete is neither to become finite nor to become infinite' but instead consists of 'an infinite moving away from itself in the infinitizing of the self, and an infinite coming back to itself in the finitizing process' (30). To be aware of ourselves as being defined as spirit thus entails an awareness of the absolute difference of infinite and finite, a difference that is synthesised by virtue of the spirit: 'Man is a synthesis of the psychical and the physical; however, a synthesis is unthinkable if the two are not united in a third. This third is spirit' (Kierkegaard 1980a, 43). As a synthesis, moreover, spirit is freedom, for it is neither reducible to the finite and determinate, to that which has already been determined to be what it is, nor is it an unchecked infinitude with no ties or connections to the finite; rather, as synthesis spirit is the possibility or infinitude inseparable from the finite. The awareness of this synthesis, the awareness of spirit, results in anxiety. As Kierkegaard puts it, 'anxiety is the dizziness of freedom, which emerges when the spirit wants to posit the synthesis and freedom looks down into its own possibility, laying hold of finiteness to support itself' (61). That is, when one comes to encounter one's self as spirit, as synthesis of finite and infinite, as freedom, then one encounters the infinite possibility that cannot be reduced to any already determined, finite and actual phenomena. The dizziness of freedom then leads us to grasp the finite for support, to latch onto a determinate signpost that will show us the way, give us a determinate sense of direction and a path to follow. For Kierkegaard this is the role fate plays in paganism, for 'in fate', he claims, 'the anxiety of the pagan has its object, its nothing', and it is nothing precisely because anxiety is the dizziness of freedom that is no thing, no determinate, finite state of affairs upon which to pin or land one's anxiety; and yet the pagan 'stands related to it (this nothing), and this relation is anxiety' (97); 'Fate is a relation to spirit as external' (96). In other words, when in paganism one does not embrace oneself as spirit, as freedom that is both the infinitising and finitising process of becoming concrete, then spirit comes to be identified with the infinite possibilities of freedom externalised as a determinate other, as fate.

Let us say, to use Kierkegaard's own example, that I have 'a mimic talent for the comical [and] ought to be an actor' (Kierkegaard 1980a, 105). To see this as one's fate, as a possibility that calls upon me, as a friend may request something of me, is to externalise the freedom and infinite possibility we are as spirit. At the same time, however, to simply identify with one's determinate talents and abilities, to take one's life as determinately given, is for Kierkegaard 'an altogether meaningless view of life, or it is rather no view at all, for it merely states what is obvious' (105). In other words, freedom for Kierkegaard is not a matter of being what one is, one with 'a mimic talent for the comical', for instance, for this is not freedom; nor does freedom consist of fleeing the determinate demands of life and the many things one encounters in life as it is offered. To grasp one's spirit as freedom is precisely to affirm the spirit as infinitising and finitising, as psyche and body, perhaps as one who is religious and with a talent for the comical. As Kierkegaard puts it, 'What profound religious reflection would be required to reach such an outward task, for example, that of becoming a comic actor!' One should therefore not take the meaningless view of life that clings simply to life as it is offered, affirming 'what is obvious', and one should not repeat the 'fault of the Middle Ages … [that] broke off too soon' (106) from life as it is given and turned towards the infinite and away from becoming concrete. For Kierkegaard the question is one of seeing whether one can, 'after having begun religious reflection, succeed in returning to himself again, whole in every respect', whereas for many in 'the Middle Ages … when an individuality was to return to himself, having encountered, for example, the fact that he possessed wit, a sense for the comic, etc., he annihilated all of this as something imperfect' (106). For Kierkegaard true freedom, a freedom without the dizziness of anxiety, occurs with faith, when one has returned to oneself again, 'whole in every respect'.

We can clarify Kierkegaard's conception of freedom – one that recurs in various ways throughout the existential tradition – if we return to the classical republican view of freedom as non-domination, as the absence of arbitrary power, and interpret Kierkegaard's understanding of freedom as compatible with classical republicanism, and thus as a view that cannot be fitted neatly into the distinction between negative and positive liberty that would come to dominate much of modern political theory. As Isaiah Berlin states this distinction (it was Berlin who made it famous), negative liberty entails being 'free to the degree to which no human being interferes with my activity' (Berlin 1969, 156). Hobbes is thought to be the first to call upon this form of freedom, where we are free to do anything within the limits laid down by the law (see §3.1.a). In other words, insofar as we act within the limits of the law we ought to be left free to do what we will. Positive liberty, by contrast, involves 'freedom as self-mastery, with its suggestion of a man divided against himself' (163). For Berlin, however, positive liberty is problematic precisely because of its tendency to promote the self-mastery one seeks through identification with a group or ideology greater than oneself. He cites the 'Jacobins and communists' as examples of those who find the freedom of self-mastery in a shared ideology, an ideology the consequences of which gave Berlin cause for concern, as they did for Camus as well (recall §4.1.c). Given that this concern was coupled with what were, at the time Berlin set forth the positive/negative liberty distinction in 1958, the fairly fresh memories of the Second World War and the atrocities of Nazi Germany – atrocities committed for the sake of a self-mastery in accord with the identity of a greater Aryan race – it is not surprising that Berlin, and many who followed in his wake, would easily embrace negative liberty as the key freedom of modernity and set aside positive liberty as a relic of a bygone era.

Touching on a number of these issues, Christoph Menke, in his recent book *Critique of Rights*, offers an innovative view on the theory of rights, including its relationship to law, and although he does not explicitly discuss Berlin's distinction between positive and negative liberty, it has clearly cast its shadow over his understanding of the modern form of rights. In particular, for Menke what is crucial is the idea that 'Modern law is law whose gap is its essence, whose essence is its gap' (Menke 2015, 88), this gap being between, on the one hand, the securing of interests, or enabling individuals to pursue their particular interests, such as becoming a comic actor for instance, and on the other hand the securing of choice, the natural freedom that is indeterminably free to act within the limits of the law. As Menke puts it, the 'securing of interests and the securing of choice are diametrically opposed' (67) in that one's interests are secured by law, by being provided with the means to realise one's *determinate* interests, and the securing of choice allows us to act without interference, and thus to pursue, within the limits of the law, an *indeterminate* range of interests. Thus whereas one's *determinate* interests are secured by law, and by determinate, established law, as Pistor has shown with respect to the creation and securing of capital wealth (5.2.c), to secure choice, by contrast, or negative liberty to use Berlin's term, is to exercise a freedom that is *indeterminate* and indeterminable with respect to the law, for the law serves as the extrinsic limit within which an infinite range of choices fall. As Menke argues, and in contrast to Berlin's emphasis upon the advantages of negative liberty over positive liberty, the modern conception of law is not simply an effort to secure negative liberty but rather attempts the paradoxical task of securing both our interests and choice at once. The result of this effort, for Menke, is that the determinate laws and rights that are established come to be problematised and rendered provisional by virtue of their paradoxical grounding. To state this in terms of the rule-following paradox with which we began (in the Introduction), and to which we will return shortly, the determinate rules and laws cannot definitively secure our interests, because the choices that support these interests can be brought into accord with an indeterminate and indeterminable number of rules. A version of this paradox, moreover, lies at the heart of Kierkegaard's project, as we have seen, and thus returning to Kierkegaard will enable us to clarify and begin to address the issues we raised regarding the paradox of rule-following – namely, what is the basis for our ability to go on in the right way, the form of life that enables us to follow rules, or the commonly shared opinion upon which, according to Hume, 'government is founded' (Hume 1985, 32)?

To take up a Kierkegaardian rethinking of the positive/negative liberty distinction, let us return to the person who has 'a mimic talent for the comical'. For such a person to simply accept that this is who they are would be, as we have seen, 'an altogether meaningless view of life, or it is rather no view at all, for it merely states what is obvious' (Kierkegaard 1980a, 105). For Kierkegaard one should not simply live life as it is actually given, with the determinate qualities and talents that come with such a life; rather one should return, religiously, to oneself as a whole, and this entails living life as spirit, as the synthesis of the finitising and infinitising processes. When Kierkegaard speaks of anxiety as the 'dizziness of freedom', therefore, the dizziness is the result of encountering the infinitising nature of ourselves, when 'freedom looks down into its own possibility' and into an infinite possibility that is not to be confused with any finite, determinate state of affairs. To this extent, therefore, Kierkegaard mirrors the negative conception of liberty in that the freedom of possibility, as a freedom that is not captured or predetermined by any determinate laws, is a freedom that is absolutely infinite and indetermin- able. At the same time, however, for Kierkegaard freedom as spirit is also a synthesis of the eternal and the temporal, the possible and the actual, and it is for this reason that returning to oneself as a whole entails, for instance, becoming a comic actor; in other words, to live a life that is meaningful is to live it as it is given, with all the determinate attributes and talents one may have, but at the same time, and paradoxically, this life embraces the eternal possibilities inseparable from these given talents and attributes. One should thus live one's life of freedom as spirit, as a synthesis of the infinitising and the eternal, and live it as it is determinately given, seeking to realise one's determinate nature and hence embrace a form of positive liberty.

Kierkegaard's comments on the nature of genius provide some clarity on the nature of this meaningful life. As he understands the nature of genius, it involves a life that is an intermediary between a 'meaningless view of life' that simply takes what is obvious and lives life as it is given, and a life wherein one returns to oneself, 'whole in every respect'. In one respect, the genius is indeed turned outward, to the temporal world as it is given in this life, and it is this outward turn that enables the genius to 'accomplish astonishing things' (Kierkegaard 1980a, 99). 'If the genius remains thus immediately determined and turned outward', Kierkegaard claims, 'he will indeed become great and his accomplishment astounding' (101). At the same time, however, what enables the genius to achieve great things is precisely the lack of significance given to the very outward, temporal world where their accomplishments come to be lauded – 'The outward as such has no significance for the genius, and therefore no one can understand him' (100). It is at this point that Kierkegaard sees the genius calling upon fate rather than returning to themselves. By turning to fate they turn to a temporal determination that is irreducible to anything temporal; fate is an objective and yet indeterminable determinant of an as yet to be actualised reality, such as the great accomplishments the genius will create. For this reason Kierkegaard claims that the genius 'is great by reason of his belief in fate'. The accomplishments of the genius, therefore, are made possible by a turn to, and belief in, an indeterminable reality that is objective and not to be confused with oneself – it may be their muse, for example. In fact, Kierkegaard argues that 'the significance of the genius to himself is nil' (100); that is, they do not engage in a full, meaningful life but rather turn to fate.

We can now return to our earlier claim that the identity that emerges in response to a problem is not predetermined but fated. In the same way that the determinate, identifiable accomplishments of the genius are not tied to the determinate phenomena of the outward, temporal world – this world 'has no significance for the genius' – but are instead tied to a fate that makes these determinate phenomena possible, so too the relationship between a problem and a solution is not one whereby a determinate solution simply realises the determinate conditions laid down by the problem, but is instead made possible by a problem that is indeterminate and not to be confused with anything determinate, including the determinate solutions it makes possible. A problem is thus very much in line with Kierkegaard's understanding of fate, but whereas Kierkegaard takes fate to be 'a relation to spirit as external' (Kierkegaard 1980a, 96), a problem is not external to the solutions it makes possible, for this presupposes the very determinate difference between an externality and that which it is external to – the self for Kierkegaard, or solutions if problems are interpreted as being external to them – and yet the determinate itself, and hence determinate differences, are made possible, as we have been arguing, by the nature of problematic Ideas that are indeterminately determinable and yet inseparable from the determinate solutions that give voice to them. For a similar reason, a problematic Idea is not to be identified with the nature of spirit as internal, as the return to oneself if this is taken to be a turning away from the determinate, temporal and worldly. This is not the type of return Kierkegaard has in mind, either, when he encourages one to return 'whole in every respect' (99), for as a synthesis of temporal and eternal, finitising and infinitising spirit is to be confused neither with the determinate nor with the indeterminate but is understood as a wholeness that is whole as existing, as becoming our concrete selves. This process of becoming ourselves, becoming 'whole in every respect', is how we have understood life as a problem, as making sense. Moreover, making sense, as we have seen, entails both de/differentiating tendencies – the move towards the indeterminate and indeterminable (dedifferentiating) and the move towards the infinitely determinate and determinable (differentiating).

If we take the works of a genius, for instance, then we can see that they are notable examples of works that express the nature of a problem, or express the process of making sense. In reference to the work of J.M.W. Turner, for example, Deleuze and Guattari claim that 'from the moment there is genius, there is something that belongs to no school, no period, something that achieves a breakthrough – art as a process without goal, but that attains completion as such' (Deleuze and Guattari 1977, 370, see also *Inquiry* §9.10). Turner's work achieves a breakthrough, or realises an identity that is fated, we could say, but it is an identity that expresses the nature of a problem and 'attains completion as such'; that is, a work of genius, as with a meaningful life for Kierkegaard, is 'whole in every respect', but it is a whole not as a determinate totality but rather as process, as process of making sense, and a process that involves both a dedifferentiating, infinitising process (it belongs to no school), and a differentiating, finitising process (Turner's paintings are determinate objects, on display in the Tate Britain, and with identifiable themes and similarities to other works). It is in this sense that a problem has the solution it deserves, 'in proportion to its sense', for a solution is simply making sense of a problematic Idea, and it makes sense in proportion to the dual de/differentiating tendencies; in other words, returning to oneself 'whole in every respect' entails 'an infinite moving away from itself in the infinitizing of the self [dedifferentiating], and an infinite coming back to itself in the finitizing process [differentiating]' (Kierkegaard 1980b, 30; recall the discussion in §4.1.c).

We should not be led astray by this discussion of genius however, concluding from it that the freedom of a meaningful life is only to be found when one is able to 'accomplish astonishing things', or when one 'achieves a breakthrough'. On this point Kierkegaard clearly moves past the genius – past the genius who fails to think religiously and aspires to temporal accomplishments. To return to oneself and one's freedom does not require great deeds and accomplishments, but can be attained in the simplest, most mundane of ways. Such is the case, Kierkegaard claims, only for one 'who is educated by possibility [and who] is educated according to his infinitude'. One who is 'educated by anxiety is educated by possibility' (Kierkegaard 1980a, 156), for in confronting the anxiety that 'is the dizziness of freedom', a 'freedom [that] looks down into its own [infinite] possibility' (62), one who becomes educated embraces the freedom of infinite possibility without 'laying hold of finiteness to support itself' (61). For one who is educated in this way, the finite and mundane become an opportunity for the embrace and exercise of freedom. As Kierkegaard puts it: 'Take the pupil of possibility, place him in the middle of the Jutland heath, where no event takes place or where the greatest event is a grouse flying up noisily, and he will experience everything more perfectly, more accurately, more thoroughly than the man who received the applause on the stage of world-history if that man was not educated by possibility' (159). To be free, therefore, is not to be left alone, to have the negative liberty to do what one will within the limits of the law, nor is it the positive liberty to pursue our determinate talents and interests, whatever they may be. For Kierkegaard, by contrast, our freedom consists of experiencing everything more perfectly, or as the expression of an infinite possibility; it is to live a life that makes sense.

A brief aside on Spinoza and Nietzsche will clarify this last point further, and in turn provide another opportunity to stress a central argument of this book – namely, that the existential tradition offers an illuminating, critical perspective upon key elements of modern society, a perspective I have called critical existentialism. The turn to Nietzsche is perhaps an obvious one to make. In numerous places Nietzsche criticised democracy as a tendency to mediocrity and hence to the denial of life (as we have seen above). More importantly, Nietzsche's account of the distinction between master and slave morality is also very much in the spirit of classical republicanism, if we interpret the latter as providing an alternative to the negative/positive conceptions of liberty. As Philip Pettit argues in his book *Republicanism*, the traditional understanding of freedom within republicanism cannot be fitted neatly into Berlin's distinction between positive and negative liberty. Although the 'standard way of reading the republican tradition', Pettit claims, is 'in conformity to the Berlin-Constant framework … as a tradition that prizes positive liberty above all else' (Pettit 1997, 27), Pettit understands the republican conception of freedom to be non-domination: one is free if one is in a position where another does not have the capacity to exert their will over one arbitrarily. Understood in this way, the republican conception of freedom is not negative liberty as non-interference, for 'it is possible', Pettit argues, 'to have domination without interference' (22), as in the case of the kindly slave-owner who does not interfere but could do so if they chose to; and neither does the republican conception of liberty completely overlap with that of positive liberty, and in particular with the self-mastery and 'liberty of democratic participation' (27) that are taken to be the key virtues of positive liberty, since one could well be subject to domination by powers that acquire their power as a result of democratic participation. As Pettit states the difference between the republican and modernist approaches to liberty: for the republican tradition 'liberty is always cast in terms of the opposition between *liber* and *servus*, citizen and slave. The condition of liberty is explicated as the status of someone who, unlike the slave, is not subject to the arbitrary power of another' (31).[7] By arguing that democratic institutions are an example of slave morality, or criticising the 'slave rebellion in morals' (Nietzsche 1966, §195, 108) where even the leaders and leading citizens (*liber*) claim to be servants (*servus*) of the people, Nietzsche is in effect adopting a crucial distinction from the republican tradition as he sets forth his own critical evaluation of modern society.

As Nietzsche develops his critique of the society of his day, his alignment with Kierkegaard becomes clear. In elaborating upon the nature of master morality, and more precisely the self-affirmation characteristic of this morality, Nietzsche calls upon the notion of eternal recurrence as a test of the extent to which one embraces and affirms one's life, or of the proportion in which one's life is affirmative rather than riddled with *ressentiment*. As Nietzsche states the notion in *The Gay Science*:

> What, if some day or night a demon were to steal after you into your loneliest loneliness and say to you: 'This life as you now live it and have lived it, you will have to live once more and innumerable times more; and there will be nothing new in it, but every pain and every joy and every thought and sigh and everything unutterably small or great in your life will have to return to you, all in the same succession and sequence...' Would you not throw yourself down and gnash your teeth and curse the demon who spoke thus? Or have you once experienced a tremendous moment when you would have answered him: 'You are a god and never have I heard anything more divine.' (Nietzsche 1974, 341)

---

7. For an even more vigorous defence of this understanding of liberty, see Skinner 1998. In laying out what he calls the 'neo-roman' theory of liberty which prevailed in the seventeenth century among writers such as Thomas More, James Harrington and Algernon Sidney, Skinner argues that it was the mere possibility of dependency on the will of another, and not just their actual interference with one's actions, that characterised this understanding of liberty, an understanding that has largely given way to the classical liberal view as found in Berlin's work. The criticisms of negative liberty developed here can be seen to be a consequence of following through on Skinner's call to 'excavate' the origins of liberal conceptions of liberty in order to determine how and whether they continue to make sense (see Skinner 1998, 115–17).

On being told that they will live their life 'once more and innumerable times more', and hence relive all the moments to infinity, the person who does not then affirm their life – who does not, as Kierkegaard's student of possibility does, see the infinite within the smallest detail – will gnash their teeth and curse the demon; but the person who affirms their life, who would live it again without editing out certain events and details, and to the extent that they affirm this unedited life – this person will have learned to embrace their fate (*amor fati*[8]), the infinite within themselves, the eternal nature of their finite, mortal life.

At this point the turn to Spinoza becomes clearer, as it already was for Nietzsche who saw in Spinoza a precursor, for he also sought, as did Nietzsche, to come to a place where one could affirm the infinite within the finite, or come to the third kind of knowledge whereby the absolutely infinite nature of God is known through one's own finite nature (recall §2.2.b). As we have seen, in a letter to his friend Franz Overbeck, Nietzsche lists some of the reasons he has a precursor in Spinoza: 'he [Spinoza] denies the freedom of the will, teleology, the moral world-order, the unegoistic, and evil' (Nietzsche 1954, 92). Much could be said about each of these (for more see Bell 2006), but for present purposes the denial of teleology is most relevant with respect to our current discussion of politics, insofar as political policymakers often take particular goals and targets as the basis and justification for their decisions and the exercise of their power. If political power is legitimised by taking that power to be exercised for the sake of the common good, then a teleological motive appears to be at the basis of much of modern politics (if not politics *in toto*). When Spinoza therefore argues, in his *Ethics*, that the mind can have no effect on the body (Spinoza 1985, 5 Preface), and thus cannot direct our bodily actions through conscious decisions to bring about a certain end, and when he argues that all our decisions are determined by our appetites (1 Appendix), there appears to be little space for thinking of politics in teleological terms, and it was precisely this critique of teleology that Nietzsche admired.

One way to think of Spinoza's critique of teleology, however, is as a critique in the Kantian tradition of setting forth the conditions for the possibility of teleological action rather than as a criticism of teleology. Admittedly a Kantian critique was not a live option for Spinoza, but he does clearly

---

8. This is a reference to the famous passage from the end of the second chapter of Nietzsche's *Ecce Homo*: 'My formula for greatness in a human being is *amor fati*; that one wants nothing to be different, not forward, not backward, not in all eternity' (Nietzsche 1969, 258).

identify appetites as the condition for the ends and goals that become the basis for our choices. As Spinoza puts it: 'By the end for the sake of which we do something I understand appetite' (Spinoza 1985, 4D7). In particular, our appetitive nature consists precisely in the attempt or striving (Spinoza's term is *conatus*) to persevere in our nature, this being understood by Spinoza as a particular ratio of motion and rest: 'If the parts composing an individual become greater or less, but in such a proportion that they all keep the same ratio of motion and rest to each other as before, then the individual will likewise retain its nature, as before, without any change of form' (2L5). Spinoza will stress this point, adding, at 3P7, the claim that 'The striving [*conatus*] by which each thing strives to persevere in its being is nothing but the actual essence of the thing.' If one is unable to maintain this 'same ratio of motion and rest', and if in encounters with other bodies one is unable to persevere in one's actual essence, then the result is death. Spinoza states this point explicitly in the *Short Treatise*: 'if other bodies act on ours with such force that the proportion of motion and rest cannot remain 1 to 3 [for example], that is death, and a destruction of the soul' (I/53). What is necessary, therefore, to persevere in our nature, to act upon our appetites, is to filter and select against excessive differences, against encounters that may undermine our striving (*conatus*) and result in death. In line with Spinoza's famous claim, made in a letter to Jarig Jelles (Letter 50) that 'all determination is negation', we can see that this holds equally for the choices and thoughts of finite beings such as ourselves, for they too are determinations that negate or exclude other differences, other possibilities, and our reason for doing so follows from our appetite and striving to persevere in our nature.

The nature of God, however, is not constrained by the necessity to select against difference, to persevere in a particular, determinate ratio of motion and rest, and this for the simple reason that God is absolutely infinite and indeterminate. In a famous letter to Lodewijk Meyer (Letter 12), Spinoza sets out to explain the difference between that which is infinite in its own kind or nature, such as the infinite nature of the attributes of thought and extension, and that which is absolutely infinite, namely God, and characteristic of God for Spinoza is 'the infinite enjoyment of existing'. The infinite enjoyment of existing is crucial to Spinoza's distinction between 'Eternity and Duration', for 'it is only of Modes', Spinoza argues, 'that we can explain the existence by Duration' (Letter 12). That is, in so far as we actively select against difference and persevere in our ratio of motion and rest, our existence is characterised by the duration of this striving. God, by contrast, as 'infinite enjoyment of existence', does not select against difference but is rather the cause and affirmation of all possible differences – 'God's power is his essence' (1P34), as Spinoza puts it – and this is the nature of Eternity for Spinoza.

With Spinoza's understanding of God as the 'infinite enjoyment of existence', we can begin to see the reasoning behind some of his more puzzling claims, such as this from the latter half of Part 5 of the *Ethics*, from which Jonathan Bennett claims we 'should in sad silence avert our eyes' (Bennett 1984, 375): 'He who has a body capable of a great many things has a Mind whose greatest part is eternal' (5P39). The difficulty Bennett and others have, including Edwin Curley, is that one would suppose that that which is eternal is not subject to change, to increasing or decreasing, and yet a body that can do more is supposed to increase the eternal part of the mind. If we understand God's nature as absolutely indeterminate and infinite, as the power and 'infinite enjoyment of existence' that is inseparable from the deter- minate modes that express this power in their own way, then even though the determinate increase is only in the determinate aspects and nature of the mind itself, nevertheless the absolutely indeterminate nature and power of God is inseparable from this increase, from this greater part that is eternal. To put this in the terms developed here, to live a meaningful life is to express the powers of making sense, including on the one hand the tendency towards differentiation, towards increased connections, relations and a reduction in the need to select against difference, and on the other hand the tendency towards dedifferentiation, towards the absolutely infinite and indeterminate nature of God, towards the 'infinite enjoyment of existence'. The more we realise our nature as expressions of God's power, of the powers of making sense, the more we can do with our determinate bodies and minds, and the more we move towards the infinite enjoyment of existing, and thus towards the realisation of our freedom, the human freedom that was precisely the title of Part 5 of the *Ethics*.

Spinoza's discussion of freedom in the *Ethics* continues and refines, with a metaphysical basis, the stress he placed on freedom in his *Tractatus Theologico- Politicus*. The key point Spinoza sets out to establish in the *Tractatus* is that not only should a republic allow for the freedom to philosophise, but more importantly it stands to benefit by allowing such freedom. That said, Spinoza is also clear that being a citizen in a republic entails a transfer of our freedom to act to those who govern and determine the limits of our actions through law. With respect to our thought and judgment, however, those who govern are 'never able to stop men from making their own judgment' (Spinoza 2016, 345; III/240). In a key passage, Spinoza echoes the republican tradition, sum- marising his earlier arguments by pointing out that 'From the foundations of the Republic explained above it follows most clearly that its ultimate end is not to dominate, restraining men by fear, and making them subject to another's control' (345; III/240). In good republican tradition, therefore, and as Pettit has argued, the purpose of a good government is to put in place institutions and practices that avoid the arbitrary domination of its citizens. More important, however, than allowing for unlimited, unimpeded freedom within the limits of the law, and hence negative liberty, a republic ought 'not to dominate', or through fear and arbitrary exercises of power make its citizens 'subject to another's control'. In setting out 'to free each person from fear, so that he can live securely, as far as possible', the goal of a proper republic, Spinoza argues, 'is not to change men from rational beings into beasts or automata, but to enable their minds and bodies to perform their functions safely, to enable them to use their reason freely' (346; III/240). In other words, the proper end of a republic is to enable us to express God's power more fully and to realise our nature as expressions of God in an 'infinite enjoyment of existence', as freedom. Allowing people 'to use their reason freely' is integral to this process and to the true ends of a republic, for 'the freedom of judgment', Spinoza argues, 'is especially necessary for advancing the arts and sciences. Only those who have a free and unprejudiced judgment can cultivate these disciplines successfully' (349; III/243). The state is thus to mirror the aspirations of the individual who seeks to attain their freedom through the intellectual love of God, or through that freedom that is nothing less than the realisation of God's essence/power, a freedom that increases as they do more with their body and mind and as they become increasingly less dependent upon selecting against difference. For the state, similarly, the task of governing is to enable citizens to reason freely, and in doing so allow for differences to become increasingly tolerated and accepted. For Spinoza this point is obvious: 'Men must be so governed that they can openly hold different and contrary opinions, and still live in harmony. There can be no doubt that this way of governing is best, and has the least disadvantages, since it's the one most compatible with men's nature' (351; III/245). It is the way of governing best suited to the attainment of human freedom, of the power of making sense of our lives. For Spinoza, however, this power and freedom is separate from the power of law. The freedom to philosophise and develop our own judgments and thoughts on things, to make sense of things, is crucial and 'necessary for advancing the arts and sciences', advances that may serve to benefit everyone in the state. But this freedom is allowed, Spinoza concludes, provided one 'takes no license from that to introduce anything into the Republic as a right, or to do anything contrary to accepted laws' (352–3; III/246). What, then, is the relationship between freedom and law, between enhancing our capacity to appreciate and tolerate differences, to express the 'infinite enjoyment of existence', and the laws that govern and restrict our actions? This is the question of the relationship between freedom and law as it has come to be understood within the liberal tradition, of which Spinoza is sometimes credited with being an early proponent. It is to this that we now turn.

Law

To clarify further the implications of the arguments in this book for understanding the nature of law, I want to return to the problem of rule-following
raised in the Introduction, and in two important and related senses. We
will first address the paradox of rule-following that Saul Kripke pinpoints
in Wittgenstein's *Philosophical Investigations*. In discussing some of the
enormous literature surrounding this problem, we will set the stage for
showing how conditions of relevance, or use as Wittgenstein might have
it, determine whether or not a rule has been applied correctly and what
it means, precisely, to be following a rule. After considering the sceptical
and anti-sceptical interpretations of the rule-following paradox that have
emerged in the course of these debates, we will extend the anti-sceptical
view as it is found in the work of ethnomethodologists. This anti-sceptical
reading will be the second sense in which we will take up the problem of
rule-following, and this will draw us closer to the practices and problems
that are inseparable from the nature of law. Where the anti-sceptics break
with the sceptics is over the assumption made by the latter that a rule is
to be thought of as separate and distinct from the practice that follows the
rule, or independently of the many actions that may be carried out in accordance with the rule. Returning to this debate will further clarify the
relationship between problems and solutions we have been developing. In
particular, our account of problematic Ideas will extend the anti-sceptical
approach by arguing that in the same way rules emerge in the midst of
practices, as ethnomethodologists argue, so too a solution emerges in the
encounter with a problem, a solution that does not exhaust the nature of the
problem that remains inseparable from it. This is why Deleuze claims that
'few philosophers have placed their trust in the question "What is X?" in
order to have Ideas' (Deleuze 1994, 188). That is, while the solutions, rules,
laws and Ideas that emerge can be seen as abstractions distinct from practices
and encounters with a problem, if one sees them in this way without also
addressing the problem they are inseparable from then one will have insuf-
ficiently understood the nature of the solutions themselves. The 'What is
X?' question is fine, Deleuze notes, when it is 'being applied in a vacuum
for propaedeutic ends' (188), when the many factors involved in constituting
the nature of a problem are excluded from the questioning, such as may be
done in simplifying for the purpose of teaching; but 'Once the dialectic
brews up', once connections, relations and determinations become increasingly manifest in exploring the nature of the problem inseparable from the
solution, then 'the questions "How much?", "How?", "In what cases?",
and "Who" abound' (188). These questions of relevance inseparable from
solutions are precisely how rules are to be understood, according to the

anti-sceptics, and once they are understood in this way then the sceptical implications of Wittgenstein's rule-following paradox dissipate.

Wittgenstein states the rule-following paradox as follows: 'This was our paradox: no course of action could be determined by a rule, because every course of action can be brought into accord with the rule' (Wittgenstein 2009, §201). As Kripke understands this paradox, it presents us with 'the most radical and original skeptical problem that philosophy has seen to date' (Kripke 1982, 60). As Wittgenstein himself elaborates upon the sceptical implications of bringing an action into accord with a rule, 'if every course of action can be brought into accord with the rule, then it can also be brought into conflict with the rule' (Wittgenstein, 2009, §201). To recall Kripke's own example (from the Introduction), let us take the action of adding the sum of 68 and 57. One person, let's say, writes down the number 125 and another writes down 5 in response to the problem. Wittgenstein's sceptical point, Kripke notes, is that both could be made to accord with a rule – either the plus rule or what Kripke calls the quus rule. In the former, an action in accord with the plus rule would give us $68 + 57 = 125$, but in the quus rule, which says that any number greater than 57 that is being added results in the answer being 5, then the action in accordance with the quus rule would be $68 + 57 = 5$. The point of Wittgenstein's sceptical paradox, as Kripke understands it, is that one would need to point to some fact in one's past usage, a fact in the head, a rule which exists prior to an action, to justify one's present usage of the plus rule as well as any future uses of this rule in novel cases. Wittgenstein, however, according to Kripke, accepts the sceptic's claim that there are no such rules, that there is no ultimate grounding or rule from which our actions follow. All we have, at bottom, is an 'ungrounded way of acting' (Wittgenstein 1972, 47): '"How am I able to follow a rule?" – If this is not a question about causes, then it is about the justification for my acting in this way in complying with the rule. Once I have exhausted the justifications, I have reached bedrock, and my spade is turned. Then I am inclined to say: "This is simply what I do"' (Wittgenstein 2009, §217).

Whether Wittgenstein's appeal to an 'ungrounded way of acting' to resolve the rule-following paradox involves the scepticism Kripke attributes to it has been the subject of tremendous debate, and a number of issues in analytic philosophy have turned on where one stands on the matter. John McDowell, for instance, pushes Hilary Putnam on the conclusions he draws from his famous Twin Earth thought experiment, conclusions with repercussions for the rule-following paradox. In particular, McDowell claims that if one pushes Putnam's central conclusion that meaning isn't in the head, then so too 'we ought to conclude [that] the mind is not in the head' (McDowell 1994, 36). If the point of Kripke's reading of Wittgenstein's paradox is that there is no fact in the head that assures us we are following a rule – plus rather than quus – then Putnam, McDowell argues, has not shaken the habit of thinking there must be such a fact tied to our mental representations. As McDowell puts it, 'Putnam's governing assumption here is that a mental state or occurrence that is representational ... must in itself consist in the presence in the mind of an item with an intrinsic nature characterizable independently of considering what it represents' (43). The lesson Putnam draws from his Twin Earth thought experiment, to be discussed in more detail shortly, is that two people, one on Earth and their twin on Twin Earth, each have the same psychological state when in the presence of what they call water, and yet what is referred to by each of them is different. Stated in McDowell's terms, both are having a 'mental state or occurrence that is representational' – namely, representational of water – and the intrinsic nature of this state, as it is 'independently' of what it represents, is the same for each of them, and yet what is referred to is indeed different. For McDowell, as we will now see, had Putnam concluded from his Twin Earth thought experiment not only that meanings are not in the head, but also that the mind is not in the head either, then he would have been open to taking a different approach to Wittgenstein's rule-following paradox.

In Putnam's thought experiment, Twin Earth is very much like earth, nearly identical in fact, with one unique exception: the liquid they call 'water' – a liquid 'indistinguishable from water at normal temperatures and pressures ... it tastes like water and it quenches thirst like water', and it fills their lakes, seas and rivers – 'is not H_2O but a different liquid whose chemical formula is very long and complicated', but which Putnam abbreviates 'simply as XYZ' (Putnam 1975, 223). The question this example helps Putnam to address is what the relation is between the meaning of water as one grasps it or understands it – its meaning as a psychological state, or its intension as Putnam also puts it – and the extension of this meaning, that which is meant when one says *this* is water. For travellers from Earth to Twin Earth, and vice versa, they would likely all be in the same state of mind as the inhabitants of the planet they visit, with the exception of those with the expertise and skills to determine that XYZ is not water for it is not H_2O. Just because people from Twin Earth and Earth are each in the same psychological state when in the presence of the liquid they call 'water', however, does not mean they are in the presence of water. In fact, the inhabitants of Twin Earth are not in the presence of water, since water is simply that which is indexically tied to what is being referred to on Earth (in a move often equated with Kripke's theory of rigid designators).[9] Moreover, if we were to

---

9. See Putnam 1975, 234: 'Kripke's doctrine that natural-kind words are rigid designators and our doctrine that they are indexical are but two ways of making the same point.'

go back in time to 1750, before anyone knew that water was H_2O, then even though everyone would be in the same psychological state this still does not mean that this state is picking out the same thing, the same extension – it is not. As Putnam pithily concludes, 'Cut the pie anyway you like, "meanings" just ain't in the head' (227).

We can bring McDowell back into the discussion at this point, and in particular his use of Wittgenstein's rule-following paradox to challenge Putnam's conclusions regarding psychological states. As we have seen, McDowell takes Putnam's 'governing assumption' to be that the psychological state associated with a representational thought about something, such as water, has an intrinsic nature distinct and independent of what is represented in this thought. The fact that everyone on Earth and Twin Earth (circa 1750) is in the same psychological state even though that which is represented differs in each case is evidence, for Putnam, of the fact that '"meanings" just ain't in the head'. The problem here, as McDowell sees it, is in determining what, if anything, connects the psychological state of grasping and understanding the meaning of a word and the extension of that word; in other words, what determines whether or not we have used the word correctly, have applied it in the right circumstances to the right sorts of things, etc.? It is just here that McDowell turns to a reading of Wittgenstein's rule-following paradox. If the grasp of a meaning is a psychological state that does not determine the extension of this meaning, as Putnam argues, then the intrinsic nature of a psychological state functions much like a sign-post, McDowell argues, that does not by itself tell you how to relate the sign-post to that which is being represented (the extension). As McDowell puts it, 'what counts as following the sign-post and what does not is not an inscribed board fixed to a post, considered in itself, but such an object under a certain interpretation – such an object interpreted as a sign-post pointing the way to a certain destination' (McDowell 1992, 41). In other words, if the psychological state, by itself, does not determine how it is related to its extension, then what does? For McDowell it is a 'certain interpretation' of the state, or the sign-post, that does so. Such an interpretation, however, is itself an act of mind, yet another psychological state or sign-post that does not determine, in itself, its relation to that which is being interpreted, its extension; and yet this interpretation needs another interpretation, and so on *ad infinitum*. To end the regress, McDowell argues that we need to move beyond thinking of meaning in terms of psychological states, following through on the promise of Putnam's argument to recognise that not only are meanings not in the head, mental states are not either. As McDowell concludes, 'What Putnam never seems to consider is the possibility of a position that holds that command of a meaning is wholly a matter of how it is with someone's mind, and combines that with the determination of extension by meaning so as to force a radically non-solipsistic conception of the mind to come to explicit expression' (McDowell 1992, 40–1). In short, to avoid the regress and resolve the paradox of rule-following, Putnam ought to have avoided the trap of calling upon a psychological state as the counterpart for a representational thought. What McDowell proposes, in short, and this is the path he says Putnam is not taking, is a non-solipsistic explanation of rule-following that avoids the regress of interpretations. This is a version of the sceptical solution to the paradox, a solution that assumes the sceptical consequences of the regress and then attempts to explain how a psychological state relates to actions done in accordance with a rule, and thus to the actions that may or may not determine the extension correctly. This solution, to rephrase Wittgenstein's point, is that the bedrock we reach is an ungrounded way of acting, or simply what we do, but it is a way of acting that is validated by the actions of the community; it is the community of fellow language-users, for instance users of the plus rule, which determines whether or not our way of acting is following the rule or not.[10]

What McDowell, Kripke and many others continue to overlook, however, as Alexander Miller observes in his overview of these debates, is that there is a non-sceptical reading of Wittgenstein's rule-following paradox. Miller notes that 'as many commentators have pointed out, the paragraph in *Philosophical Investigations* which follows [the famous one which states the rule-following paradox] shows that contrary to what Kripke claims, Wittgenstein does not accept the skeptical paradox that there is no such thing as a fact about meaning' (Miller 2004, 132). For Wittgenstein, facts about meaning entail rules that are inseparable from the actions that are or are not done in accordance with the rules, interpretations that are inseparable from that which is interpreted. It is only by beginning with this determinate difference between rules (facts in the head) and actions, interpretations and interpretants, that we end up with the sceptical consequences of the rule-following paradox. Wittgenstein alludes to just this point in the paragraph Miller mentions, when he claims 'there is a way of grasping a rule which is not an interpretation, but which is exhibited in what we call "obeying the rule" and "going against it" in actual cases' (Wittgenstein 2009, §201). Wittgenstein anticipates this move a couple pages earlier when he claims that 'Any interpretation still hangs in the air along with what it interprets, and cannot give it any support. Interpretations

---

10. It should be noted that there are a number of philosophers who neither accept the para-
    doxical implications of the rule-following paradox nor the communitarian solution to it.
    In a series of related thought experiments concerning an isolated Robinson Crusoe, Jody
    Azzouni (2017) offers a dispositional account of rule-following that relies neither on facts
    in the head nor on a community of fellow language-users.

by themselves do not determine meaning' (§198). In other words, for Wittgenstein it is simply a mistake to think in terms of the distinction between an interpretation and that which is interpreted, such as a rule for instance – according to Wittgenstein there are simply actions that can be said, in actual cases, to be cases of obeying or going against the rule.

In the Introduction, as we reached this point, we noted that Wittgenstein left us largely without an explanation for what these cases of obeying or going against a rule were like, other than to say that they involve an agreement of some type, a form of life. We can now begin to see why Wittgenstein does not offer an explanation, since to do so would simply be to resurrect the problematic relations between an explanans and an explanandum, an interpretation and an interpreted. It was for this reason that Wittgenstein abandoned explanation in philosophy and claimed that description should take its place ('All *explanation* must disappear, and description alone must take its place' [Wittgenstein 2009, §109; emphasis in original]). We can further clarify Wittgenstein's position here by drawing on our earlier discussion of the cartographic illusion (see §5.1.b). As Ingold argued with respect to mapmaking, the cartographic illusion is the result of processes of wayfinding that give rise to the abstract distinction between a map and the territory this map represents. This illusion gives one the sense that because a map represents an already complete and determinate space, one can simply use it to navigate from where one is on the map to any other place one may want to go. The cartographic illusion, according to Ingold, entails thinking that the map is complete in itself and that mapmaking accurately accounts for the process of wayfinding, when in fact wayfinding involves a heterogeneous sequence of wayfindings that give rise, as abstractions from this process, to the distinction between a map, as a representation, and the territory mapped, the represented. Even maps themselves, as Denis Wood has argued, presuppose a code which enables us to connect the diagrams and marks on the maps with the physical objects, locations and other phenomena that are being mapped. Different codings can give rise to vastly different representations, as we saw with the different maps of the 2016 presidential election results (see §5.1.c). In other words, and to return to Wittgenstein's point, grasping the correct action by way of an interpretation of a rule is analogous to plotting one's course by looking at a map. This would be comparable to the cartographic illusion, but just as it is a mistake, according to Ingold, to assume that mapmaking is a straightforward process of simply representing the space that is to be mapped, so too for Wittgenstein it is a mistake to think that rule-following is a straightforward process of following an already established and determinate rule, whether as a fact in the head or as a norm, rule or law of one's society. Mapmaking presupposes a heterogeneous series of wayfindings, or a heterogeneous series of actions, some of them being cases of 'going the right way', others cases of 'going the wrong way', from which a map comes to be abstracted (through the dedifferentiating tendency); so too rule-following for Wittgenstein entails a heterogeneous series of actions, some cases of 'obeying the rule', and others cases of 'going against it', and the rules-as-rails are abstractions from this multiplicity (again through dedifferentiation).

To further clarify this reading of Wittgenstein, what has come to be called the anti-sceptical reading, we can return to Putnam. The key lesson Putnam draws from his Twin Earth thought experiment is that two assumptions that were widely thought to be unquestionable with respect to the meaning of 'meaning', are incompatible. The first is that 'knowing the meaning of a term is just a matter of being in a certain psychological state' (Putnam 1975, 219). We have seen how Putnam's thought experiment led to the conclusion that the meaning of '... is water' is not to be identified with a psychological state, for the same state could mean two different things. Meanings, Putnam concluded, 'just ain't in the head'. The second assumption is that 'the meaning of a term determines its extension' (219). Putnam will 'keep this assumption', arguing that meaning does determine extension, but 'by construction, so to speak' (270). What he means by 'construction' here is that it is no longer meaning as grasped by an individual that determines extension, but rather 'the sociolinguistic state of the collective linguistic body to which the speaker belongs that fixes the extension' (229). This collective linguistic body also has a division of labour whereby some have the skills and conceptual repertoire to differentiate H_2O from XYZ, whereas most will simply see and say water, and mean it. It is the theory of the experts, a theory Putnam takes to be tracking the nature of reality, that determines and fixes extension. This gets us to the heart of Putnam's internal realism, for the phrase '... is water' does determine the extension of something real, namely H_2O, and this extension is not determined by social or cultural factors, but by a theory that seeks to represent reality. Putnam claims that, if Archimedes were to refer to a substance X we now know is not gold, but refer to it as gold, then he would not be *correctly* fixing the extension of X as gold, even if he were using the best theories and understanding of his day. If one counters with the question 'who is to say Archimedes is wrong?', Putnam has a ready answer: '*we are* (using the best theory available today)' (236). Stated in terms of the anti-sceptical reading of Wittgenstein's rule-following paradox, Putnam's internal realism argues that it is an illusion to think of reality, as the metaphysical realist does, as that which is independent of and distinct from the theories humans create to represent this reality at particular times and places, and within particular cultural settings. There are simply the many efforts to account for, track and represent phenomena in our theories, and the notion of a reality distinct from these theories is an effect of, and an abstraction from, these many efforts. Putnam's internal realism, therefore, is very much in line with the anti-sceptical understanding of Wittgenstein's rule-following paradox.

Returning to our earlier discussion of Harold Garfinkel's ethno-methodological approach to sociology, which we pointed to as an example of the symptomatological approach to revealing the expectations, values and structures of everyday life (see 4.2.a), we can now see that this approach is compatible with the anti-scepticism reading of Wittgenstein. Michael Lynch has made this point explicitly, arguing that what makes the ethnomethodological approach to the study of scientific practice unique, for instance, is precisely this anti-sceptical reading of the rule-following paradox. In contrasting his own ethnomethodological studies of work in the sciences and mathematics (or ESW) with studies done in the sociology of scientific knowledge (SSK) by the likes of David Bloor, Barry Barnes and Harry Collins, among others, Lynch argues that 'the key differences between the ESW and SSK research programs can be illuminated by reference to a familiar debate in philosophy over Wittgenstein's discussion of actions in accord with rules'. As he goes on to clarify: the 'crux of my argument will be that SSK offers a skepticist extension of Wittgenstein … Ethnomethodology, contrary to what is often said about its program, offers a nonskepticist, but not a realist or rationalist, extension of Wittgenstein' (Lynch 1992, 217). We will say more below about Lynch's hesitation to pursue a realist or rationalist extension of Wittgenstein, but for the moment the key point is that a rule, according to ethnomethodologists, is not separate or distinct from the actions done in accordance with the rule, and thus the determinate difference that generates the sceptical consequences of the rule-following paradox is rejected from the start. Lynch understands the sceptical take on Wittgenstein as follows:

> The critical move in the skepticist strategy is to isolate the formulation of the rule from the practice it formulates (its extension). Once the rule statement is isolated from the practices that extend it to new cases, the relation between the two becomes problematic … Such indeterminacy is then remedied by a skepticist solution, in which extrinsic sources of influence are used to explain the relation between rules and their interpretations. (Lynch 1992, 226)

The problem in following the plus rule, we saw, was in determining what assures that the rule is followed into the future rather than some other rule, such as quus. The skepticist solution turns to the reinforcement and expectations of the community as the causal factor in accounting for the following of rules. The SSK program will rely on just such an account. In his well-known symmetry arguments, for example, David Bloor contended that just as we often turn to sociological factors as external causes of error in scientific practice, we also need to do the same in accounting for what is taken to be true, for without this external factor at work we cannot spell out why a theory was accepted when, and, following the sceptical reading of Wittgenstein, the same phenomena and events could have been interpreted to be in accordance with any number of other rules or theories (see Bloor 1983). The mistake in this approach, Lynch argues, is to 'presuppose the independence of the rule and its extension, as though the rule were external to the actions performed in accord with it' (Lynch 1992, 227). Lynch claims that it was Wittgenstein himself who alerted us to this mistake when, in response to the question '"But are the steps not determined by the algebraic formula?"', his terse reply was that 'The question contains a mistake' (Wittgenstein 2009, §189). The algebraic formula, in other words, is taken to be a rule external to the actions and steps it determines, either as a fact in the mind (which was Wittgenstein's primary target) or as the social factors Bloor and the SSK programme credits (which is Lynch's target). In both cases, Lynch claims, we have 'The skepticist interpretation [that] retains the quasi-causal picture of rule following, since it never abandons the search for explanatory factors beyond or beneath the rule-following practice' (Lynch 1992, 227). This search is a mistake, and hence Lynch and the ESW programme will follow Wittgenstein's anti-scepticist lead.

The key anti-sceptical move, according to Lynch, is to shift the account of rule-following from the presupposition that there is an external, quasi-causal relation between a rule and the actions that follow and extend this rule, to 'an "internal" relation [that] holds between rule and extension' (Lynch 1992, 227). Put simply, rather than rely on 'extrinsic social factors' as is done in the SSK programme, Lynch argues that the 'nonskepticist reading [of the rule-following paradox] treats the rule as an expression in, of, and as the orderly activity in which it occurs' (242). To state this in the terms that have been used here, the relation between universals and particulars, or between rules and the actions done in accordance with those rules, are abstractions of a process of making sense; rules and the actions done in accordance with them are each abstractions of the de/differentiating tendencies of making sense. These abstractions or solutions become possible, as we have argued, as a heterogeneous series of elements, or actions in this case, come to constitute a 'consistence and uniformity' which then allows for the possibility of a solution, or for learning. The disruptive experiments Garfinkel performed highlight precisely the importance of the 'consistence and uniformity' of everyday actions. Let us return to the example discussed earlier (4.2.a):

> The victim waved his hand cheerily
> (S) How are you?

(E) How am I in regard to what? My health, my finances, my school work, my peace of mind, my … ?

(S) (Red in the face and suddenly out of control.) Look! I was just trying to be polite. Frankly, I don't give a damn how you are. (Garfinkel 1967, 44).

As experiments such as these demonstrated, what is often unnoticed until disrupted is the extent to which our daily lives fit in with numerous patterns that others expect us to follow. When disrupted, the connections and relationships that are maintained by way of these patterns may also become disrupted and frayed, as was the case in the experiment cited above. The rule one is expected to follow in cases such as this – saying 'fine, how are you?' in response to the subject's initial query – is not an external rule but, to repeat Lynch's way of putting it, 'an expression in, of, and as the orderly activity in which it occurs'. Our routine ways of interacting with one another, or the expectations and rules one could say these interactions are in accordance with, are not external to the interaction but are expressed in the interaction itself, which, as it occurs in actual cases, is simply an instance of the pattern, much as for Wittgenstein there is 'a way of grasping a rule which is not an interpretation, but which is exhibited in what we call "obeying the rule" and "going against it" in actual cases' (Wittgenstein 2009, §201). What Garfinkel's disruption experiments revealed was precisely the orderliness of the connections involved in an interaction, their rule-following nature so to speak, but also their contingent status, or the fact that their orderly status is not immune to challenge (although challenges are clearly resisted, as many of Garfinkel's experiments showed).

Before turning to another example to help clarify Lynch's Wittgensteinian approach to understanding the nature of rule-following, we can first restate Lynch's arguments in the context of Spinoza's understanding of freedom. As we saw earlier, our appetite, the end towards which we strive (*conatus*) to persevere, is a particular ratio of motion and rest that is the actual essence of the individual who strives. These ratios of motion and rest, in short, are the rules that are expressed in, of, and as the very individual that is striving, rather than rules, or natural laws as many Spinoza commentators argue, that are external to the individuals that act in accordance with them. Inseparable from this striving is the necessity to select against difference, against disrupters so to speak, as Garfinkel's experiments illustrated. And yet freedom, for Spinoza, consists of the intellectual love of God, or what he calls the third kind of knowledge whereby one recognises oneself as an expression of God's infinite enjoyment of existing, and hence as a power that affirms absolutely infinite difference and does not select against difference – and as absolutely infinite and indeterminate, God entails no determinations, and thus no negations. As finite beings, however, beings who must persevere in a particular ratio of motion and rest, the true nature of our freedom comes to light as we encounter and embrace life as a problem. When encountering a problem, the established relations, patterns and expectations become dedifferentiated – one unlearns certain habits as a precondition for creating the new habits and relations (differentiation) that come with learning. Encountering and embracing life as a problem is thus a condition for enhancing one's relations and activities so that one can do many things; our freedom is tied to living life as a problem, for then one can become, as Spinoza suggests, one 'who has a body capable of a great many things [and therefore] has a Mind whose greatest part is eternal' (5P39). One positive use of Garfinkel's experiments, then – the symptomatological use they may be put to we might say – is to reveal the problematic nature inseparable from the determinate rules, habits and values that are expressed in, of, and as the everyday life we live. Doing this entails developing a taste for the problematic inseparable from solutions, the relevance questions inseparable from abstract rules, and so on; in other words, it entails engaging in critical existentialism as understood here.

We are now better placed to return to the theme with which we began, in the Introduction: thinking in accordance with a rule. As we saw, in his studies of villagers in Uzbekistan and Kirghizia, Aleksandr Luria discovered that those who could not read also had difficulties thinking in accordance with formal rules, such as the syllogism. They often had trouble with problems such as the following: 'In the Far North, where there is snow, all bears are white. Novaya Zemlya is in the Far North. What color are bears there?' (Luria 1976, 107). Rather than think in accordance with the rules of syllogistic reasoning, the villagers' typical response to this question was to say that they 'had never been in the North and had never seen bears; to answer the question you would have to ask people who had been there and seen them' (107). The conclusion Luria drew from this and many other examples like it was that 'the formal operation of problem-solving presents major, sometimes insurmountable difficulties for these subjects' (132). Luria's working hypothesis appears to have been that literacy gives one a handle on abstract categories and concepts, categories that serve as rules to guide us in determining what does or does not fall under a general concept. This was particularly evident for Luria in cases where villagers were asked to group silk strips of various colours into distinct groupings, with the assumption being that they would group the strips in accordance with certain categorial colours – e.g., as a particular shade of blue for instance. What Luria found was that those with some education and reading ability 'had no difficulty in classifying colors by partitioning them into several groups' (26). For a group of illiterate ichkari women, however, Luria found that 'the instruction to divide the colors into groups created compete confusion and called forth responses such as, "It can't be done", "None of them are the same", "They're not at all alike'" (27).

Sylvia Scribner's more recent work on the role literacy plays in our cognitive development has led her to conclude that Luria's conclusions were mistaken. For Scribner (1977) the problem for the villagers was not one of being unable to follow a rule because their lack of literacy left them without a repertoire of abstract categories and rules to follow in their thinking; rather, drawing explicitly on Wittgenstein at this point, Scribner argues that they were simply unfamiliar with the closed nature of certain formal language-games. As James Glick pointed out in one of his studies of Kpelle tribesmen (cited earlier in the Introduction), it was not a lack of ability that accounted for why they did not group objects in accordance with certain abstract categories – for instance, potato and orange with food; hoe and knife with tool – but rather that such ordering principles were not relevant to their daily life. It was for this reason that the tribesmen, when asked by Glick 'how a fool would do it?' (Glick 1975, 635), had no problem in immediately grouping the food together and the tools together. This is not to say that the tribesmen possessed the extensive repertoire of language-games that those with higher levels of education have, but it does highlight the fact that following rules is part and parcel of the process of making sense of things in actual situations, situations where relevance questions dominate.

The rules that come to the fore as solutions to the problems encountered in the processes of making sense are thus not abstract, pre-existent rules simply awaiting discovery by those who either act in accordance with such rules or apply them to other things, like algebraic formulas are applied to algebra problems, to recall Wittgenstein's example. This is the reason for Lynch's hesitation to accept a realist and rationalist extension of Wittgenstein's project. Rules and reasons do play an important role in our everyday lives, just as maps and laws do, but the mistake for Lynch, as with the cartographic illusion Ingold identifies in the case of maps, is to understand the nature of rules as solutions without a problem, as rules that determine in advance the manner in which solutions are to be achieved – just follow the rules, one might say, and all will work out well. But this is an illusion; it is the mistake Wittgenstein alerts us to and that Lynch and his fellow ethnomethodologists such as Garfinkel are also keen to avoid. It is thus an illusion to think that rules and laws have a reality distinct from that which acts in accordance with them. As Jack Sidnell found in his study of Indo-Guyanese villagers, they have a very specific rule that they invoke all the time – the rule that 'Big brother can't talk to little brother's wife' (Sidnell 2003, 432) – but they nonetheless find various ways of making sense of situations with this rule, with the rule being an element in the very process of making sense. As Sidnell puts it, 'In following, violating, or otherwise orienting to rules ... [the villagers] are not simply matching the specifics of a rule to an encountered situation, rather, they are proposing that a rule bears on a social situation in a particular way and in that sense proposing that the situation has a determinate set of features' (434).

We found this process very clearly at work in the coding of capital that lawyers perform, coding that has contributed to the capital wealth and in- equalities that are so prominent in today's society. As we saw, lawyers rely on a number of key laws and statutes to create capital, most notably, 'contract law, property rights, collateral law, trust, corporate, and bankruptcy law' (Pistor 2019, 3 [recall §5.2.c]). These laws, moreover, are not simply rules lawyers follow and act in accordance with while performing their task as lawyers; to the contrary, it is in the very nature of coding, as Pistor argues, to use the law in the process of making sense of a particular situation and proposing that this situation has certain qualities and features – in the case of assets, for instance, legal coding proposes that certain assets have 'strong priority rights for the assets of their choice, durability over and above the life expectancy of competing assets, the option to convert financial assets into cash at will, and all of the above with legal force against the world' (161). The highly prized results of legal coding are not, as Pistor makes clear, simply the result of applying the law in a straightforward manner such that it is clear the coding is simply being done in accordance with the law. Legal coding is inseparable from the problematic nature of making sense, and thus the process of legal coding itself may well undermine and problematise the very laws that are employed in the process of making sense of capital in given situations. It is for this reason that many lawyers 'go to great lengths to avoid giving a court an opportunity to render a negative ruling on the legal coding they have employed for the benefit of hundreds, if not thousands, of clients' (180). A corporate lawyer could thus identify with the Indo-Guyanese villagers who make use of rules in particular ways in order to make sense of a given situation, and in order to justify their own rule-following behaviour. The lawyer does much the same with their use of various laws, but their legal coding efforts may be negated by the courts if challenged, and with this possibility we come to the institutional powers that act on behalf of, and as expressions of, law.

At an important moment in her book, Pistor accounts for why the legal coding of capital has been able to proceed without much scrutiny or criticism: 'Law is taken as a given, as exogenous to the assets that are the harbingers of wealth; and enormous deference is given to the claim that one's actions are "legal", that they are based on rights' (Pistor 2019, 222). As she goes on to argue, in the Foucauldian manner of problematising what previously went without question (again, see 5.2.c), the law is not exogeneous to capital wealth but is very much integral to the processes involved in legal coding, and hence to the creation of capital wealth itself, which is why lawyers will do whatever they can to avoid the risk of a negative legal decision that could wipe out the wealth they have created through their coding efforts. The decisions of the court that could affect the status of legal codings are themselves based on written law and previous decisions (*stare decisis*), but the law that comes into play here ought not to be understood as a rule separate from the actions and persons to whom the rule may apply. This is indeed the common understanding of the relation, which again follows the understanding of negative liberty whereby laws are thought to be external to actions that are to be left alone (non-interference) to the extent they are conducted within the limits of the law. The anti-sceptical understanding of rules set forth here, however, is more in line with the classical republican conception of freedom whereby the role of law is not to leave us alone, or to promote our own fullest potential and self-governance, but rather to ensure a situation where one does not fall under the arbitrary domination of another. Law is not external and exogenous to the non-domination that is being sought, but is inseparable from practices that maintain non-domination. As Pettit put it:

> When non-domination is promoted by certain political and other institutions – when people are guarded against possibilities of arbitrary interference in their lives – that effect is not causally distinct from the institutions; like the immunity produced by antibodies in the blood, the non-domination is constituted by such institutional arrangements: it has an inherently institutional existence. (Pettit 1997, 274)[11]

On this point Pettit echoes Hume, who also recognised the inseparability of institutions from the behaviours, actions and habits these institutions help to constitute. As we saw earlier, Hume argues that with a well-structured set of institutions, and with a good 'system of laws to regulate the administration of public affairs to the latest posterity', the result will be a civil society that no longer needs to rely 'on the humors and education of particular men, [and hence] the one part of the same republic may be wisely conducted, and another weakly, by the very same men, merely on account of the difference

---

11. See Pettit 2012 for a more extensive discussion of the ways in which the ideas of classical republicanism could become manifest in various democratic institutions. See also Pettit 1990 for his discussion of rule-following. There, Pettit accounts for rule-following by arguing that a series of actions may exemplify a rule (Pettit 1990, 11). This argument has a strong resonance with the approach offered here, where rules are understood to be abstractions made possible by a dedifferentiating tendency immanent to processes of making sense.

of the forms and institutions, by which these parts are regulated' (Hume 1985, 24). To state Hume's point in Lynch's terms, institutions with good systems of laws are not external to the subjects who become part of, or are affected by, these institutions, but the systems of laws become expressions in, of, and as the orderly behaviour of the institutions themselves. If we understand the relations between governing institutions and the individuals governed as themselves being expressions in, of, and as the orderly behaviour that supports these institutions, then we can offer an account of the mystery with which Hume began his essay 'On the First Principles of Government', and the question with which we closed the Introduction.

> Nothing appears more surprizing to those, who consider human affairs with a philosophical eye, than the easiness with which the many are governed by the few; and the implicit submission, with which men resign their own sentiments and passions to those of their rulers. When we enquire by what means this wonder is effected, we shall find, that, as Force is always on the side of the governed, the governors have nothing to support them but opinion. It is therefore, on opinion only that government is founded; and this maxim extends to the most despotic and most military governments, as well as to the most free and most popular. (Hume 1985, 32)

The mystery and surprise that the few are able to maintain their power to govern despite 'Force [being] always on the side of the governed', vanishes once we recognise, on the reading of Hume offered here, that those who govern do not have a transcendent, exogenous power whereby their rule of law is external to and forced upon those who are ruled; rather, their power is, to repeat, simply the expression in, of, and as the orderly expectations and opinions of those who are governed, and this was precisely Hume's point.[12] Hume's lesson, however, has not been widely acknowledged, and the tendency remains one of continuing to envision political institutions, and in particular the institutions of government that are the source of law, authority and power, as exogenous and external to the subjects that are governed. This tendency is yet another instance of the hegemony of the concept of negative liberty in thinking about law and legal institutions.

In her recent book, *Private Government*, Elizabeth Anderson can be seen to be showing precisely what happens when we do not take Hume's point

---

12. This is not to say that 'the orderly expectations and opinions of those who are governed' are beyond reproach. Were the orderly expectations and opinions of everyday non-Jewish Germans in 1933 'orderly'? In short, yes, but the task of critical existentialism as set forth here, and of the symptomatological approach it employs, is to push the narratives that make sense of and are expressions of these orderly expectations. As with the conspiracy theories discussed earlier, the narratives that support these expectations will be seen to be forced rather than authentic. I thank Paul Livingston for raising this issue.

seriously, or consider it at all – to wit, we become increasingly subject, in the workplace, to various forms of private government. As Anderson puts it, 'We are told that our choice is between free markets and state control, when most adults live their working lives under a third thing entirely: private government' (Anderson 2017, 6). The basic point for Anderson is that government is not just what we tend to think of as government – the exogenous institutions disconnected from our daily lives and tucked away in capital cities – but is also what we encounter in our daily lives at work. According to Anderson, if 'government exists wherever some have the authority to issue orders to others, backed by sanctions, in one or more domains of life' (42), then the workplace is one of the places where government exists. What makes a government private or not is the manner in which decisions are made by those with authority to issue orders to others. If the decision-making process is transparent and open to public debate, then the government is public. As Anderson notes, however, 'the association of the state [government] with the public sphere is not inherent. It is a contingent social achievement of immense importance' (44). In the corporations and businesses where most people work, the situation is very different. Not only is 'the state kept out of decision-making in these governments [i.e., workplaces] … the governed are kept out of decision-making as well' (45). In private governments we thus have a situation where 'The most highly ranked individual takes no orders but issues many. The lowest-ranked may have their bodily movements and speech minutely regulated for most of the day' (37). Anderson details some of the countless instances where this occurs, where we become subject to decisions, surveillance and regulation with little or no say regarding the decision-making processes that approve these policies. For Anderson this has all the earmarks of authoritarian government, which leads her to conclude that 'public and academic discourse has largely lost sight of the problem that organized workers in the nineteenth century saw clearly: the pervasiveness of private government at work. Here most of us are toiling under the authority of communist dictators, and we do not see the reality for what it is' (62).

Anderson's claim that most people work for communist dictators is not a random, hyperbolic claim, but rather reflects her genuine belief that we are indeed not seeing 'reality for what it is'. She is quite explicit that 'the modern workplace is communist, because the government – that is, the establishment – owns all the assets, and the top of the establishment hierarchy designs the production plan, which subordinates execute' (Anderson 2017, 39). Since these forms of government are private, neither those governed (the employees) nor the state has a voice in the decision-making processes of the company. If they had such a voice we would be on our way to public government, which is precisely the task Anderson sets before us: 'The task is to replace private government with public government' (65). To pursue this task effectively we must first take heed of Hume's lesson, or of the anti-sceptical reading of laws and rule-following we have been developing here. Anderson is clear on this point: 'we need to reject the false narrowing of the scope of government to the state, recognizing that one's liberty can be constrained by private governors in domains of activity kept private from the state' (48). Instead of thinking of government as exogenous to our daily lives we need to begin to see the many ways in which we are not only subjected to forms of public government, but moreover to forms of private government over which we have no say. Once we begin to replace private government with public government, as Anderson hopes, then we may well realise 'that increased state constraints on people's negative liberties can generate massive net gains in individual positive and republican freedoms. It can even generate net gains in their negative liberties, to the extent that the people being constrained by the state are private governors over others' (48). In other words, through law and state regulation, that is, through public government, corporations ought to become subject to regulations and constraints that will prevent private governors from being able to exercise arbitrary domination over their employees. Anderson recognises the parallels with the republican conception of liberty, though following Pettit we would see this not as a positive liberty, nor as negative liberty – the latter being partly responsible for the failure to recognise the pervasiveness of private government – but rather liberty as non-domination, which is inseparable from the institutions and laws that secure this liberty. For Anderson, therefore, the work of attaining liberty through law, or the project of liberalism we might say, continues. What are the prospects for success or progress in this regard, and is progress really what we want? It is to this question that I now turn, in closing.

Progress

The modern conception of progress is in many ways a natural fit with and outgrowth of the emerging emphasis on negative liberty beginning in the seventeenth century (with Hobbes [recall 3.1.a]). If in the political realm law is external to the infinite, indeterminate freedom of subjects, subjects who are left alone insofar as they remain within the limits of the law, then a correlate to this would be to view nature itself as being infinitely determinable and yet subject to laws – i.e., natural laws – that are external to these determinable processes. In many ways this modern view recalls the Stoics' conception of natural law, and their well-known mandate that one should live in accordance with one's nature. In contrast to the Stoic view, however, whereby one needs simply to live in accordance with a nature one already is, if only potentially, the modern conception views our nature as determinable but infinitely so, and hence the more we know about our nature, the more determinations of our determinable nature we can catalogue, the more we progress towards the full realisation and understanding of our determinable nature.

This contrast becomes clearer if we note the differences between St Augustine and Spinoza. Admittedly the differences are numerous, but on one crucial issue we could say they agree – for both, the key to our happiness and blessedness is grasping the truth of God. Discussing those who deliver sermons and aspire to teach their fellow human beings, Augustine argues that with respect to the highest truths, teachers can do little more than remind us of the truth that already abides within us: 'Now He who is consulted and who is said to "dwell in the inner man", He it is who teaches us, namely, Christ, that is to say, "the unchangeable Power of God and everlasting wisdom"' (Augustine 1968, 51). For Augustine this is no infinite task but rather relies on the grace of God for the ever-present truth to be revealed to us, or for us to recollect the truth that dwells within us. For Spinoza as well, our freedom is attained when we come to the intellectual recognition of ourselves as expressions of the power of God, the infinite enjoyment of existing. For Spinoza, however, what comes to be known is a singular, absolutely infinite power that is infinitely determinable, and thus although we ourselves are finite, the intellectual knowledge of God (the third kind of knowledge) reveals an infinitely determinable reality inseparable from our finite, determinate mind and body. The key for Spinoza, as it was for Kierkegaard (see §4.1.a), is to embrace the nature of ourselves as finite and infinite: an infinite that is finite and a finite that is infinite; a dedifferentiating that is differentiating and a differentiating that is dedifferentiating; in short, a life as making sense, a problematic Idea.

With the shift to the more prominent embrace of negative liberty, if only implicitly, the paradoxical nature of the problem as finitising and infinitising comes to be thought in terms of a solution that is separate and distinct from the problem, a solution without a problem and that dissolves the problem that gave rise to it. In this context the infinitising process becomes an infinite progression to a limit, to a solution that resolves the progression as the truth of the process. This was Leibniz's response to the fear of Spinozism, the fear of pantheism (see §1.2.c). Rather than embrace the inseparability of the infinite power of God from each and every determinate thing, including ourselves, Leibniz separated God from the infinitely determinate and determinable world, and it was this separate God who decided to create the best of all possible worlds that in turn serves as the solution that guarantees the harmony of all processes, the guarantor that infinite processes will progress to the limit. With Leibniz, therefore, we can see the formalisation of the process that will come to be understood simply as progress, as the movement towards what is better and, ideally, to the best itself. The process of progressing is infinite, but it is guaranteed of success by freely following the infinite task thought lays out before us, following it to the limits, at which point the truth that comes at the end of this progress, at the limit, will be revealed.

We can now appreciate more fully why Russell was so keenly drawn to Leibniz, writing a full monograph on his philosophy early in his career. At one level, it is easy to see why this should be so: given Russell's own background in philosophy of mathematics and the work he was developing that would become logical atomism, it is not surprising that he was drawn to Leibniz, whose advances in the calculus and use of infinitesimals and limits in developing his own theory of monads was very much in line with Russell's own philosophical sympathies. At the same time, however, and less obviously, Russell is drawn to the intellectual tradition of liberalism that gets an early formalisation in Leibniz. This can be seen in Russell's relatively early work, *The Problems of Philosophy* (1912), where he confronts the difficulty of thinking of philosophy in terms of progress:

> If you ask a mathematician, a mineralogist, a historian, or any other man of learning, what definite body of truths has been ascertained by his science, his answer will last as long as you are willing to listen. But if you put the same question to a philosopher, he will, if he is candid, have to confess that his study has not achieved positive results such as have been achieved by other sciences. It is true that this is partly accounted for by the fact that, as soon as definite knowledge concerning any subject becomes possible, this subject ceases to be called philosophy, and becomes a separate science. (Russell 2001, 90)

The sciences, in other words, can list the progressive accumulation of established facts and knowledge their respective disciplines have attained over the years; they have truly progressed and have a better understanding of their subject now than they did in the past. Philosophers, by contrast, can point to precious little they have done in the way of progressing within the discipline. For Russell, however, philosophers can take credit for the questions that, once they can be addressed through the tools of the empirical sciences, become questions for those sciences – at which point definite knowledge and progress becomes possible. Philosophy is thus an incubator of the sciences, and as such it works best when it allows for uncertainty, when it allows for the questions that may disrupt and problematise current habits and expectations. 'The man who has no tincture of philosophy', Russell claims, 'goes through life imprisoned in the prejudices derived from common sense, from the habitual beliefs of his age or his nation ... To such a man the world tends to become definite, finite, obvious; common objects rouse no questions, and unfamiliar possibilities are contemptuously rejected' (Russell 2001, 91). By contrast, if we turn to philosophy, or develop a taste for the problematic nature inseparable from common sense – from what has 'become definite,

finite, obvious' – then this will 'enlarge our thoughts and free them from the tyranny of custom'; in the process, 'while diminishing our feeling of certainty as to what things are, it greatly increases our knowledge as to what they may be' (91). In the spirit of liberalism Russell embraced, moreover – more precisely in the liberal tradition that sought, as Elizabeth Anderson noted, for public forms of government – Russell is also seeking a public form of knowledge, a 'free intellect [that] will see as God might see ... [a] knowledge as impersonal, as purely contemplative, as it is possible for man to attain' (93). By challenging the obvious and customary, by problematising our biases and prejudices, most of which are reflections and expressions of our private, imprisoned conceptions of the world, Russell credits philosophy with the replacement of private knowledge by public knowledge and with the 'enlargement of the not-Self' (93), or with how God might see. The end result of this process may be science, and the accumulation of scientific knowledge, but it is philosophy, according to Russell, that gets the process going.

In the thirty-three years that passed between the publication of *The Problems of Philosophy* and his *History of Western Philosophy*, Russell witnessed many significant challenges to his dream of liberalism, and even to the Spinozist dream whereby a government that allows the freedom to philosophise will in the end benefit from the advances in knowledge such freedom brings about. This was also John Stuart Mill's dream, who saw in the case of China a cautionary tale. With all the advances and institutional achievements the Chinese had made – a long written history, institutions of learning, respect for sages, etc. – it would seem, as Mill put it, that 'Surely the people who did this have discovered the secret of human progressiveness' (Mill 1991, 80). But they did not progress, and the reason they had 'become stationary', Mill argues, is because they did not encourage the free development of people's individual natures, up to the limit of the law, and as a result they succeeded 'in making a people all alike, all governing their thoughts and conduct by the same maxims and rules' (80). The threat to liberalism and the freedom it unleashes that allows for human progressiveness, Mill worried, is that other powers, whether public opinion, the state or a ruling party, may interfere with and prevent the free development of thought and individuality. For Mill, China was an example of the risk such interference entails. Russell, writing his *History of Western Philosophy* while the Second World War was ongoing, had more immediate examples to consider. In the preface to this book, Russell writes that throughout history there has been a perpetual pendulum swing from periods where 'civilizations start with a rigid and superstitious system' to periods where anarchy and tyranny reign. Between these two, Russell finds there are times when there appears 'a period of brilliant genius, while the good of the old tradition remains and the evil inherent in its dissolution has not yet developed'. 'The doctrine of liberalism', Russell continues, 'is an attempt to escape from this endless oscillation. The essence of liberalism is an attempt to secure a social order not based on irrational dogma, and insuring stability without involving more restraints than are necessary for the preservation of the community' (Russell 1972, xiii). Having himself had come into immediate and direct contact with such irrational forces – he was imprisoned for a time for his anti-war views in 1916 – Russell believed that to counter those forces what is needed, again, is the not-self of philosophy. Here is how he stated his concerns in 1945:

> I feel a grave danger, the danger of what might be called cosmic impiety. The concept of 'truth' as something dependent upon facts largely outside human control [i.e., not-Self] has been one of the ways in which philosophy hitherto has inculcated the necessary element of humility. When this check upon pride is removed, a further step is taken on the road towards a certain kind of madness – the intoxication of power which invaded philosophy with Fichte, and to which modern men, whether philosophers or not, are prone. I am persuaded that this intoxication is the greatest danger of our time, and that any philosophy which, however unintentionally, contributes to it is increasing the danger of vast social disaster. (Russell 1972, 737)

Philosophy had thus taken on a new task since Russell wrote *The Problems of Philosophy*. In addition to instilling uncertainty into the common sense beliefs of one's day that may be taken to be obvious, the philosopher needs to avoid contributing to the intoxication of power. In other words, the move beyond the self to the not-Self that Russell encourages with the pursuit of philosophy, and the sense of progressing towards a greater understanding of the truth that comes with this, risks becoming confused with an intoxication of power, a doubling down on private prejudices and fears, the result being the type of 'vast social disaster' the world had witnessed at the time Russell was writing. For Russell, the best way to avoid this dangerous intoxication of power to which 'modern men, whether philosophers or not, are prone', is to tie one's 'truth', and hence that which makes sense of what one is doing in life and why, to facts that are 'largely outside human control'. The encounter with a fact we cannot control, with something that resists our will or desire for it to be other than it is, is thus the check on arbitrary power Russell seeks. As did Mill, who also believed that there are truths independent of human passions, customs and prejudices, Russell wants to balance the freedom of thought and enquiry with the truths that provide the foundation and basis for justifying our thoughts. The problem here, however, is that whatever is appealed to as the given or the foundation that justifies one's beliefs and thoughts presupposes the processes of making sense, and thus the infinitising, dedifferentiating process that may undermine this foundation. As we have been arguing, one's thoughts always involve the narrativising that makes sense of these thoughts, and the task of the critical existentialism we have been developing here is to set out to understand the de/differentiating tendencies that are involved in this process of making sense.

We could return again to the research of Luria, Scribner, Stenning and Lambalgen, among many other examples brought in to this work, in order to recall the importance of determining precisely what is determinately given as that upon which one's thoughts and justifications are to be based, the rule or interpretation of the rule which allows us to proceed. As Stenning and Lambalgen argue, reasoning entails the dual process of reasoning to an interpretation and reasoning from an interpretation. Glick's case of the Kpelle tribesman who reasoned from an interpretation based on the relevance of their situation, in contrast to one with a formal education, is a good example of how different reasonings to an interpretation could lead to different conclusions or solutions. Foucault begins his book *The Order of Things* with a fictional example, but one no less relevant to the point we have been stressing. The passage Foucault quotes is from Borges, about 'a certain Chinese encylopedia'

> in which it is written that 'animals are divided into: (a) belonging to the Emperor, (b) embalmed, (c) tame, (d) sucking pigs, (e) sirens, (f) fabulous, (g) stray dogs, (h) included in the present classification, (i) frenzied, (j) innumerable, (k) drawn with a very fine camelhair brush, (l) et cetera, (m) having just broken the water pitcher, (n) that from a long way off look like flies'. (Foucault 1973, xvi; citing Borges 1964, 103)

Foucault's response to this taxonomy is that 'the thing we apprehend in one great leap, the thing that, by means of the fable, is demonstrated as the exotic charm of another system of thought, is the limitation of our own, the stark impossibility of thinking that' (xvi). Stated differently, we lack the narrative (system of thought) to make sense of the relations and interconnections of the taxonomy, why this list is relevant and meaningful, for whom it is meaningful, and in what cases and circumstances, rather than thinking of it as insignificant and meaningless. As we have been arguing, narratives are themselves processes of making sense, hence the term narrativising, processes that draw together elements into planes of consistency (as Deleuze and Guattari put it) such that solutions become possible, with a rule that then predetermines the relationship between elements being one such solution. Some narratives are expressions of our freedom, with freedom understood here, on the existential reading, as encountering the nature of life as a problem. Other narratives, by contrast, will themselves become solutions without problems, narratives distinct from the events and elements they make sense of. A conspiracy theory, as we saw, is an extreme case of such a narrative (see §3.2.b), though Russell's and Mill's appeal to a fact or truth beyond the control of human prejudices and biases will authorise in its own way the embrace of narratives or 'truths' that are taken to be solutions without problems. It was for this reason that Foucault challenged the hegemony of scientific knowledge, not because he was anti-science but because the narratives that make sense of science tend to present it as the privileged form of knowledge, as a solution without a problem, and thus as a standard or narrative external to the social practices concerned with making sense of things. Foucault's task, as he saw it, was thus one of 'detaching the power of truth from the forms of hegemony, social, economic and cultural, within which it operates at the present time' (Foucault 1980, 133). We could read Foucault here as offering his own indictment of the sceptical reading of Wittgenstein's rule-following paradox. In this context, the paradox could be stated as follows: no event or fact can be made sense of by a narrative because all events or facts can be made sense of by this narrative, or the same events and facts can be made sense of by conflicting narratives. In taking the anti-scepticist reading of narratives, or of systems and regimes of truth, Foucault rejects the idea that a scientific narrative is external to scientific practice, or founded in a reality external to theories and 'truths', insisting instead that these theories and 'truths' are themselves expressions in, of, and as the orderly behaviour of scientific practices. This Foucauldian reading of scientific narratives thus converges, surprisingly perhaps, with Putnam's internal realism. In another sense, however, this is not surprising, since both Foucault and Putnam sought to avoid metaphysical realism and cultural relativism, though each brought their own terms and examples to the effort, their own solutions to the problem of making sense.

In living a narrative that makes sense of things, and in embracing the freedom that involves encountering the problem of living, we need to rethink the nature of progress itself, and in turn rethink the role this notion plays within contemporary understandings of society and liberalism. Without falling back into the hegemony of narratives that present solutions without problems, intoxicating as these solutions may be, we need to think of progress not in terms of a goal that is already determined and waiting to be realised – an ultimate theory of everything, the final progression to the limit and ideal, etc. – but in terms of a narrative that will have no determinate goal or end outside the process of making sense itself, though it will, if a good faith rather than a bad faith narrative, increase what the body can do, increase our joy in Spinoza's sense. There are also times, however, where the narratives that make sense of things in our daily encounters stop making sense, when an encounter disrupts us in the manner of Garfinkel's experiments. These disruptions and encounters that stop making sense are symptomatic of the problem that is inseparable from what had always simply made sense and went without question. It is in situations such as these where we learn the most, where the conditions of the problem allow for the enhancement of connections and relations, for affirming the infinite enjoyment of existing. As the ethnomethodologist Kenneth Liberman discovered in his studies of coffee tasters, this moment of learning in the encounter with a problem occurs when a taster comes upon a taste that stops making sense, that refuses to be identified according to the already determinate set of descriptors they have been using. As one taster whispered to Liberman during such an encounter, "'This is where I learn the most about coffee taste'" (Liberman 2013, 247 [see *Inquiry*, 14.5]). Progress, therefore, is not a path to a determinately better future, or towards a better future with determinate markers that will help us along our way to this future, but it is a life of freedom, a life that is embraced even when, and especially when, it stops making sense. Stated differently, in order to avoid the risks associated with liberalism – the 'vast social disaster' that can come with bad faith narratives, passions and the intoxicating power of solutions without problems – we ought to embrace the possibility of becoming lost in liberalism.

Conclusion

As we come to the end of this project to think and rethink some of the key notions that populate discourses about modern society and politics – namely, freedom, law and progress – it will be helpful to recall where we began, with the apartment manager whose thinking, in the wake of his daughter's death, had undermined him to the point where he took his own life. For Camus, as we saw, this was not just a tragic turn of events in a person's life but reflected a basic human condition that Camus expressed, famously, in a single sentence: 'There is but one truly serious philosophical problem, and that is suicide' (Camus 1955, 3). When it comes to matters of life and death – whether the fateful choice of the person committing suicide, or the actions of a state, or those acting on its behalf, in carrying out what it takes to be justified murder – Camus argued that no set of determinate facts could ultimately justify the lives that are taken, nor, and more importantly, could a determinate set of facts justify or ground the meaning of life itself. It is this confrontation with the limits to our justifications, our search for reasons, that becomes, for Camus, the 'one truly serious philosophical problem'.

As we developed the implications of Camus' insight, his undermining thought, we stressed a distinction that was crucial to Deleuze's own philosophy. This was the distinction between what I called truth questions – 'What is X?' questions, where one looks to a determinate fact or state of affairs for an answer, to give us the truth of a situation – and relevance questions, the 'how?', 'why?', 'who?' and 'in what case?' questions that forever threaten to undermine the security and stability of the answers to our truth questions. In the case of the apartment manager Camus discusses, for instance, we saw that no determinate facts could end the undermining thinking he was engaged in, and this for the very reason that this thinking was motivated by problems and questions that no determinate facts could satisfy. This was why Camus saw such questions regarding life and death, questions concerning why, how, and in what cases one should live, to be the true philosophical questions. Deleuze will echo Camus' sentiments and speak more broadly about the nature of philosophy: 'It should be noticed how few philosophers have placed their trust in the question "what is X?" in order to have Ideas.' For Deleuze, 'Once it is a question of determining the problem or the Idea as such, once it is a question of setting the dialectic in motion, the question "What is X?"

gives way to other questions, otherwise powerful and efficacious, otherwise imperative: "How much, how and in what cases?'" (Deleuze 1994, 188). In other words, and as we have seen throughout this book, when it comes to the nature of problematic Ideas, truth questions no longer suffice and it is relevance questions that become imperative.

As we developed the arguments regarding problematic Ideas in the *Inquiry*, the companion work to this project, we saw how relevance questions allowed us to address a number of important metaphysical questions that have persisted throughout the history of philosophy, questions that remained problematic precisely because the answers were often sought by way of 'What is X?' truth questions. In this book our focus has been upon the type of thinking and questioning with which the apartment manager was engaged – that is, with the problem of making sense of one's life. A motif that recurred throughout this questioning was that the dual de/differentiating tendencies of making sense forever threaten and undermine the stable answers one has in response to a 'What is X?' question. Believing a truth question to have been definitively answered is to assume that we have a solution without a problem, and it is this assumption, or illusion, that runs throughout the effort to make sense of life. It is in fact one of the inevitable tendencies of that effort, and it was precisely for this reason that I turned to the existential philosophers, who repeatedly challenge our tendency to rely upon solutions as if they were solutions without a problem. Picking up on this critical line of thought throughout this book, and linking it to the Deleuzian arguments regarding problematic Ideas, I have brought the two together to develop what I have called a critical existentialism.

In setting forth and deploying this critical existentialist approach, we addressed and expanded upon Bertrand Russell's concerns regarding the fate of liberalism. Although Russell need not be considered the canonical spokesperson for liberalism, his views have been widely shared and his philosophical project has also been important both to this work and to the *Inquiry*. That said, the overarching task of the critical existentialism at work here is not to provide yet another justification of, or perhaps criticism of, liberalism; rather, the task has been one of setting forth the manner in which the determinate ways in which we make sense of our lives, including our political situations, come to be. It was here that problematic Ideas as problems of making sense were helpful in showing both the reasons for the illusions we succumb to – why solutions are taken to be solutions without a problem – and the implications of problems persisting and subsisting within solutions. With respect to the latter point, we called upon a symptomatological approach to revealing the problematic Ideas (or relevance questions) that persist in our unquestioned assumptions and narratives. Drawing from Nietzsche, Goffman,

Garfinkel and others, we began to show what a critical existentialism might look like in practice.

In the final chapters our focus returned to Russell's concerns regarding liberalism, or more precisely his concerns for the fate of freedom, law and progress in society. Bringing Wittgenstein's rule-following paradox into the discussion, we stressed the anti-scepticist reading of the paradox, arguing that rules are to be seen as inseparable from the actions that are themselves done in a rule-like way; as Wittgenstein put it, 'there is a way of grasping a rule which is not an interpretation, but which is exhibited in what we call "obeying the rule" and "going against it" in actual cases' (Wittgenstein 2009, §201). In clarifying this point and extending it to an understanding of the rule of law in society, we argued that the mistake is to think of the rule as separate from that which is done in accordance with the rule. Rules are to be understood, rather, as abstractions from a heterogeneous multiplicity of actions (drawing from Ingold's work here). Bringing critical existentialism to bear on the assumption that rules, or in this case the laws and those who govern, are extrinsic to acts in accordance with the rules, or to those who are governed, we showed that recognising the inseparability of governance from our everyday lives is critical to making sense of politics, and thereby to facilitating the potential to transform our political situation. This is one of the tasks of critical existentialism as it is understood here, and Elizabeth Anderson's important work, as we saw, points us in just this direction. Anderson takes Hume's lesson to heart – the lesson that the power the institutions which govern us have is in large part inseparable from the habits and opinions that support those institutions and their power; or, as Michael Lynch puts it, these institutions are simply 'an expression in, of, and as the orderly activity in which it occurs' (Lynch 1992, 242). Hume thus provides the answer to his own question as to how and why the many allow themselves to be governed by the few, especially when 'Force is always on the side of the governed.' For Hume the answer is opinion: it is 'on opinion only that government is founded' (Hume 1985, 32). With the anti-scepticist reading of Wittgenstein offered here, we have a better understanding of how this opinion, itself inseparable from processes of making sense, has given rise to the sense of rule or law as a solution without a problem. We have also, by developing our critical existentialist approach, begun to sketch some of the ways in which we can encounter the problems that are inseparable from solutions, problems that bring with them many questions – of how, who, when, in what case – that are part and parcel of philosophy and its effort to make sense of life.

Bibliography

Addison, Joseph. 1713. *Cato: A Tragedy*. London: Longman.

Adkins, Brent. 2007. *Death and Desire in Hegel, Heidegger and Deleuze*. Edinburgh: Edinburgh University Press.

Adorno, Theodor W. 1973 [1964]. *The Jargon of Authenticity*. Translated by Knut Tarnowski and Frederic Will. Evanston: Northwestern University Press.

Adorno, Theodor W., and Max Horkheimer. 1969. *Dialectic of Enlightenment*. London: Continuum.

Adorno, Theodor W., Hans Albert, Ralf Dahrendorf, Jürgen Habermas, Harald Pilot and Karl R. Popper. 1976. *Positivist Dispute in German Sociology*. Translated by Glyn Adey and David Frisby. New York: Harper & Row.

Alchian, Armen A. 1950. 'Uncertainty, Evolution, and Economic Theory'. *The Journal of Political Economy* 58 (3):211–21.

Althusser, Louis. 1969. *For Marx*. Translated by Ben Brewster. London: Allen Lane.

Althusser, Louis, Étienne Balibar, Roger Establet, Pierre Macherey and Jacques Rancière. 2016 [1972]. *Reading Capital*. Translated by Ben Brewster and David Fernbach. Edited by Ben Brewster. London: Verso.

Amadae, S.M. 2003. *Rationalizing Capitalist Democracy: The Cold War Origins of Rational Choice Liberalism*. Chicago: University of Chicago Press.

Anderson, Benedict. 1991. *Imagined Communities*. New York: Verso.

Anderson, Elizabeth. 2017. *Private Government*. Princeton: Princeton University Press.

Anderson, Perry. 1974a. *Passages from Antiquity to Feudalism*. London: New Left Books.

Anderson, Perry. 1974b. *Lineages of the Absolutist State*. London: New Left Books.

Annas, Julia. 2011. *Intelligent Virtue*. Oxford: Oxford University Press.

Anthony, Third Earl of Shaftesbury. 2001 [1711]. *Characteristicks of Men, Manners, Opinions, Times*. Indianapolis: Liberty Fund.

Arcese, Peter. 1987. 'Age, intrusion Pressure and Defense Against Floaters by Territorial Male Song Sparrows.' *Animal Behaviour* 35:773–84.

Aristotle. 1984. *The Complete Works of Aristotle*. 2 vols. Princeton: Princeton University Press.

Arrighi, Giovanni. 1994. *The Long Twentieth Century: Money, Power, and the Origins of Our Times*. New York: Verso.

Arrighi, Giovanni. 2009. *Adam Smith in Beijing: Lineages of the 21st Century*. London: Verso.

Arrow, Kenneth J. 1951. 'Alternative Approaches to the Theory of Choice in Risk-Taking Situations'. *Econometrica* 19 (4):401–37.

Arrow, Kenneth J. 1977. 'Extended Sympathy and the Possibility of Social Choice'. *The American Economic Review* 67 (1):219–25.

Arrow, Kenneth J. 1982. 'Risk Perception in Psychology and Economics'. *Economic Inquiry* 20 (1):1–9.

Artaud, Antonin. 1948. 'Van Gogh: The Man Suicided by Society'. *Horizon* 17 (79):46–50.

Augustine, St. 1968. *The Teacher; The Free Choice of The Will; Grace and Free Will*. Translated by Robert P Russell. Washington, DC: The Catholic University of America Press.

Ayache, Elie. 2015. *The Medium of Contingency: An Inverse View of the Market*. New York: Palgrave.

Azzouni, Jody. 2017. *The Rule-Following Paradox and its Implications for Metaphysics*. Cham: Springer.

Baier, Annette C. 1991. *A Progress of Sentiments: Reflections on Hume's Treatise*. Cambridge, MA: Harvard University Press.

Baran, Paul, and Paul Sweezy. 1966. *Monopoly Capital: An Essay on the American Economic and Social Order*. New York: Modern Reader Paperbacks.

Baudry, Jean-Louis, and Alan Williams. 1974–1975. 'Ideological Effects of the Basic Cinematographic Apparatus'. *Film Quarterly* 28 (2):39–47.

Bauman, Richard. 1986. *Story, Performance, and Event: Contextual Studies of Oral Narrative*. Cambridge: Cambridge University Press.

Becker, Gary S. 1964. *Human Capital: A Theoretical and Empirical Analysis, with Special Reference to Education*. Chicago: University of Chicago Press.

Becker, Gary S., and Kevin M. Murphy. 1988. 'A Theory of Rational Addiction'. *Journal of Political Economy* 96 (4):675–700.

Bell, Jeffrey A. 2006. *Philosophy at the Edge of Chaos: Gilles Deleuze and the Philosophy of Difference*. Toronto: University of Toronto Press.

Bell, Jeffrey A. 2016. *Deleuze and Guattari's* What is Philosophy? *A Critical Introduction and Guide*. Edinburgh: Edinburgh University Press.

Bellah, Robert. 2005. 'What is Axial about the Axial Age?' *European Journal of Sociology* 46 (1):69–89.

Benes, Jaromir, and Michael Kumhof. 2012. 'The Chicago Plan Revisited'. *IMF Working Paper* (WP/12/202):1–70.

Bennett, Jonathan. 1984. *A Study of Spinoza's Ethics*. New York: Hackett Publishing Company.

Berg, Joyce, John Dickhaut and Kevin McCabe. 1995. 'Trust, Reciprocity, and Social History'. *Games and Economic Behavior* 10:122–42.

Berlin, Isaiah. 1969. 'Two Concepts of Liberty'. In *Four Essays on Liberty*. Oxford: Oxford University Press, 155–65.

Bjerg, Ole. 2014. *Making Money: The Philosophy of Crisis Capitalism*. London: Verso.

Black, Jeremy. 1997. *Maps and Politics*. London: Reaktion Books.

Bloor, David. 1983. *Wittgenstein: A Social Theory of Knowledge*. London: Macmillan Press.

Blyth, Mark. 2002. *Great Transformations: Economic Ideas and Institutional Change in the Twentieth Century*. Cambridge: Cambridge University Press.

Boldyrev, Ivan. 2019. 'The Ontology of Uncertainty in Finance: The Normative Legacy of General Equilibrium'. *Topoi* 40: 725–31.

Borges, Jorge Luis. 1964. *Other Inquisitions, 1937–1952*. Translated by L.C. Ruth. Austin: University of Texas Press.

Borsay, Peter. 1989. *The English Urban Renaissance: Culture and Society in the Provincial Town, 1660–1770*. Oxford: Clarendon Press.

Borsay, Peter, ed. 1990. *The Eighteenth-Century Town: A Reader in English Urban History, 1688–1820*. New York: Longman.

Bourdieu, Pierre. 199a0. *In Other Words: Essays Towards a Reflexive Sociology*. Stanford: Stanford University Press.

Bourdieu, Pierre. 1990b [1977]. *Reproduction: In Education, Society and Culture*. Beverly Hills: SAGE.

Braverman, Harry. 1998 [1974]. *Labor and Monopoly Capital: The Degradation of Work in the Twentieth Century*. New York: Monthly Review Press.

Bréhier, Émile. 1908. *Théorie des Incorporels dans L'Ancien Stoïcisme*. Paris: Librairie Alphonse Picard & Fils.

Bréhier, Émile. 1958 [1928]. *The Philosophy of Plotinus*. Chicago: University of Chicago Press.

Brenner, Robert. 1976. 'Agrarian Class Structure and Economic Development in Pre-Industrial Europe'. *Past and Present* 70:30–75.

Brenner, Robert. 2003 [1993]. *Merchants and Revolution: Commercial Change, Political Conflict, and London's Overseas Traders, 1550–1653*. London: Verso.

Brooke, Christopher. 2012. *Philosophic Pride: Stoicism and Political Thought from Lipsius to Rousseau*. Princeton: Princeton University Press.

Brotton, Jerry. 2014. *A History of the World in 12 Maps*. New York: Penguin Books.

Brouwer, René. 2014. *The Stoic Sage: The Early Stoics on Wisdom, Sagehood and Socrates*. Cambridge: Cambridge University Press.

Burchell, Stuart, Colin Clubb and Anthony G. Hopwood. 1985. 'Accounting in its Social Context: Towards a History of Value Added in the United Kingdom'. *Accounting, Organizations and Society* 10 (4):381–413.

Burge, Tyler. 1984. 'Frege on Extensions of Concepts'. *Philosophical Review* 93 (1):3–34.

Camerer, Colin F. 2003. *Behavioral Game Theory: Experiments in Strategic Interaction*. Princeton: Princeton University Press.

Camus, Albert. 1955 [1942]. *The Myth of Sisyphus and Other Essays*. New York: Knopf.

Camus, Albert. 1989 [1942]. *The Stranger*. New York: Vintage.

Camus, Albert. 2000 [1951]. *The Rebel*. London: Penguin Classics.

Cencini, Alvaro, and Sergio Rossi. 2015. *Economic and Financial Crises: A New Macroeconomic Analysis*. London: Palgrave Macmillan.

Chalmers, David. 2002. 'Does Conceivability Entail Possibility?' In *Conceivability and Possibility*. Edited by Tamar Szabó Gendler and John Hawthorne. Oxford: Oxford University Press, 145–200.

Chang, Hasok. 2004. *Inventing Temperature: Measurement and Scientific Progress*. Oxford: Oxford University Press.

Cheney, Dorothy L., and Robert M. Seyfarth. 2007. *Baboon Metaphysics: The Evolution of a Social Mind*. Chicago: University of Chicago Press.

Chomsky, Noam. 1995. *The Minimalist Program*. Cambridge: Cambridge University Press.

Chomsky, Noam. 2013. *On Anarchism*. New York: The New Press.

Chomsky, Noam, and Edward S. Herman. 1988. *Manufacturing Consent: The Political Economy of the Mass Media*. New York: Pantheon Books.

Chrysostom, Dio. 1932. *Discourses 1–11*. Vol. 257, *Loeb Classical Library*. Cambridge, MA: Harvard University Press.

Clark, Peter, ed. 1976. *The Early Modern Town: A Reader*. New York: Longman.

Clarke, Stephen V.O. 1967. *Central Bank Cooperation 1924–31*. New York: Federal Reserve Bank of New York.

Cole, Michael, J. Gay, J.A. Glick, and D.A. Sharp, eds. 1971. *The Cultural Context of Learning and Thinking: An Exploration in Experimental Anthropology*. New York: Basic Books.

Cole, Michael, and Sylvia Scribner. 1974. *Culture and Thought*. New York: Wiley.

Constant, Benjamin. 1988 [1819]. 'The Liberty of Ancients Compared with that of Moderns'. In *Benjamin Constant: Political Writings*. Edited by Biancamaria Fontana. Cambridge: Cambridge University Press, 309–28.

Cooper, Melinda. 2017. *Family Values: Between Neoliberalism and the New Social Conservatism*. New York: Zone Books.

Corbusier, Le. 1987 [1929]. *The City of To-morrow and its Planning*. Translated by Frederick Etchells. New York: Dover.

Counihan, Marian. 2008. 'Looking for Logic in All the Wrong Places: An Investigation of Language, Literacy and Logic in Reasoning'. Institute for Logic, Language and Computation, University of Amsterdam (ILLC Dissertation Series DS-2008–10).

Cronon, William. 1992. *Nature's Metropolis: Chicago and the Great West*. New York: William Norton & Co.

Davidson, Graham. 1982. 'The City as a Natural System: Theories of Urban Society in Early Nineteenth-Century Britain'. In *The Pursuit of Urban History*. Edited by Derek Fraser and Anthony Sutcliffe. London: Edward Arnold.

Davies, Robert, and Stephen Wheatcroft. 2009. *The Years of Hunger: Soviet Agriculture, 1931–1933*. London: Palgrave Macmillan.

Davis, Mike. 2001. *Late Victorian Holocausts: El Niño Famines and the Making of the Third World*. London: Verso.

de Beauvoir, Simone. 2011 [1949]. *The Second Sex*. Translated by Constance Borde and Sheila Malovany-Chevalier. New York: Vintage Books.

de Bruin, Boudewijn. 2015. *Ethics and the Global Financial Crisis: Why Incompetence is Worse than Greed*. Cambridge: Cambridge University Press.

Deleuze, Gilles. 1990a. *Expressionism in Philosophy: Spinoza*. Translated by Martin Joughin. New York: Zone Books.

Deleuze, Gilles. 1990b. *The Logic of Sense*. Translated by Mark Lester, with Charles Stivale. New York: Columbia University Press.

Deleuze, Gilles. 1994. *Difference and Repetition*. Translated by Paul Patton. New York: Columbia University Press.

Deleuze, Gilles. 1995. *Negotiations*. Translated by Martin Joughin. New York: Columbia University Press.

Deleuze, Gilles. 2001. *Pure Immanence*. Translated by Anne Boyman. New York: Zone Books.

Deleuze, Gilles. 2004. *Desert Islands and Other Texts 1953–1974*. Translated by Michael Taormina. New York: Semiotext(e).

Deleuze, Gilles, and Félix Guattari. 1977. *Anti-Oedipus: Capitalism and Schizophrenia*. Translated by Mark Seem, Robert Hurley and Helen R. Lane. Minneapolis: University of Minnesota Press.

Deleuze, Gilles, and Félix Guattari. 1987. *A Thousand Plateaus: Capitalism and Schizophrenia*. Translated by Brian Massumi. Minneapolis: University of Minnesota Press.

Deleuze, Gilles, and Félix Guattari. 1994. *What is Philosophy?* Translated by Hugh Tomlinson and Graham Burchell. New York: Columbia University Press.

Deneen, Patrick J. 2018. *Why Liberalism Failed*. New Haven: Yale University Press.

Descartes, René. 1984 [1641]. 'Meditations on First Philosophy'. In *The Philosophical Writings of Descartes*. Cambridge: Cambridge University Press.

Dewey, John. 1910. *How We Think*. Lexington, MA: D.C. Heath.

Dostoyevsky, Fyodor. 1992 [1864]. *Notes from Underground*. Translated by M. Ginsburg. New York: Bantam Books.

Dreyfus, Hubert L. 2005. 'Overcoming the Myth of the Mental: How Philosophers Can Profit from the Phenomenology of Everyday Expertise'. *Proceedings and Addresses of the American Philosophical Association* 79: 47–65.

Durkheim, Émile. 1965 [1915]. *The Elementary Forms of Religious Life*. Translated by Joseph Ward Swain. New York: Basic Books.

Durkheim, Émile. 2013 [1892]. *The Division of Labour in Society*. Translated by W.D. Halls. London: Palgrave Macmillan.

Edelman, Lee. 2004. *No Future: Queer Theory and the Death Drive*. Durham, NC: Duke University Press.

Eichengreen, Barry. 2008. *Globalizing Capital: A History of the International Monetary System*. Princeton: Princeton University Press.

Elden, Stuart. 2013. *The Birth of Territory*. Chicago: University of Chicago Press.

Fama, Eugene F. 1970. 'Efficient Capital Markets: A Review of Theory and Empirical Work'. *The Journal of Finance* Papers and Proceedings of the Twenty-Eighth Annual Meeting of the American Finance Association, 383–417.

Federici, Silvia. 2004. *Caliban and the Witch: Women, the Body and Primitive Accumulation*. New York: Autonomedia.

Filmer, Sir Robert. 1680. *Patriarcha; or the Natural Power of Kings*. London: Richard Chiswell.

Finnegan, Ruth. 1973. 'Literacy versus Non-literacy: The Great Divide?' In *Modes of Thought, Essays on Thinking in Western and Non-Western Societies*. London: Faber and Faber.

Fisher, Irving. 1932. *Booms and Depressions*. New York: Adelphi.

Fisher, Irving. 1933. 'The Debt-Deflation Theory of Great Depressions'. *Econometrica* 1 (4):337–57.

Fisher, Mark. 2009. *Capitalist Realism: Is There No Alternative?* London: Zero Books.

Flandreau, Marc, Carl-Ludwig Holtfrerich, and Harold James, eds. 2003. *International Financial History in the Twentieth Century: System and Anarchy*. Cambridge: Cambridge University Press.

Foucault, Michel. 1973. *The Order of Things*. New York: Vintage Books.

Foucault, Michel. 1980. *Power/Knowledge: Selected Interviews & Other Writings, 1972–1977*. New York: Pantheon Books.

Foucault, Michel. 2001. *Fearless Speech*. Los Angeles: Semiotext(e).

Foucault, Michel. 2008. *The Birth of Biopolitics: Lectures at the Collège de France*. London: Palgrave Macmillan.

Frandsen, Ann-Christine, and Keith W. Hoskin. 2014. '"After Accounting": Re-thinking Accounting's Historical-Theoretical Beginnings "Before Writing"'. Critical Perspectives on Accounting, Toronto.

Frege, Gottlob. 1960. *Translations from the Philosophical Writings of Gottlob Frege*. Oxford: Basil Blackwell.

Fricker, Miranda. 2007. *Epistemic Injustice: Power and the Ethics of Knowing*. Oxford: Oxford University Press.

Friedman, Milton. 1966. 'The Methodology of Positive Economics'. In *Essays in Positive Economics*, Chicago: University of Chicago Press, 3–43.

Friedrichs, Christopher R. 1965. *The Early Modern City, 1450–1750*. New York: Longman.

Fritz, Paul, and David Williams. 1973. *City and Society in the 18th Century*. Toronto: University of Toronto Press.

Fustel de Coulanges, Numa Denis. 1980. *The Ancient City*. Baltimore: Johns Hopkins University Press.

Garfinkel, Harold. 1967. *Studies in Ethnomethodology*. Englewood Cliffs: Prentice-Hall.

Gauthier, David. 1986. *Morals by Agreement*. Oxford: Oxford University Press.

Geddes, Patrick. 1915. *Cities in Evolution: An Introduction to Town Planning Movement and to the Study of Civics*. London.

Gellner, Ernest. 1983. *Nations and Nationalism*. Oxford: Basil Blackwell.

Gellner, Ernest. 1998. *Language and Solitude: Wittgenstein, Malinowski and the Habsburg Dilemma*. Cambridge: Cambridge University Press.

Gendler, Tamar Szabó, and John Hawthorne, eds. 2002. *Conceivability and Possibility*. Oxford: Oxford University Press.

Geoghegan, Bernard Dionysius. 2011. 'From Information Theory to French Theory: Jakobson, Lévi-Strauss, and the Cybernetic Apparatus'. *Critical Inquiry* 38 (1):96–126.

Gibson, James J. 2014 [1979]. *The Ecological Approach to Visual Perception*. New York: Routledge.

Gintis, Herbert, and Dirk Helbing. 2015. '*Homo Socialis*: An Analytical Core for Sociological Theory'. *Review of Behavioral Economics* 2:1–59.

Girouard, Mark. 1990. *The English Town: A History of Urban Life*. New Haven: Yale University Press.

Gleick, James. 2011. *The Information: A History, a Theory, a Flood*. New York: Pantheon.

Glick, James. 1975. 'Cognitive Development in Cross-cultural Perspective'. In *Review of Child Development Research*. Edited by J. Horowitz. Chicago: Chicago University Press.

Godfrey-Smith, Peter. 2017. *Other Minds: The Octopus, the Sea, and the Deep Origins of Consciousness*. New York: Farrar, Straus and Giroux.

Goffman, Erving. 1956. *The Presentation of Self in Everyday Life*. New York: Anchor Books.

Goldstick, D. 1979. 'Why is There Something Rather than Nothing?' *Philosophy and Phenomenological Research* 40 (2):265–71.

Goodman, Dena. 1992. 'The Hume-Rousseau Affair: From Private Querelle to Public Process'. *Eighteenth-Century Studies* 25 (2):171–201.

Green, T.H. 1881. 'Lecture on "Liberal Legislation and Freedom of Contract"'. In *Miscellaneous Works*. Edited by R.L. Nettleship. Cambridge: Cambridge University Press, 365–86.

Greenwald, A.G. 1980. 'The Totalitarian Ego: Fabrication and Revision of Personal History'. *American Psychologist* 35:603–18.

Griggs, Richard A., and James R. Cox. 1982. 'The Elusive Thematic-Materials Effect in Wason's Selection Task'. *British Journal of Psychology* 73:407–20.

Grotius, Hugo. 2004 [1609]. *The Free Sea*. Translated by Richard Hakluyt. Indianapolis: Liberty Fund.

Guala, Francesco. 2006. 'Has Game Theory Been Refuted?' *The Journal of Philosophy* 103 (5):239–63.

Hall, Peter Geoffrey. 1998. *Cities in Civilization*. New York: Random House.

Hansen, Mogens Herman. 2006. *Polis: An Introduction to the Ancient Greek City-State*. Oxford: Oxford University Press.

Harlow, Harry F. 1949. 'The Formation of Learning Sets'. *Psychological Review* 56 (1):51–65.

Harlow, Harry F. 1959. 'Learning Set and Error Factor Theory.' In *Psychology: A Study of a Science*, edited by Sigmund Koch. New York: McGraw-Hill Book Company, 492–537.

Havelock, Eric. 1963. *Preface to Plato*. Cambridge, MA: Harvard University Press.

Hayek, Friedrich August von. 1945. 'The Use of Knowledge in Society'. *The American Economic Review* 35 (4):519–30.

Hayek, Friedrich August von. 1948a. 'The Meaning of Competition'. In *Individualism and Economic Order*. Edited by Friedrich August von Hayek. Chicago: University of Chicago Press.

Hayek, Friedrich August von. 1948b. *Individualism and Economic Order*. Chicago: The University of Chicago Press.

Hayek, Friedrich August von. 1978. *New Studies in Philosophy, Politics, Economics and the History of Ideas*. New York: Routledge.

Hayek, Friedrich August von. 1988. *The Fatal Conceit: The Errors of Socialism*. Chicago: University of Chicago Press.

Hayek, Friedrich August von. 2011. *The Constitution of Liberty: The Definitive Edition (Book 17), The Collected Works of F.A. Hayek*. Chicago: University of Chicago Press.

Heft, Harry. 1996. 'The Ecological Approach to Navigation: A Gibsonian Perspective'. In *The Construction of Cognitive Maps*. Edited by Juval Portugali. Dordrecht: Kluwer Academic Publishers, 105–32.

Heidegger, Martin. 1962 [1927]. *Being and Time*. Translated by John Macquarrie and Edward Robinson. New York: Harper & Row.

Heinrich, Michael. 2012. *An Introduction to the Three Volumes of Karl Marx's Capital*. Translated by Alex Locascio. New York: Monthly Review Press.

Hempel, Carl. 1965. *Aspects of Scientific Explanation and Other Essays*. New York: Free Press.

Hilberg, Raul. 1985 [1961]. *The Destruction of the European Jews*. New Haven: Yale University Press.

Hilton, R.H., ed. 1976. *The Transition from Feudalism to Capitalism*. London: Verso.

Hobbes, Thomas. 1994 [1651]. *Leviathan*. Edited by Edwin Curley. Indianapolis: Hackett.

Hobsbawm, Eric. 1990. *Nations and Nationalism Since 1780*. Cambridge: Cambridge University Press.

Hobsbawm, Eric, and Terence Ranger, eds. 1983. *The Invention of Tradition*. Cambridge: Cambridge University Press.

Hochschild, Adam. 1998. *King Leopold's Ghost: A Story of Greed, Terror, and Heroism in Colonial Africa*. New York: Houghton Mifflin Company.

Hochschild, Arlie. 2016. *Strangers In Their Own Land: Anger and Mourning On the American Right*. New York: The New Press.

Hoffmeyer, Jesper. 1996. *Signs of Meaning in the Universe*. Translated by Barbara J. Haveland. Bloomington: Indiana University Press.

Hohenberg, Paul M., and Lynn Hollen Lees. 1995 [1985]. *The Making of Urban Europe: 1000–1994*. Cambridge, MA: Harvard University Press.

Horkheimer, Max. 2002 [1972]. *Critical Theory: Selected Essays*. Translated by Matthew J. O'Connell. London: Continuum.

Hoskin, Keith W., and Richard H. Macve. 1986. 'Accounting and the Examination: A Genealogy of Disciplinary Power'. *Accounting, Organizations and Society* 11 (2):105–36.

Huber, Joseph. 2017. *Sovereign Money: Beyond Reserve Banking*. London: Palgrave Macmillan.

Hull, David. 1986. 'On Human Nature'. *PSA: Proceedings of the Biennial Meeting of the Philosophy of Science Association* 1986:3–13.

Hume, David. 1978 [1739]. *A Treatise of Human Nature*. Edited by L.A. Selby-Bigge. Oxford: Clarendon Press.

Hume, David. 1983 [1754–62]. *The History of England in Six Volumes*. 6 vols. Indianapolis: Liberty Fund.

Hume, David. 1985 [1741–42]. *Essays, Moral, Political, and Literary*. Edited by Eugene Miller. Indianapolis: Liberty Fund.

Hume, David. 1999 [1751]. *Enquiry Concerning the Principles of Morals*. Oxford: Oxford University Press.

Hume, David. 2005 [1748]. *An Enquiry Concerning Human Understanding*. Edited by Tom Beauchamp. Oxford: Oxford University Press.

Hume, David. 2007 [1779]. *Dialogues Concerning Natural Religion*. Cambridge: Cambridge University Press.

Humphrey, Caroline, and Stephen Hugh-Jones. *Barter, Exchange and Value: An Anthropological Approach*. Cambridge: Cambridge University Press.

Husserl, Edmund. 1983 [1913]. *Ideas Pertaining to a Pure Phenomenology and to a Phenomenological Philosophy, First Book*. The Hague: Martinus Nijhoff.

Huxley, Julian S. 1934. 'A Natural Experiment on the Territorial Instinct'. *British Birds* 27:270–7.

Hyppolite, Jean. 1997. *Logic and Existence*. Translated by Leonard Lawlor and Amit Sen. Albany: State University of New York Press.

Ingham, Geoffrey. 2004. *The Nature of Money*. Cambridge: Polity Press.

Ingold, Tim. 2000. *The Perception of the Environment: Essays on Livelihood, Dwelling and Skill*. New York: Routledge.

Innes, A. Mitchell. 1914. 'The Credit Theory of Money'. *Banking Law Journal* January:151–68.

Inwood, Brad. 1999 [1985]. *Ethics and Human Action in Early Stoicism*. Oxford: Clarendon Press.

Inwood, Brad. 2008. *Reading Seneca: Stoic Philosophy at Rome*. Oxford: Oxford University Press.

Istomin, Kirill V., and Mark J. Dwyer. 2009. 'Finding the Way: A Critical Discussion of Anthropological Theories of Human Spatial Orientation with Reference to Reindeer Herders of Northeastern Europe and Western Siberia'. *Current Anthropology* 50 (1):29–49.

Jacobs, Jane. 1961. *The Death and Life of Great American Cities*. New York: Random House.

Jacobs, Jane. 1969. *The Economy of Cities*. New York: Random House.

Jacoby, Matthew Gerhard. 2002. 'Kierkegaard on Truth'. *Religious Studies* 38 (1):27–44.

Jakobson, Roman. 1978. *Six Lectures on Sound and Meaning*. Translated by John Mepham. Cambridge, MA: The MIT Press.

Jansen, Harry. 2001. *The Construction of an Urban Past: Narrative and System in Urban History*. Translated by Feike de Jong. Oxford: Berg.

Jensen, Michael C., and William H. Meckling. 1976. 'Theory of the Firm: Managerial Behavior, Agency Costs and Ownership Structure'. *Journal of Financial Economics* 3 (4):305–60.

Jones, Emily. 2017. *Edmund Burke and the Invention of Modern Conservatism, 1830–1914*. Oxford: Oxford University Press.

Judt, Tony. 2011. *Ill Fares the Land*. New York: Penguin Books.

Kafka, Franz. 1964. *The Trial*. Translated by Edwin Muir and Willa Muir. New York: Schocken Books.

Kafka, Franz. 1971. *The Complete Stories*. Translated by Edwin Muir and Willa Muir. New York: Schocken Books.

Kahneman, Daniel. 2003. 'A Psychological Perspective on Economics'. *The American Economic Review* 93 (2):162–8.

Kahneman, Daniel. 2011. *Thinking, Fast and Slow*. New York: Farrar, Straus and Giroux.

Kant, Immanuel. 1983. *Perpetual Peace and Other Essays*. Indianapolis: Hackett.

Keynes, John Maynard. 1930. *A Treatise of Money*. New York: Harcourt, Brace and Company.

Keynes, John Maynard. 1936. *The General Theory of Employment, Interest, and Money*. London: Palgrave.

Kierkegaard, Søren. 1968. *Concluding Unscientific Postscript*. Translated by David F. Swenson and Walter Lowrie. Princeton: Princeton University Press.

Kierkegaard, Søren. 1980a [1844]. *The Concept of Anxiety*. Translated by Reidar Thomte. Princeton: Princeton University Press.

Kierkegaard, Søren. 1980b [1849]. *The Sickness Unto Death*. Translated by Howard Vincent Hong and Edna Hatiestad Hong. Princeton: Princeton University Press.

Kierkegaard, Søren. 2006 [1843]. *Fear and Trembling*. Translated by C. Stephen Taylor. Cambridge: Cambridge University Press.

Kindleberger, Charles. 2005. *Manias, Panics, and Crashes: A History of Financial Crises*. Hoboken: John Wiley & Sons, Inc.

Klein, Peter. 1998. 'Foundationalism and the Infinite Regress of Reasons'. *Philosophy and Phenomenological Research* 58 (4):919–25.

Klein, Peter. 1999. 'Human Knowledge and the Infinite Regress of Reasons'. *Philosophical Perspectives* 13:297–325.

Klein, Peter. 2003. 'When Infinite Regresses are *Not* Vicious'. *Philosophy and Phenomenological Research* 66 (3):718–29.

Klein, Peter. 2004. 'Closure Matters: Academic Skepticism and Easy Knowledge'. *Philosophical Issues* 14 (1):165–84.

Klein, Peter. 2007. 'Human Knowledge and the Infinite Progress of Reasoning'. *Philosophical Studies* 134 (1):1–17.

Knight, Frank H. 1921. *Risk, Uncertainty and Profit*. New York: Sentry Press.

Knight, Frank H. 1923. 'The Ethics of Competition'. *The Quarterly Journal of Economics* 37 (4):579–624.

Knight, Frank H. 1935a. *The Ethics of Competition and Other Essays*. Freeport: Books for Libraries Press.

Knight, Frank H. 1935b [1924]. 'The Limitations of Scientific Method in Economics'. In *The Ethics of Competition and Other Essays*, Freeport: Books for Libraries Press, 105–47.

Köhler, Wolfgang. 1927. *The Mentality of Apes*. Translated by Ella Winter. New York: Harcourt, Brace and Company.

Kripke, Saul. 1982. *Wittgenstein on Rules and Private Language: An Elementary Exposition*. Oxford: Blackwell.

Kronfeldner, Maria. 2018. *What's Left of Human Nature? A Post-Essentialist, Pluralist, and Interactive Account of a Contested Concept*. Cambridge, MA: The MIT Press.

Latour, Bruno. 1987. *Science in Action: How to Follow Scientists and Engineers Through Society*. Cambridge, MA: Harvard University Press.

Lefebvre, Henri. 1991 [1974]. *The Production of Space*. Translated by Donald Nicholson-Smith. Oxford: Basil Blackwell.

Lefebvre, Henri. 1996. *Writings on Cities*. Translated by Eleonore Kofman and Elizabeth Lebas. Oxford: Blackwell Publishers.

Lefebvre, Henri. 2003 [1970]. *The Urban Revolution*. Translated by Robert Bononno. Minneapolis: University of Minnesota Press.

Leibniz, Gottfried Wilhelm. 1988. *Discourse on Metaphysics; Correspondence with Arnauld; Monadology*. Translated by George Montgomery. La Salle: Open Court.

Liberman, Kenneth. 2013. *More Studies in Ethnomethodology*. Albany: State University of New York Press.

Lindsey, Brink, and Steven M. Teles. 2017. *The Captured Economy: How the Powerful Enrich Themselves, Slow Down Growth, and Increase Inequality*. Oxford: Oxford University Press.

Locke, John. 1988 [1689]. *Two Treatises of Government*. Cambridge: Cambridge University Press.

Losurdo, Domenico. 2014. *Liberalism: A Counter-history*. London: Verso.

Lukács, Georg. 1971a. *The Theory of the Novel: A Historico-philosophical Essay on the Form of Great Epic Literature*. Translated by Anna Bostock. Cambridge, MA: The MIT Press.

Lukács, Georg. 1971b. *History and Class Consciousness: Studies in Marxist Dialectics*. Translated by Rodney Livingstone. London: Merlin Press.

Luria, Aleksandr. 1976. *Cognitive Development: Its Cultural and Social Foundations*. Cambridge, MA: Harvard University Press.

Lynch, Kevin. 1960. *The Image of the City*. Cambridge, MA: The MIT Press.

Lynch, Michael, ed. 1987. *The Early Modern Town in Scotland*. London: Croom Helm.

Lynch, Michael. 1992. 'Extending Wittgenstein: The Pivotal Move from Epistemology to the Sociology of Science'. In *Science as Practice and Culture*. Edited by Andrew Pickering. Chicago: University of Chicago Press.

McCauley, Robert N., and Joseph Henrich. 2006. 'Susceptibility to the Müller-Lyer Illusion, Theory-Neutral Observation, and the Diachronic Penetrability of the Visual Input System'. *Philosophical Society* 19 (1):79–101.

McCormick, John P. 1997. *Carl Schmitt's Critique of Liberalism: Against Politics as Technology*. Cambridge: Cambridge University Press.

McDowell, John. 1992. 'Putnam on Mind and Meaning'. *Philosophical Topics* 20 (1):35–48.

McDowell, John. 1994. *Mind and World*. Cambridge, MA: Harvard University Press.

MacGilvray, Eric. 2011. *The Invention of Market Freedom*. Cambridge: Cambridge University Press.

MacIntyre, Alasdair. 1981. *After Virtue*. South Bend: University of Notre Dame Press.

Mackay, Robin, ed. 2014. *#Accelerate: The Accelerationist Reader*. Falmouth: Urbanomic.

Marshall, Alfred. 1890. *Principles of Economics*. New York: Macmillan and Co.

Marshall, Peter. 2010 [1992]. *Demanding the Impossible: A History of Anarchism*. Oakland: PM Press.

Marx, Karl. 1988 [1844]. *Economic and Philosophic Manuscripts of 1844*. Translated by Martin Milligan. New York: Prometheus Books.

Marx, Karl. 1990. *Capital: A Critique of Political Economy, Volume One*. Translated by Ben Fowkes. New York: Penguin Books.

Marx, Karl. 1993 [1858]. *Grundrisse: Foundations of the Critique of Political Economy*. Translated by Martin Nicolaus. New York: Penguin Classics.

Maynard Smith, John. 1982. *Evolution and the Theory of Games*. Cambridge: Cambridge University Press.

Maynard Smith, John, and David Harper. 2003. *Animal Signals*. Oxford: Oxford University Press.

Maynard Smith, John, and G.A. Parker. 1976. 'The Logic of Asymmetric Contests'. *Animal Behaviour* 24 (1):159–75.

Menke, Christoph. 2015. *Critique of Rights*. London: Polity.

Mercier, Hugo, and Dan Sperber. 2011. 'Why Do Humans Reason? Arguments for an Argumentative Theory'. *Behavioral and Brain Sciences* 34:57–111.

Mercier, Hugo, and Dan Sperber. 2017. *The Enigma of Reason*. Cambridge, MA: Harvard University Press.

Mill, John Stuart. 1991. *On Liberty and Other Essays*. Edited by John Gray. Oxford and New York: Oxford University Press.

Miller, Alexander. 2004. 'Rule-Following and Externalism'. *Philosophy and Phenomenological Research* 68 (1):127–40.

Miller, Peter. 2003. 'Management Accounting Practices and Assemblages'. Eighth Biennial Management Accounting Research Conference, Sydney, Australia, 21/22 February.

Miller, Peter, and Michael Power. 2013. 'Accounting, Organizing, and Economizing: Connecting Accounting Research and Organization Theory'. *The Academy of Management Annals* 7 (1):557–605.

Mills, Charles W. 2005. '"Ideal Theory" as Ideology'. *Hypatia* 20 (3):165–84.

Minsky, Hyman P. 2008. *Stabilizing an Unstable Economy*. New York: McGraw Hill.

Montes, Leonidas, and Eric Schliesser, eds. 2006. *New Voices on Adam Smith*. London: Routledge.

Mumford, Lewis. 1961. *The City in History*. New York: Harcourt Brace.

Nagel, Ernest. 1961. *Structure of Science: Problems in the Logic of Scientific Explanation*. New York: Harcourt, Brace & World.

Naimark, Norman. 2010. *Stalin's Genocides*. Princeton: Princeton University Press.

Nederman, Cary J. 2009. *Lineages of European Political Thought: Explorations along the Medieval/ Modern Divide from John of Salisbury to Hegel*. Washington, DC: The Catholic University of America Press.

Neu, Dean, Jeff Everett, and Abu Shiraz Rahaman. 2009. 'Accounting Assemblages, Desire, and the Body without Organs'. *Accounting, Auditing & Accountability Journal* 22 (3):319–50.

Nice, M.M. 1937. *Studies in the Life History of the Song Sparrow I*. New York: Transactions of the Linnaean Society.

Nice, M.M. 1943. *Studies in the Life History of the Song Sparrow II*. New York: Transactions of the Linnaean Society.

Nietzsche, Friedrich. 1954. *The Portable Nietzsche*. Translated by Walter Kaufmann. New York: Penguin Books.

Nietzsche, Friedrich. 1966 [1886]. *Beyond Good and Evil*. Translated by Walter Kaufmann. New York: Vintage Books.

Nietzsche, Friedrich. 1969 [1887]. *On the Genealogy of Morals; Ecce Homo*. Translated by Walter Kaufmann. New York: Vintage Books.

Nietzsche, Friedrich. 1974 [1887]. *The Gay Science*. Translated by Walter Kaufmann. New York: Vintage Books.

Nietzsche, Friedrich. 1996 [1879]. *Human, All-Too-Human: A Book for Free Spirits*. Translated by R.J. Hollingdale. Cambridge: Cambridge University Press.

Nietzsche, Friedrich. 2011 [1881]. *Dawn: Thoughts on the Presumptions of Morality*. Translated by Brittain Smith. Edited by Alan Schrift, Keith Ansell Pearson and Duncan Large, in *The Complete Works of Friedrich Nietzsche*. Stanford: Stanford University Press.

Nozick, Robert. 1998 [1974]. *Anarchy, State, and Utopia*. New York: Basic Books.

O'Meara, Dominic J. 2000. 'Scepticism and Ineffability in Plotinus'. *Phronesis* 45 (3):240–51.

Oestreich, Gerhard. 1982. *Neostoicism and the Early Modern State*. Translated by David McLintock. Cambridge: Cambridge University Press.

Ohlsson, Stellan. 2011. *Deep Learning: How the Mind Overrides Experience*. Cambridge: Cambridge University Press.

Olson, David R. 1994. *The World on Paper: The Conceptual and Cognitive Implications of Writing and Reading*. Cambridge: Cambridge University Press.

Ortmann, Andreas, John Fitzgerald and Carl Boeing. 2000. 'Trust, Reciprocity, and Social History: A Re-examination'. *Experimental Economics* 3 (2):81–100.

Östling, Johan. 2018. *Humboldt and the Modern German University: An Intellectual History*. Lund: Lund University Press.

Peirce, Charles S. 1955. *Philosophical Writings of Peirce*. New York: Dover Publications.

Perkins, David. 2000. *The Eureka Effect: The Art and Logic of Breakthrough Thinking*. Cambridge, MA: Harvard University Press.

Pettit, Philip. 1990. 'The Reality of Rule-Following'. *Mind* 99 (393):1–21.

Pettit, Philip. 1997. *Republicanism: A Theory of Freedom and Government*. Oxford: Oxford University Press.

Pettit, Philip. 2012. *On the People's Terms: A Republican Theory and Model of Democracy*. Cambridge: Cambridge University Press.

Pierce, John R. 1960. *An Introduction to Information Theory: Symbols, Signals and Noise*. New York: Dover Publications.

Piketty, Thomas. 2014. *Capital in the Twenty-First Century*. Cambridge, MA: Belknap Press.

Pirenne, Henri. 1939. *Medieval Cities: Their Origins and the Revival of Trade*. Princeton: Princeton University Press.

Pistor, Katharina. 2019. *The Code of Capital: How the Law Creates Wealth and Inequality*. Princeton: Princeton University Press.

Plato. 1939. *Parmenides*. Translated by Harold North Fowler, Loeb Classical Library, Vol. 167. Cambridge, MA: Harvard University Press.

Plato. 1986. *Statesman*. Edited by Seth Benardete. Chicago: University of Chicago Press.

Plato. 2006. *Philebus*. Translated by Harold North Fowler and W.R.M. Lamb, *Loeb Classical Library*, Vol. 164. Cambridge, MA: Harvard University Press.

Plato. 2016. *Laws*. Translated by Tom Griffith. Edited by Malcolm Schofield, *Cambridge Texts in the History of Philosophy*. Cambridge: Cambridge University Press.

Plutarch. 1919. *Lives*. Translated by Bernadotte Perrin. Cambridge, MA: Harvard University Press.

Polanyi, Karl. 2001 [1944]. *The Great Transformation: The Political and Economic Origins of Our Time*. New York: Beacon Press.

Popkin, Richard. 1952. 'David Hume and the Pyrrhonian Controversy'. *The Review of Metaphysics* 6 (1):65–81.

Popkin, Richard. 1978. 'Did Hume or Rousseau Influence the Other?' *Revue Internationale de Philosophie* 32 (124):297–308.

Popkin, Richard. 1979. *The History of Scepticism from Erasmus to Spinoza*. Berkeley: University of California Press.

Popkin, Richard. 2003 [1960]. *The History of Scepticism from Savonarola to Bayle*. Oxford: Oxford University Press.

Postone, Moishe. 1996. *Time, Labor, and Social Domination*. Cambridge: Cambridge University Press.

Protevi, John. 2009. *Political Affect: Connecting the Social and the Somatic*. Minneapolis: University of Minnesota Press.

Proust, Marcel. 2003 [1923]. *In Search of Lost Time: The Prisoner and the Fugitive*. Translated by Carol Clark. London: Penguin Classics.

Putnam, Hilary. 1975. *Mind, Language and Reality: Philosophical Papers, Volume 2*. Cambridge: Cambridge University Press.

Ramsay, Maureen. 1996. *What's Wrong with Liberalism?* London: Bloomsbury.

Rancière, Jacques. 1991. *The Ignorant Schoolmaster*. Translated by Kristin Ross. Stanford: Stanford University Press.

Rancière, Jacques. 1999. *Dis-agreement: Politics and Philosophy*. Translated by Julie Rose. Minneapolis: University of Minnesota Press.

Rancière, Jacques. 2014. *Hatred of Democracy*. Translated by Steve Corcoran. London: Verso.

Read, Jason. 2003. *The Micro-Politics of Capital: Marx and the Prehistory of the Present*. Albany: State University of New York Press.

Richards, Richard A. 2010. *The Species Problem: A Philosophical Analysis*. Cambridge: Cambridge University Press.

Ricoeur, Paul. 1980. 'Narrative Time'. *Critical Inquiry* 7 (1):169–90.

Roberts, William Clare. 2017. *Marx's Inferno: The Political Theory of Capital*. Princeton: Princeton University Press.

Romer, Paul. forthcoming. 'The Trouble With Macroeconomics'. *The American Economist*.

Rose, Gillian. 1978. *The Melancholy Science*. London: Verso.

Rose, Gillian. 1993. 'Of Derrida's Spirit'. *New Literary History* 24 (2):447–65.

Rose, Gillian. 2017. *Judaism and Modernity: Philosophical Essays*. New York: Verso.

Roth, Paul A. 2017. 'Essentially Narrative Explanations'. *Studies in History and Philosophy of Science* 62:42–50.

Rousseau, Jean-Jacques. 1979. *Emile or On Education*. Translated by Allan Bloom. New York: Basic Books.

Rousseau, Jean-Jacques. 2002. *The Social Contract and The First and Second Discourses*. Translated by Susan Dunn. New Haven: Yale University Press.

Russell, Bertrand. 1905. 'On Denoting'. *Mind* 14 (56):479–93.

Russell, Bertrand. 1950. *Unpopular Essays*. New York: Simon and Schuster.

Russell, Bertrand. 1972 [1945]. *A History of Western Philosophy*. New York: Simon and Schuster.

Russell, Bertrand. 1996 [1928]. *Sceptical Essays*. London: Routledge.

Russell, Bertrand. 2001 [1912]. *The Problems of Philosophy*. Oxford: Oxford University Press.

Sabl, Andrew. 2012. *Hume's Politics: Coordination and Crisis in the History of England*. Princeton: Princeton University Press.

Sandbrook, Richard. 2014. *Reinventing the Left in the Global South: The Politics of the Possible*. Cambridge: Cambridge University Press.

Sartre, Jean-Paul. 1956 [1943]. *Being and Nothingness*. Translated by Hazel Barnes. New York: Washington Square Press.

Sassoon, Donald. 1998. *One Hundred Years of Socialism: The West European Left in the Twentieth Century*. New York: The New Press.

Schacht, Hjalmar. 1967. *The Magic of Money*. Translated by Paul Erskine. London: Oldbourne.

Schelling, Thomas. 1963. *The Strategy of Conflict*. Cambridge, MA: Harvard University Press.

Schlick, Moritz. 1939 [1930]. *Problems of Ethics*. Translated by David Rynin. New York: Prentice-Hall.

Schliesser, Eric. 2012. What Happened to Knightian (and Keynesian) Uncertainty Post WWII? A Philosophic History. *SSRN*, at <https://papers.ssrn.com/sol3/papers.cfm?abstract_id=2033117>.

Schliesser, Eric. 2017. *Adam Smith: Systematic Philosopher and Public Thinker*. Oxford: Oxford University Press.

Schliesser, Eric. 2018. 'Hume on Affective Leadership'. In *Hume's Moral Philosophy and Contemporary Psychology*. Edited by P.A. Reed and R. Vitz. New York: Routledge, 311–33.

Schmandt-Besserat, Denise. 1992. *Before Writing, Volume I: From Counting to Cuneiform*. Austin: University of Texas Press.

Schmitt, Bernard. 2014. 'The Formation of Sovereign Debt: Diagnosis and Remedy'. *SSRN*. https://papers.ssrn.com/sol3/papers.cfm?abstract_id=2513679.

Schmitt, Carl. 2008 [1932]. *The Concept of the Political*. Chicago: University of Chicago Press.

Schofield, Malcom. 1991. *The Stoic Idea of the City*. Cambridge: Cambridge University Press.

Schumpeter, Joseph A. 1939. *Business Cycles: A Theoretical, Historical, and Statistical Analysis of the Capitalist Process*. New York: McGraw-Hill.

Scribner, Sylvia. 1977. 'Modes of Thinking and Ways of Speaking: Culture and Logic Reconsidered'. In *Thinking: Readings in Cognitive Science*. Edited by P.N. Johnson-Laird and P.C. Wason. Cambridge: Cambridge University Press, 483–500.

Searcy, William A., Çağlar Akçay, Stephen Nowicki and Michael D. Beecher. 2014. 'Aggressive Signaling in Song Sparrows and Other Songbirds'. In *Advances in the Study of Behavior*. New York: Elsevier, 89–125.

Seneca. 1928. *Moral Essays, Volume 1*. Translated by John William Basore. Cambridge, MA: Harvard University Press.

Sextus Empiricus. 1933. *Outlines of Pyrrhonism*. Translated by R.G. Bury. Cambridge, MA: Harvard University Press.

Shackle, G.L.S. 1955. *Uncertainty in Economics and Other Reflections*. Cambridge: Cambridge University Press.

Shannon, Claude E., and Warren Weaver. 1949. *The Mathematical Theory of Communication*. Urbana: University of Illinois Press.

Sheldahl, Lea A., and Emilia P. Martins. 2000. 'The Territorial Behavior of the Western Fence Lizard, *Sceloporus Occidentailis*'. *Herpetologica* 56 (4):469–79.

Sherman, David K., and Geoffrey L. Cohen. 2006. 'The Psychology of Self-Defense: Self-Affirmation Theory.' *Advances in Experimental Social Psychology* 38:183–242.

Sidnell, Jack. 2003. 'An Ethnographic Consideration of Rule-Following'. *The Journal of the Royal Anthropological Institute* 9 (3):429–45.

Simondon, Gilbert. 2013. *L'individuation: à la lumière des notions de forme et d'information*. Grenoble: Millon.

Sjoberg, Gideon. 1960. *The Preindustrial City: Past and Present*. New York: Free Press.

Skinner, Quentin. 1998. *Liberty Before Liberalism*. Cambridge: Cambridge University Press.

Slobodian, Quinn. 2018. *Globalists: The End of Empire and the Birth of Neoliberalism*. Cambridge, MA: Harvard University Press.

Smith, Adam. 1976a [1759]. *The Theory of Moral Sentiments*. Indianapolis: Liberty Fund.

Smith, Adam. 1976b [1776]. *An Inquiry into the Nature and Causes of the Wealth of Nations*. Indianapolis: Liberty Press.

Smith, Andrew. 2015. 'Between Facts and Myth: Karl Jaspers and the Actuality of the Axial Age'. *International Journal of Philosophy and Theology* 76 (4):315–34.

Smith, Vernon L., and Bart J. Wilson. 2019. *Humanomics: Moral Sentiments and the Wealth of Nations for the Twenty-First Century*. Cambridge: Cambridge University Press.

Southall, Aidan. 1998. *The City in Time and Space*. Cambridge: Cambridge University Press.

Spinoza, Benedict de. 1985. *The Collected Works of Spinoza, Volume I*. Translated by Edwin Curley. Princeton: Princeton University Press.

Spinoza, Benedict de. 2016. *The Collected Works of Spinoza, Volume II*. Translated by Edwin Curley. Princeton: Princeton University Press.

Spinoza, Benedictus. 1925. *Opera*, 4 vols. Edited by Carl Gebhardt. Heidelberg: C. Winter.

Sprintzen, David A., and Adrian van den Hoven, eds. 2004. *Sartre and Camus: A Historic Confrontation*. Amherst: Humanity Books.

Sraffa, Piero. 1960. *Production of Commodities: Prelude to a Critique of Economic Theory*. Cambridge: Cambridge University Press.

Stamps, J.A., and V.V. Krishnan. 1994a. 'Territory Acquisition in Lizards: I. First Encounters'. *Animal Behaviour* 47:1375–85.

Stamps, J.A., and V.V. Krishnan. 1994b. 'Territory Acquisition in Lizards: II. Establishing Social and Spatial Relationships'. *Animal Behaviour* 47:1387–400.

Stamps, J.A., and V.V. Krishnan. 1995. 'Territory Acquisition in Lizards: III. Competing for Space'. *49*:679–93.

Stamps, J.A., and V.V. Krishnan. 1998. 'Territory Acquisition in Lizards. IV. Obtaining High Status and Exclusive Home Ranges'. *Animal Behaviour* 55:461–72.

Stanley, Jason. 2015. *How Propaganda Works*. Princeton: Princeton University Press.

Stasavage, David. 2003. *Public Debt and the Birth of the Democratic State: France and Great Britain, 1688–1789*. Cambridge: Cambridge University Press.

Stasavage, David. 2015. *States of Credit: Size, Power, and the Development of European Polities*. Princeton: Princeton University Press.

Steele, Claude M. 1988. 'The Psychology of Self-Affirmation: Sustaining the Integrity of the Self.' In *Advances in experimental social psychology*, edited by L. Berkowitz, 261–302. New York: Academic Press.

Stenning, Keith, and Michiel van Lambalgen. 2008. *Human Reasoning and Cognitive Science*. Cambridge, MA: The MIT Press.

Steuart, Sir James. 1767. *An Inquiry Into the Principles of Political Economy*. London: A. Millar and T. Cadell.

Stewart, M.V. 1973. 'Tests of the "Carpentered World" Hypothesis by Race and Environment in America and Zambia'. *International Journal of Psychology* 8:83–94.

Strauss, Leo. 1953. *Natural Right and History*. Chicago: University of Chicago Press.

Strawson, P.F. 1985. *Scepticism and Naturalism: Some Varieties*. New York: Columbia University Press.

Streeck, Wolfgang. 2014. *Buying Time: The Delayed Crisis of Democratic Capitalism*. Translated by Patrick Camiller. London: Verso.

Streeck, Wolfgang. 2016. *How Will Capitalism End? Essays on a Failing System*. London: Verso.

Sudnow, David. 1978. *Ways of the Hand*. Cambridge, MA: Harvard University Press.

Sweezy, Paul, Maurice Dobb, H.K. Takahashi, Rodney Hilton, and Christopher Hill. 1963. 'The Transition From Feudalism to Capitalism: A Symposium'. *Science & Society*.

Thoburn, Nicholas. 2003. *Deleuze, Marx, and Politics*. New York: Routledge.

Tolman, Edward C. 1948. 'Cognitive Maps in Rats and Men'. *The Psychological Review* 55 (4):189–208.

Tucker, Aviezer, ed. 2009. *A Companion to the Philosophy of History and Historiography*. London: Blackwell Publishing.

Tuomela, Raimo. 2009. 'Collective Intentions and Game Theory'. *The Journal of Philosophy* 106 (5):292–300.

Ullman-Margalit, Edna. 1977. *The Emergence of Norms*. Oxford: Oxford University Press.

Vance, J.E. 1977. *This Scene of Man: The Role and Structure of the City in the Geography of Western Civilization*. London: Blackwell.

Vanderschraaf, Peter. 2008. 'Game Theory Meets Threshold Analysis: Reappraising the Paradoxes of Anarchy and Revolution'. *The British Journal for the Philosophy of Science* 59 (4):579–617.

Varoufakis, Yanis. 1993. 'Modern and Postmodern Challenges to Game Theory'. *Erkenntnis* 38 (3):371–404.

Vehrencamp, Sandra L., Jesse M. Ellis, Brett F. Cropp, and John M. Koltz. 2014. 'Negotiation of Territorial Boundaries in a Songbird'. *Behavioral Ecology* 25 (6):1436–50.

Vitruvius. 1960. *The Ten Books on Architecture*. New York: Dover Publications, Inc.

Wason, P.C. 1968. 'Reasoning About a Rule.' *Quarterly Journal of Experimental Psychology* 20:273–81.

Weber, Max. 1968. *Economy and Society*. New York: Bedminster Press.

Weisberg, Robert W. 2015. 'Toward an Integrated Theory of Insight in Problem Solving'. *Thinking & Reasoning* 21 (1):5–39.

Werner, Richard A. 2014. 'How Do Banks Create Money, and Why Can Other Firms Not Do the Same? An Explanation for the Coexistence of Lending and Deposit-taking'. *International Review of Financial Analysis* 36:71–7.

Widder, Nathan. 2008. 'Foucault and Power Revisited'. *European Journal of Political Theory* 3 (4):411–32.

Widder, Nathan. 2012. *Political Theory After Deleuze*. London: Continuum.

Widder, Nathan. 2018. 'Deleuze and Guattari's "War Machine" as a Critique of Hegel's Political Philosophy'. *Hegel Bulletin* 39 (2):304–25.

Williams, James. 2016. *A Process Philosophy of Signs*. Edinburgh: Edinburgh University Press.

Wilson, Mark. 1982. 'Predicate Meets Property'. *The Philosophical Review* 91 (4):549–89.

Wilson, Mark. 1985. 'This Thing Called Pain'. *Pacific Philosophical Quarterly* 66 (3–4):227–67.

Winston, Patrick Henry. 2011. 'The Strong Story Hypothesis and the Directed Perception Hypothesis'. Advances in Cognitive Systems: Papers from the 2011 AAAI Fall Symposium.

Wittgenstein, Ludwig. 1972. *On Certainty*. Translated by G.E.M. Anscombe. New York: Harper & Row.

Wittgenstein, Ludwig. 2009 [1953]. *Philosophical Investigations*. Edited by G.E.M. Anscombe. Oxford: Basil Blackwell.

Wood, Denis. 2010. *Rethinking the Power of Maps*. London: Guilford Press.

Wood, Ellen Meiksins. 1986. *The Retreat from Class: A New 'True' Socialism*. London: Verso.

Wood, Ellen Meiksins. 2002. *The Origin of Capitalism: A Longer View*. London: Verso.

Wright, Crispin. 2002. 'Critical Notice of Colin McGinn's *Wittgenstein on Meaning*'. In *Rule-Following and Meaning*. Edited by Alexander Miller and Crispin Wright. Chesham: Acumen, 108–28.

Zuboff, Shoshana. 2019. *The Age of Surveillance Capitalism*. New York: PublicAffairs.

Index